SOME LETTERS FROM BURMA

SOME LETTERS FROM BURMA

The Story of the 25th Dragoons at War

Tom Grounds

Foreword by
Brigadier H.M.H. Ley CBE

PARAPRESS LTD
Tunbridge Wells · Kent

In the same series:

Came the Dawn – 50 Years an Army Officer by Brigadier Paul Cook
Dual Allegiance – From the Punjab to the Jordan (WW2) by Monty Green
Haul Taut & Belay – Memoirs of a Flying Sailor by Rear Admiral Sir Donald Gibson
Keep Your Head Down – Falklands Notes by Cmdr Bernie Bruen
Let Go Aft – The Indiscretions of a Salthorse Commander by Cmdr H.G. de Chair
Letters from the Front – Letters of Lt Brian Lawrence, Grenadier Guards (WW1) by Ian Fletcher
Ordinary Naval Airmen by Jim Spencer
The Perilous Road to Rome Via Tunis (WW2) by Edward Grace
Soldier On! by Brigadier Joe Starling
They Gave me a Seafire by Cmdr Mike Crosley
Triumph and Disaster – The Autobiography of Naval Officer by Cmdr Victor Clark
Wren's Eye View – The Adventures of a Visual Signaller (WW2) by Stephanie Batstone

ISBN 1-898594-11-2

First published in the UK in 1994 by
PARAPRESS LTD
12 Dene Way
Speldhurst
Tunbridge Wells
Kent TN3 0NX

British Library Cataloguing-in-Publication Data:
A catalogue record for this book is available
from the British Library

Typeset by Vitaset, Paddock Wood, Kent
Printed and bound by The Ipswich Book Co Ltd, Suffolk

Contents

Acknowledgements vii
Abbreviations ix
Chain of Command x
Order of Battle xii
Units in the Admin Box xiv
Foreword xvii
Prologue: November 1941. The Rev. W.F. Cox xix
Introduction: India 1
1 Journey to the Jungle 22
2 Blooding the Hounds 38
3 Panic in the Parlour 50
4 Rendezvous for Battle 70
5 Besieged 85
6 ODTAA 104
7 Signs of Relief 123
8 Last Days of Siege 141
9 The Fall of Buthidaung 162
10 Across the River 181
11 Battle for the Monsoon Line 199
12 The Way Back 218
Postscript: 'A' Squadron at Meiktila 234
Epilogue: February 1947. Compton Mackenzie 243
Appendices 249
Glossary 260
Sources 261
Index of Persons 262

Maps

	page
The operational area, Arakan, Jan–June 1944	36
The Razabil Fortress and environs	44
The Admin Box at Sinzweya, February 1944	83
The road from the tunnels to Buthidaung	166
Pt 551 and the Maungdaw–Buthidaung road	202
The approaches to Kalaw, June 1945	239

Acknowledgements

This book has its origins in my letters home from India and Burma. The first draft was intended for reading by family and friends, but some of these urged publication. When fresh and important material became available I found it difficult to resist the argument that some sort of history of the 25th Dragoons was needed. The book is not an official or complete history but it does follow through the story of the Regiment's involvement in the Burma war.

Many people have contributed and made it possible and I am indebted to all of them. Some are mentioned here by name but I am aware of the many others who in one way or another have kept me on the track.

I must first express my gratitude to Mrs Jean Frink for allowing me to see and quote from the papers of her late husband, Brigadier H.R.C. Frink DSO, so giving added depth and authenticity to the story.

My very sincere thanks go also to Brigadier H.M.H. Ley CBE, DL, firstly for reading my drafts and offering many helpful comments and much interesting detail, and secondly for generously writing a Foreword to the book.

I have been fortunate to see some unpublished mémoires of the events in Arakan 1944 and am particularly grateful to Dr Christopher Houghton Brown for permission to reproduce substantial passages from *Farmer-Soldier* by his brother the late Lt Col J. Houghton Brown DSO; also to Mr Peter Ascham for passages from his *The Turning Point*; also to Mr J.D. Daligan for passages from Mr Bill Harding's *Story of 139 Jungle Field Regiment R.A.* and from R.Q.M.S. Murgatroyd's *History of the Admin. Box*; to the Museum of the Royal Corps of Signals for the account by Brigadier Patrick Hobson DSO of the Japanese attack on the Headquarters of the 7th Indian Division and its defence; to Major O.C. Horne for passages from his article *The Story of 25th Dragoons*; to Mr William Nicholson for passages from his *Here and There*; and not least to Captain the Rev W.F. Cox for the use of part of his address in November 1941 as prologue.

I would like to record the help and encouragement I received from the late Major K. Spooner who read the first draft and offered comments. I am grateful to Lt Col R. McCaig, Major H.G. Ablett, Major J. McVicker, Mr John Leyin, Mr Charles Fairweather, Mr Norman Hamer, the late Mr John Monger MM and Mr A.D. Carse, for much detail and incident.

For the Postscript I am indebted to Mr Tom Thompson MBE, Mr Geoffrey Anlezark and Mr James Tiley, all of 'A' Squadron, and to the Museum of the Worcestershire and Royal Sherwood Foresters Regiment regarding the taking of Kalaw.

For the photographs I have to thank more especially Lt Col C. Auchinleck, as well as the late Major K. Spooner, Mrs J. Frink, the Tank Museum, Borington, and the Imperial War Museum.

I must also acknowledge the value of the books listed under 'Sources' in completing the historical background. Where extracts have been quoted, I regret it has not always been possible to trace the publishers or authors.

Last but far from least I want to thank Mrs Elizabeth Crabtree, Mrs Janice Pettiford and my daughter for their miraculous work in turning my sometimes chaotic manuscript into neat tidy pages. I am very grateful to my daughter for help in proof-reading and preparing the index. All of which would have been of no avail without the willingness of Mr Ian Morley-Clarke of Parapress to see the book through publication.

Austwick, North Yorkshire Tom Grounds
May 1994

Abbreviations

AA	Anti-aircraft
AT	Anti-tank
AFV	Armoured Fighting Vehicle
AML	Airmail Letter Card
AP	Armour-piercing
Bde	Brigade
Batt, Bn	Battalion
BO	British Officer
BOR	British Other Rank
Brig	Brigadier
CO	Commanding Officer
Coy	Company
Cpl	Corporal
CRA	Commander Royal Artillery
Div	Division
25D	25th Dragoons
DD	Duplex Drive (amphibious tanks)
DSO	Distinguished Service Order
ENSA	Entertainments National Service Association
FFR	Frontier Force Rifles
FOO	Forward Observation Officer
FUP	Forming-up Position
Gen	Major General/Lieutenant General/General
GHQ	General Headquarters
Gnr	Gunner
GOC	General Officer Commanding
HE	High Explosive
HMT	His Majesty's Troop-ship
I	Intelligence
IE	Indian Engineers
INA	Indian National Army
IOR	Indian Other Rank
IO	Indian Officer
IEME	Indian Electrical and Mechanical Engineers
JIFS	Japanese Indian Forces
KOSB	King's Own Scottish Border Regiment
LAD	Light Aid Detachment
L/Cpl	Lance Corporal
LMG	Light Machine Gun
LST	Landing Ship, Tank
Lt	Lieutenant
MC	Military Cross
MDS	Main Dressing Station
MG	Machine Gun
MMG	Medium Machine Gun
MI	Medical Inspection
MO	Medical Officer
MM	Military Medal
OC	Officer Commanding
OP	Observation Post
POL	Petrol, Oil, Lubrication
POW	Prisoner of War
QMS	Quarter Master Sergeant
RA	Royal Regiment of Artillery
RAP	Regimental Aid Post
RAC	Royal Armoured Corps
RAMC	Royal Army Medical Corps
RE	Royal Engineers
Recce	Reconnaissance
RIASC	Royal Indian Army Service Corps
RQMS	Regimental Quarter Master Sergeant
RSM	Regimental Sergeant Major
RTR	Royal Tank Regiment
REME	Royal Electrical and Mechanical Engineers
SSM	Squadron Sergeant Major
SS	Steam Ship
Sqn	Squadron
SEAC	South East Asia Command
TDT	Tank Delivery Troop
Tpr	Trooper
Trp	Troop
VCO	Viceroy's Commissioned Officer
VE	Victory in Europe
VJ	Victory over Japan
WO	Warrant Officer

CHAIN OF COMMAND DURING THE ARAKAN CAMPAIGN 1943-1944

South East Asia Command (SEAC):
Admiral Lord Louis Mountbatten

11th Army Group:
General George Giffard

XIVth Army:
Lt Gen William Slim

14th Army

The XVth Corps:
Lt Gen Philip Christison

XV Ind Corps

5th Indian Division:	Maj Gen Harold R. Briggs
7th Indian Division:	Maj Gen Frank W. Messervy
25th Indian Division:	Maj Gen Davies
26th Indian Division:	Maj Gen C.E.N. Lomax
36th British Division:	Maj Gen F.W. Festing
81st West African Division:	Maj Gen C.G. Woolner

Corps Armoured Group

Col S.H. Persse

25th Dragoons RAC
1 Troop, 401 Field Squadron, IE
1 Company, 3rd/4th Bombay Grenadiers (Motorized)
Detachment 254 Bridging Troop, IE
81st West African Reconnaissance Regt
3rd Gwalior Lancers (Mechanized Wing)

(This group was reorganized 27th Feb 1944)

25th Dragoons RAC

Commanding Officer:	Lt Col H.R.C. Frink
Second in Command:	Major H.M.H. Ley
Squadron Leaders:	
A Squadron	Major W.C.W. Sloan
B Squadron	Major N.C. Johnstone
C Squadron	Major O.C. Horne
Reserve Squadron	Major S.B. Youens
Adjutant:	Captain C.D. Anderson
Technical Adjutant:	Captain E.G. Winters
Medical Officer:	Captain B. Gaunt, RAMC
Quartermaster:	Captain E.W. Manners
Padre:	Captain W.F. Cox, CF

ORDER OF BATTLE

(Infantry Regiments involved in the defence and relief of the Box and/or with whom 25th Dragoons co-operated)

5th Indian Division

9 Brigade:	2nd Batt West Yorkshire Regt
	3rd Batt 9th Jats
	3rd Batt 14th Punjab
123 Brigade:	2nd Batt Suffolk Regt
	2nd Batt 1st Punjab
	1st Batt 17th Dogra
161 Brigade:	4th Batt Queen's Own Royal West Kent Regt
	1st Batt 1st Punjab
	4th Batt 7th Rajput

7th Indian Division

33 Brigade:	1st Batt Queen's Royal Regt
	4th Batt 15th Punjab
	4th Batt 1st Gurkha Rifles
89 Brigade:	2nd Batt King's Own Scottish Borderers
	7th Batt 2nd Punjab
	4th Batt 8th Gurkha Rifles
114 Brigade:	1st Batt Somerset Light Infantry Regt
	4th Batt 14th Punjab
	4th Batt 5th Gurkha Rifles
HQ Defence:	1st Batt 11th Sikh

26th Indian Division

4 Brigade:	1st Batt Wiltshire Regt
	2nd Batt 13th Frontier Force
	2nd Batt 17th Rajput
71 Brigade:	1st Batt Lincolnshire Regt
	5th Batt 1st Punjab
	1st Batt 18th Royal Garwhali Rifles
36 Brigade:	8th Batt 13th Frontier Force Regt
	5th Batt 16th Punjab
	1st Batt 8th Gurkha Rifles

36th British Division

This Division was in Calcutta at the time of the Japanese attack on the 4th February 1944. It was brought up to Chittagong to replace 26th Indian Division as reserve and was then brought to Arakan and took a late part in the Battle of the Box.

25th Indian Division

This Division was also brought up after the Battle of the Box to replace 5th Division. It included the 6th Battalion of the Oxford and Bucks Light Infantry with whom Lt Arthur's Special Troop co-operated at the end of April 1944.

81st West African Division

This consisted of 2 Brigades in the Kaladan Valley, supplied entirely by air. It did not directly take part in the Battle. During the siege, General Christison pulled them back to the eastern bank of the Kalapanzin river.

UNITS PRESENT IN THE ADMIN BOX 6th-24th FEB 1944

Royal Armoured Corps

25th Dragoons: Regimental HQ
A Squadron (part of the time)
B and C Squadrons

Royal Artillery

139 Jungle Field Regt, 362 Mortar Battery (3″)
6 Medium Regt, 1 Battery
136 Field Regt, B Echelon
24 Anti-Tank Regt, 2 Batteries and Regimental HQ
8 Belfast (Heavy) Anti-Aircraft Regt, 1 Section

Royal Indian Artillery

24 Mountain Regt 2 Sections
Regimental HQ

British Infantry

2nd Battalion, West Yorkshire Regt A, B and C Companies, Carrier Platoon, Admin and HQ
2nd Battalion, King's Own Scottish Borderers (less detachments) (part of the time)

Indian Infantry

4th Battalion, 8th Gurkha Rifles, 2 Companies (part of the time)
7th Battalion, 2nd Punjab Regt (part of the time)
3rd Battalion, 4th Bombay Grenadiers, 1 Company

Royal Indian Army Service Corps

2 Supply and Issue Sections
Field Supply and Depot Personnel
20th Mule Company
Motor Transport Company (elements of)
Officers' Shop

Indian Army Ordnance Corps

Ordnance Field Park

Indian Engineers

303rd Field Park Coy
Bridging Train, 1 Section (part of the time)

5th Indian Division

9 Brigade, HQ and B Echelon

7th Indian Division

Headquarters
Rear Headquarters
Signals (Rear)
'Admin Box' HQ
33 Brigade, B Echelon
89 Brigade, B Echelon

Dressing Station

66th Indian Field Ambulance
12 Mobile Surgical Unit
48 Indian Dental Unit
28 Indian Blood Transfusion Unit

TO THE MEMORY OF ALL RANKS
OF
25th DRAGOONS
and other units
in
XV CORPS ARMOURED GROUP
who lost their lives during the
campaign in Arakan, Burma, in 1944
or during the expeditions to Kalaw
and Toungoo in 1945.

Foreword

by Brigadier H.M.H. Ley CBE

The 25th Dragoons were the 'war-formed' regiment parented by the 3rd Carabiniers (Prince of Wales' Dragoon Guards) who were at the outbreak of war stationed in the Punjab, NW India.

The Carabiniers provided a cadre of specially selected officers, WOs, NCOs and men – I believe about 25% of the required strength – and the remainder was drawn from volunteers from other regiments in India (mainly infantry) and from trained drafts and postings from the UK.

The first batch of officers from the UK arrived fitted out by the Cavalry hatter, Herbert Johnson, of Bond Street, with service caps bearing a badge depicting some sort of elephant; for apparently, unknown to us, it was by no means a 'new' regiment, having served at the time of the Peninsular War and disbanded around 1818. However, we had already devised our own new cap badge of crossed cavalry sabres surmounted by a 'xxv' with an appropriate motto – and we kept it!

I joined the Regiment, at the end of a tour as instructor at the Staff College, as 2nd-in-Command. They were undergoing intensive training en route for the Arakan at a place called Ranchi, in Bihar and Orissa, which I can only remember now for the poor quality of the local gin and the enormous blue-bottles which infested the place.

Within a short time we set off for the Arakan. This, in itself, was a formidable operation. We were disguised as a workshops, wearing REME badges. Tank landing craft had to be found to land us on the coast as the existing road and rail facilities would not take medium tanks and we were landed on the east coast of the Bay of Bengal north of Cox's Bazaar and thence special pontoons had to be constructed and bridges built to take us down to the battle front in the Arakan.

While all this was going on we were hidden in the jungle on the coast so that the Jap would be completely taken by surprise at the arrival of so powerful a weapon as the LEE medium tank. The year before a troop or so of Valentine tanks had been used against him without much success, having inadequate fire power.

The Regiment had since late 1941 been commanded by Lt Col H.R.C. Frink (late 4/7 Dragoon Guards), or 'Frinkie' as he was affectionately known throughout the British Cavalry, and was much loved and respected by his new command. No better officer could have been chosen to take over and weld together a new unit formed from such wide and varied elements of the army.

As a result he had a first class outfit to take to war for the first time. Training was excellent and morale high; and they knew they had a weapon that was going to give the Jap a sharp shock.

The fortuitous timing of its arrival, to coincide with the Japanese attempt to outflank XV Corps and to penetrate into India via Cox's Bazaar and Chittagong, turned out, in fact, to be the first turning point in the Burma campaign, to be closely followed by their failure at Imphal where the parent regiment of the 25th played so distinguished a part.

There is no doubt that without the presence and the fire power of the LEE tanks the heroic actions of the other units of the 7th and 5th Indian Divisions in the 'Admin Box' might well have been to no avail and we might have had a very different war on our hands in Burma.

Sometime after the Battle of the Box, I left the Regiment to take up a senior staff appointment and the next year I was appointed to command the Carabiniers, to continue the war in Malaya (which of course never happened). So my armoured war service was with the 25th Dragoons for whom I retain to this day a deep admiration and affection.

It is naturally of great interest to me now to read, through the medium of Tom Grounds' letters home, the view of the tank crew of the operations that I had been through and I hope it will give others the same pleasure.

Burrow, Lancashire H.M.H.L.

Prologue 1941

From a sermon preached by the Reverend Wallace F. Cox, Chaplain to the Forces, in Skipton Parish Church in the West Riding of Yorkshire, on Remembrance Sunday 1941. (As reported in the *Craven Herald and Pioneer*, November 1941.)

We have short memories and I think it is true to say that, in all our secular history, there are only two dates we can remember easily and both of them are in November – November 5th and November 11th. On this second date our thoughts turn to the men who gave their lives during the years 1914-1918 and to the men who have fallen in the present war. 'How are the mighty fallen'. That is true of those men of whom we have been shorn who should have been the light of our generation. Because they loved freedom and honour and because they hated oppression, they gladly gave their lives and the words of my text could apply to each one of them.

This war can be divided into two parts. There is the actual fighting which we must win and, secondly, there is winning the peace. By the sacrifice of the men we are remembering this day, we won the actual fighting in the last war, but we did not win the peace. I believe that, when historians come to write the history of our times, they will say that the peace of 1918 was no peace, and that cruelty, hatred, selfishness, misunderstanding, class war and economic war were continued. How should we prepare ourselves for the winning of the next peace?

I think there are four cardinal virtues that should be practised – wisdom, temperance, fortitude and justice. Temperance we must have in its full meaning, which is that men should have full control of themselves. Fortitude we shall have to practise if we are to endure happiness, and there must be justice, for if there is no justice we can never have a lasting peace. There is no favouritism in justice and there must be no favouritism for class or nation if we want a real peace after the war.

In this way we would pay our debt to those men who have died and when we come to our last hours we should be able to say, 'I have fought the good fight. I have finished the course. I have kept the faith'.

(Padre Cox died on 17th June 1994, aged 81 years, as this book was going to publication.)

Introduction: India

Bengal 1943

Cities paved with bones
And dying hands . . .
Pass them by.
Leave them in their rags.

Who is the microscopic I
Who can defy such death,
Such desolation?

Who am I,
The microscopic I,
In all this desolation and despair?
Eat while I can,
For there are others there,
Hanging from breasts long dried,
Hanging from hope that died.

Tara Ali Baig
Bombay Women's Service

B Squadron, 25th Dragoons,
RAC India Command

(Airmail) 16th August 1943

My Dear Mother and Dad,

Here I am at last on leave in Calcutta. I am with L– B–. We left in a great rush on Saturday midday and arrived yesterday morning. It is eight months since I last had any leave, so it is a marvellous feeling to be free again to do exactly what one likes, and for three weeks too!

As a city I prefer Calcutta to Bombay. (I am referring to the 'show' quarter. The poverty and utter wretchedness of the Indian quarters are much the same.) There are many stretches of parkland or 'maidan' with lakes, both natural and ornamental. You come across these squares quite unexpectedly round corners. The general tone of the architecture, although rather artificial, being brick with a lot of ornamental stucco to make it look like stone, is not so hard as Bombay. It is all European and many of the Government buildings, such as the GPO, are very pretentious, having domes and Grecian columns etc., out of place in India, which has its own architectural tradition . . .

(Sea mail) 24th August 1943

We are staying in a clean, pleasant little hotel. It is in one way more of a hostel for servicemen on leave since most rooms have more than two beds in them. However, there is no one else in our room and we have almost exclusive use of the washing place and shower attached. We are only paying for bed and breakfast so that we do not have to rush back for every meal. There are plenty of European restaurants in Calcutta which manage to provide excellent food despite the severe prevailing shortage. The Chinese restaurants we find the most preferable. They are always scrupulously clean and the food is always good and perfectly cooked.

It is rather difficult walking about the streets at night, as the black-out prevents you seeing the many people who sleep on the pavements, some dying of starvation. You do not want to tread on the bodies of these people who are forced to live and die on the streets.

I went to Evensong at the cathedral on Sunday. It was a good service. There was a strong appeal made by the minister, on behalf of the bishop, for funds for the opening of Relief Food Kitchens in a certain area. It is intended to keep these going for two months at a cost of 15,000 rupees to be contributed by the cathedral congregation. It is a little late because all the Indian charitable organizations opened food centres sometime back and even the Government has, at least, issued orders for the opening of controlled shops. The cathedral canon is taking a party to see the kitchens working, of which I intend to be a member. It will be like going to the zoo to see the animals fed.

Everyday it is said 30 to 60 people are admitted to hospital in a state of collapse due to hunger and 8 or 9 generally die.

Our room overlooks a delightful lake, surrounded by trees and grass, a very pleasant sight to get up for in the morning.

We saw 'Gone with the Wind' last week. I was rather disappointed that such a terrific effort in spectacle should have been wasted on a poor story.

The Bengal Famine of 1943 was now at its height. For a long time the Government had refused officially to recognize its existence. Eventually *The Statesman*, the main English language newspaper of Calcutta, published reports and photos because it was simply impossible to ignore it any more. This was the reason the church had not, until then, opened a public appeal of any sort.

Estimates of the number who died in the famine vary greatly. The Famine Enquiry Commission concluded that one and a half million deaths occurred as a result of the famine and the epidemics that followed in its train. Philip Ziegler, Lord Mountbatten's biographer, put the figure at two million and Indian historians speak of three to three and a half million. Exact figures would be impossible because of the movement of population and the haphazardness of death.

St Paul's Cathedral, Calcutta, is ideally situated on the green maidan to the east of Chowringhee. It was completed in 1847 and is in the early Victorian Gothic style. As with many other British buildings in India, the architect was a military engineer. Nevertheless, I remember thinking at the time, it was a fine and beautiful building, though the association of British Victorian architecture with Christianity in India might have become something of a liability by then.

Two months or so later Cecil Beaton was in Calcutta as a war photographer. He wrote of his experience at the end of the war:

> Today Calcutta, so recently recovered from famine, is thriving. Fortunes are being made. It is now a sort of oriental Clapham Junction. Air commodores, generals and celebrities of every kind and race spend the night at one of the overcrowded hotels. Most of the men of the 14th Army spend their leave here. In their bush-hats and shorts they crowd out the hostels, canteens, cinemas, cafes, milk-bars and 'attractions' along Chowringhee. Calcutta provides plenty of noise; the tick-ticking and thunder-rolling of the trams, the honking of taxis – for Sikhs always drive with the horn – the bells of the rickshaws and the incessant caw-cawing of the crows which circle above.

(Sea mail) 28th August 1943

Here is one more letter from Calcutta, 'City of Palaces'. There are just another six days before we have to return to the regiment.

We have made several Indian friends. One of them invited us to his house the other day. It was actually a small lodging at the top of a rather cramped building. After going through a number of narrow winding passages and up a narrow spiral staircase, experiencing a great variety of smells, we eventually came upon a small clean apartment. Being on the top floor it had all the light and fresh air. There was, of course, no furniture and we were invited to sit down on some linoleum mats spread on the floor. We met his wife and little boy. He insisted on giving us a meal cooked by his wife. It consisted of a pile of rice with small quantities of two different curries and juice of pulse and mango, served on a plate.

We ate this in correct Indian fashion, with our fingers, washing our hands afterwards. The flavour and taste were far from European dishes. They were poor people compared to English standards but many people in India have no standard of living at all. Had I been to the house of anyone of a higher class, I should have received a false impression. Though there was little decoration in the room, everything was very neatly kept. Our host was an educated man and could speak English fairly well. Had it been otherwise, conversation would have been impossible as neither of us could speak Hindi or Bengali.

Several times he has insisted on taking us into Indian sweet shops and making us partake of a few of the many different types of Indian sweetmeats. Most of these are round balls, the shape of a golf ball, although some are elongated. They vary in colour. They have the most exotic and extraordinary flavours, each one different from the last. Our friend told us that there are a hundred or more different kinds. At weddings guests eat large numbers of these sweetmeats and, not infrequently, suffer afterwards! We found them heavy and slow to digest; they took away our appetites for sometime afterwards.

Our friend comes to the hotel for breakfast with us some mornings, when we make him struggle with a knife and fork and fried eggs. Through him we have come to meet a number of other Indians, including an assistant editor of an important paper in Calcutta. Most of them are deeply concerned about the political situation in India and we have learnt a good deal about it. They are all very friendly and treat us as very honourable guests.

One thing I notice is their exuberant sense of humour. You can never tell when it is going to bubble over and their faces change to a broad smile. Also their complete freedom from bitterness towards the British in general or to us in particular, although some of them have been in prison for their principles . . .

British soldiers were not encouraged to mix with Indians, especially political ones, neither were they forbidden to do so. Absolutely nothing was done to interest the thousands of British troops in the country to which they had come or its people, let alone to suggest that decent behaviour be observed towards them. The police had a network of agents who kept an eye on active politicians (those who were not already in prison). If a British soldier was seen associating with an 'undesirable element' he might be reported to his unit. As for us, we were in India to fight the Japs, we were not breaking the rules and it was well understood that we could talk of nothing pertaining to ourselves or military matters.

The 'important paper' in Calcutta mentioned in the above letter was probably the *Amrita Bazaar Patrika*. It was an English-language paper edited from the nationalist view-point. The Government imposed censorship of the press in the interests of the war but this was applied to items about the famine which was greatly resented. The *Patrika* would leave blank spaces marked 'censored' which it claimed would have been filled by news items about the famine which it was not allowed to publish.

Cecil Beaton also paid a visit to a residential apartment in a neighbourhood of modern honeycomb tenement buildings that seemed so unsuitable for the climate of India. He visited the house of an Indian writer and was struck by its peaceful beauty and simplicity. Transparent dhotis and saris, freshly laundered, were hanging from the landings and balcony; the golden ewers sparkled in the washroom; the stark almost empty bedroom with the children asleep was innocent of all the unnecessary and stuffy impedimenta of a similar room in the Western world. Here were no cluttered drawers, here were the essentials alone; and yet, when he wanted a tripod, the writer was able to produce it.

He also visited some factories:

> In a gun and shell factory, where supplies are made for the war in Burma, the atmosphere is little different from that in any such factory throughout England: it is as clean, no more no less, the manager as impersonal; but the Indian workers seem more suited to precise and continuous tasks than workers of a more volatile and restless temperament. One 16 year old boy was at work planing and filing a small part of a gun. The delicacy and sympathy of his hands, the coolness of his gestures and the meek intensity with which he laboured, were very touching to watch.
>
> The employees here are given periodic propaganda talks, but few of them have any hatred for the Japs or any real idea about the war. Most of them are working because they are paid good money. As workers they do what they are told with prodigious powers of application.

In another huge factory, in the heart of Calcutta, precision instruments, optical lenses, telescopes and gun-sights are made. Some of those employed here are fourth-generation employees, descendants of those who were associated with the firm since its inception.

Apart from some visits to the cinema, we found an amateur British company putting on performances of Bernard Shaw's 'The Doctor's Dilemma'. It was well done and a nice reminder of civilisation.

On another occasion we visited the home of an Indian musician. How this came about I cannot remember. He was a professional who sung and played on All-India radio. He sang for us, accompanying himself on a short keyboard with one hand, producing a sound from a small cluster of notes which usually elicits the term 'whining' from an inexperienced European. As I listened to the music (and it may have been a modern song), it seemed to come from many centuries ago, perhaps thousands of years, an ancient sound from the depths of human civilisation.

(Airmail) 1st September 1943

My Dear Auntie Gwen and Auntie Lillian,

I am writing to you both while on 3 weeks leave in Calcutta. It is almost over now and we are not looking forward to returning to camp. We are continually being told to cut down our kit to the minimum and I am finding it increasingly difficult to keep even a few books with me. So I hope you will not mind if I ask you not to send any more.

Cheerio and all my love.

(Airmail) 2nd September 1943

My Dear Mother and Dad,

This is my last day in Calcutta. We start on our return journey tomorrow and shall be in camp by Saturday afternoon. It has been three weeks of blessed freedom. Naturally none of your letters have been sent on from camp, so there should be quite a pile awaiting my return.

I am getting such a pile of books that I am finding it increasingly difficult to look after them. We have to carry all our kit wherever we go now, whether it be on leave or to hospital or on a course. We have also been told to get rid of all unnecessary kit.

In view of the widespread famine here I sent a subscription of 30 rupees to the cathedral fund towards the maintenance of relief food kitchens.

Cheerio for the moment.

While L– B– and I were wallowing in our leave in Calcutta, at another level Admiral Lord Louis Mountbatten accompanied the Prime Minister Winston Churchill and the other chiefs of staff to the Allied Conference in Quebec. There Churchill offered Mountbatten the job of Supreme Allied Commander South East Asia. Lord Louis asked for 24 hours to think it over and then accepted.

The Japanese at this time occupied almost the whole of South East Asia including Burma up to its frontier with India. As yet they had not suffered any serious defeat on any front. Our morale was said to be low because we were still smarting from the humiliation of our defeat and evacuation of Burma in 1942. No doubt Churchill felt that Mountbatten's powers of decision together with his flamboyant personality and ability to get on with people would revitalize the whole situation. There was also the implication which, as will be seen, was not altogether followed through that, with the new appointment, more equipment would be made available.

Military secrecy being what it was, I could not tell my parents what we were doing in the Regiment. In fact, in the early days of August, some 40 General Lee M3 medium tanks had reached the Regiment, all Stuarts being returned. We had begun training on these tanks fairly hard, as is implied by my remark about working all Saturdays and some Sundays in my next letter.

(Airmail) 12th September 1943

This is my first letter since I returned to camp. There was quite a large pile of mail waiting for me on my return which I will now endeavour to answer.

The cutting about Sir Gerald Wollaston and the concert programme were very interesting. I am glad to hear you enjoyed the music. I expect Mrs Holmes and the Van Somerons had a hand in getting up the concert. I had a letter from David Gilling in which he said that the Holmes were back in Hoddesdon. If John West is stationed in Calcutta, he would hardly require leave very badly, being within easy range of all that India's 'City of Palaces' can provide. If I ever get the chance I shall, of course, like Richard Jones go to Kashmir, but the journey takes rather a hole out of the leave unless you are stationed not too far away.

My letters will get scarce and less I am afraid. We work all day Saturdays now and one Sunday per month (if no other jobs turn up!).

Love.

(Airmail) 24th September 1943

I had already heard from Joyce of MacDonald being a POW. She is going to send me his address as soon as possible.

Thank you for sending on copies of the Beveridge Report. I have seen so many articles about it in the papers and now the Army propaganda dept have started sending round pamphlets about it, so I wanted to get the 'pukka dope'.

Why is Dr West against a state medical service? It is very difficult to find another answer to the problem.

I hope Dad got away to Llandeilo and enjoyed his holiday and came home with the coveted salmon. I also hope you will get away Mother, if only for a few days.

On Sunday, the day after tomorrow, the Bishop is visiting the camp to consecrate our new church. After the war, when the military have gone, it will be used as a missionary church.

(Airmail) 2nd October 1943

Last Sunday our church was consecrated and dedicated to St Peter by the Bishop. It had been built by the Garrison Engineer, for the most part, free of charge I understand. In fact, practically all the brick and cement work and general construction were carried out by Indian labour with an Indian contractor supervising. The detailed painting of the altar and the making of the altar ornaments were done by one of the regimental carpenters, together with some other small jobs.

This is not to say that the Padre did not have to bear most of the responsibility and anxiety. There were several hitches. On one occasion, when the Padre was on leave in Calcutta, the contractor was ill and the workmen were not paid on time, so they went on strike. As they were paid an average of 8 annas per day (about 9d) this was not surprising. However, as soon as the pay turned up they went back to work. It was interesting to know that they were sufficiently organized to be able to strike.

The day of consecration had eventually to be postponed for a week. On the very morning the doors did not turn up until half-an-hour before the service was due to begin. As you will see from the service sheet, these form a necessary part of the ceremony. Unfortunately the roof had to be thatched but it will probably be tiled later.

I sang bass in the choir. The ceremony went very well. The Bishop sprinkled holy water with a mango branch on the walls. John (Bradberry) was an acolyte and carried the holy water. The B knocked on the doors (see service sheet) and from inside Keith (Fox) made the response. The singing had to be unaccompanied as we had no piano or harmonium. Nevertheless it went quite well.

The entry of the Soviet Union into the war against Germany seems to have let loose a whole field of literature, art and music. A new composer has come into the limelight, Shostakovich, whose music is played at the Proms and recorded by HMV, not to mention the flood of Soviet literature which has overflowed even into Indian bookshops.

* * *

On 29th September the whole Regiment with tanks moved to the Lohardaga area for a 10 day Scheme or Exercise. The tanks, which were American, required a 7 man crew consisting of Driver, Wireless Operator, 75mm Gunner and Loader in the hull and a 37mm Gunner and Loader together with the Tank Commander in the turret. Maximum speed was about 25 mph and weight about 27 tons. Armour was from ½ inch to 2 inches thick. A machine-gun was mounted co-axially with the 37mm gun in the turret.

The No 19 wireless set consisted of two quite separate transmitter/receivers in the same chassis called A and B sets. The A set was used for communication at squadron level whilst the B set operated on very high frequency for short distances between the three tanks of a single troop. The latter was considered very secure (secret) because the signals travelled only a short distance over land. Both Operator and Tank Commander could talk and receive on these two frequencies by the operation of switches on the set. If the Commander was on one net, the Operator had to be on the other.

In theory, every member of a crew was to be capable of doing the jobs of all the others but, in practice, people were lucky to be trained-up on two jobs. Trades were Driver/Mechanic, Driver/Operator and Gunner/Operator. Members of a crew were each responsible for maintenance of their own pieces of equipment.

Intercommunication amongst the crew was run through the wireless, all members having head-sets and microphones. Many a rude remark, intended solely for the benefit of the crew, was broadcast to the whole squadron, inviting a sharp and probably ribald reply from Control Station (the squadron leader).

We were still stationed at Ratu, near Ranchi, in the province of Bihar and Orissa, together with other components of XVth Corps, commanded by Lt Gen Christison. The place was still as unpleasant as ever and Major O.C. Horne described it as 'a ghastly

FORM OF SERVICE

FOR

The Consecration of the Church of St. Peter, RATU
in the Lines of the 25th Dragoons R. A. C.

(By kind permission of Lt. Col. H. R. C. FRINK.)

By THE BISHOP of Chota Nagpur

ON

Sunday 26th September 1943

AT

9.30 a. m.

The Bishop accompanied by the Chaplain shall proceed to the West End of the Church

The Commanding Officer shall then request the Bishop to dedicate the Church.

Reverend Father in God, I request you to dedicate this Church which we have build for the glory of God and the service of His people.

After the Bishop has signified his consent, a procession will be formed which will proceed round the Church. During the circuit Hymn 162 'We love the place, O God' shall be sung.

On arrival at the West door the Bishop shall say :—

We beseech Thee O Lord, graciously enter Thy House, within the hearts of Thy faithful people establish for Thyself an everlasting habitation, that they may be glorified by the Indwelling of Him, by Whose building we live: Through Jesus Christ Our Lord Amen.

The Bishop shall then knock on the door of the Church with his staff and say :—

Bishop. Lift up your heads, O ye gates, and be ye lift up, ye everlasting doors, and the King of Glory shall come in.

Response. (from within) Who is the King of Glory ?

Bishop. It is the Lord strong and mighty, even the Lord mighty in battle.

The door shall then be opened and the Bishop shall make the sign of the Cross with his staff on the threshold and with his thumb on the door-post.

The Bishop and the Congregation shall then enter the Church. On entering, the Bishop shall say :—

Peace be to this House...from God our heavenly Father, amen.
Peace be to this House...from Christ who is our Peace, amen.
Peace be to this House...from the Holy Ghost the Comforter, amen.

As the people enter they shall sing Hymn 24
'Come, Holy Ghost, our souls inspire'

The Hymn being ended the Bishop standing at the chancel steps shall say:—

Lord, have mercy upon us.
Christ, have mercy upon us.
Lord, have mercy upon us.

V. Our help is in the Name of the Lord.
R. Who hath made Heaven and Earth.
V. Blessed be the Name of the Lord.
R. Henceforth world without end.
V. Lord, hear our prayer.
R. And let our cry come unto Thee.
V. The Lord be with you.
R. And with thy spirit.

Let us pray.

O God, Who hallowest places dedicated to Thy Name, pour Thy Grace, we beseech Thee, upon this House of Prayer, sanctify and bless it that all who call upon Thee here may feel the comfort of Thy gracious mercy and protection, through Jesus Christ, Thy Son, O Lord, amen

O God of all sanctification, Omnipotent Spirit, whose loving kindness never faileth, who rulest both in Heaven and in Earth, keeping mercy for Thy people who walk before the presence of Thy glory: Hear the prayers of Thy servants, that Thine Eyes may be upon this building day and night: Graciously accept this House which we set apart to Thy honour and glory and in memory of Thy servant, St. Peter, and illumine and brighten it with Thine own glory. Favourably receive every soul who comes in humility and love to worship here. For the glory of Thy holy and ever blessed Name and of Thy mighty and exalted arm, protect, hear and everlastingly keep and defend all who make their prayer unto Thee in this place, that they abiding in peace and ever rejoicing in Thy true religion may hold fast the faith, and being endued with heavenly virtues, may draw the Gentiles to believe in Thee: Through Jesus Christ our Lord, Who with Thee and the Holy Ghost liveth and reigneth one God world without end, amen

The Bishop shall then ascend to the altar while Hymn 143

'The King of Love my Shepherd is' is sung. After which he shall say two prayers, the second of which will be preceded by the following versicles and responses.

V. Peace be with you.
R. And with thy spirit.
V. Lift up your hearts.
R. We lift them up unto the Lord.
V. Let us give thanks unto our Lord God.
R. It is meet and right so to do.

The Bishop shall then declare the Church to be duly dedicated to the service of God and set apart from common uses.

Then shall the ornaments be placed on the altar and the Bishop shall bless them.

Then shall follow the sermon after which shall be sung Hymn 140. 'The Church's one foundation'

After the Hymn the Bishop shall recite the Collect of St. Peter to whose honour the Church is dedicated and shall bless the congregation.

The Service of Dedication will be followed by celebration of the Holy Communion at which Revelation 21 verses 2 to 5 shall be read as the Epistle and St. Matthew 21 verses 12 to 16 as the Gospel.

---

place, remembered for its evil-tasting Indian gin and giant bluebottles'. Personally I found the place bad enough without drinking the gin, though I don't remember any of the stuff coming my way!

I remember Ranchi for the incredible number of ants who overnight built tiny mud tunnels up the posts of the bashas in which we lived, the legs of the charpoys on which we slept and our kit bags. If part of the tunnel was knocked away, it revealed two processions of ants, one moving upwards with materials to extend the tunnel and the other downwards making the return journey. They discovered a tiny hole in my kit bag and took their tunnel through it, so my clothes got infested with ants and mud.

It was perhaps more depressing than it might have been in that the monsoon was in full flood for a lot of the time we were there. The roofs of the bashas were thatched with dried palm leaves which, sooner or later, let the rain in and nothing could be fully dried out for weeks.

(Airmail) 13th October 1943

Since my last AML of the 2nd Oct, I have received yours of Sept 22nd. As you say, I think newspapers and magazines are the best things to send. They are always appreciated and can be passed on easily. Send anything from the *Times* to the *Daily Worker*.

It was hardly to be expected that the Bengal famine would not eventually appear in the English papers. But judging from Mr Amory's speech in the parliamentary debate on the subject, you are given a different view of the situation to the one I formed from what I saw and heard and read in Calcutta. My letter to Aunts L and G was censored apparently. I mentioned the famine but, as far as I remember, in quite mild terms.

By the way, we are only allowed to send one of these AMLs each week, added to which we have not been issued with any for the last few weeks. There is no limitation on airgraphs, sea mail, etc.

(Airgraph) 15th October 1943

We have been out on a Scheme for the past fortnight and that must be my excuse for not writing last weekend.

I have had a letter from (Sister) Margaret Churchill. She is spending a leave on a houseboat in Kashmir and enjoying it.

* * *

Wednesday 6th October 1943
We took off at 06.30 at first light of dawn, and landed at 06.45 with a burnt-out solenoid in the variable pitch gear of one of our propellers. It took 2 hours to mend and when we left at 09.30 we realized we were due to land in Karachi in the dark.

I could not help getting a certain thrill at the moment when we crossed the coast of India, to feel that it had fallen to me to be the outward and visible symbol of the British Empire's intention to return to the attack in Asia and regain our lost empire.

We landed in the dark at 20.30 and were met by a vast concourse of officers. The whole party was put up in the brand-new Governor's house at Karachi, where our host was Sir Hugh Dow, Governor of the newly-created Sind province.

(Mountbatten: Diary 1943-1946)

So Lord Louis Mountbatten made his entry into India and took up the Supreme Command of South-East Asia. His headquarters were in Delhi. No time was wasted. A round of interviews and conferences began immediately. He then flew off over the 'Hump' (the eastern end of the Himalayas in North Burma) to see Generalissimo and Madame Chiang Kai-shek at Chungking. The Generalissimo was not at all an easy man to deal with and the situation in China was complicated. Part of it was occupied by the Japanese, part was governed by Chiang Kai-shek and yet another part, in the north, was under Mao-Tse-Tung and the Communists.

The troops under Mountbatten's command were Indian, British, Gurkha, African, Australian, Burmese, French, Dutch and, last but not least, American and Chinese. With hindsight it is difficult to think of any other figure who could have filled the position. With his energy and enthusiasm, his quick thinking and decisiveness, his patience and meticulous attention to detail, his modern outlook and, with it all, his charm (which, at any rate for the time being, disarmed his critics) he was able to oil the differences of national temperament and personal ambition and ensure they worked together towards the great objective.

(Airmail) 25th October 1943

I am writing this whilst in hospital with a slight attack of jaundice. It is quite prevalent in our particular district apparently, but I have not got it very severely. I am not nearly so yellow as some of the people in this ward. I hope to be out fairly shortly.

I have noticed in the paper recently that London has had several alerts. I hope the planes do not come near Broxbourne and keep you awake at nights as they did once upon a time.

I have just had a visit from what seemed like half the unit. Actually it was John, Cliff, Jim, Frank Hill and the Padre. They had all been to the cathedral (which is next to the hospital) to see Cliff confirmed. It takes some moral courage to do these things in the Army. It was good to see them all again, even if only for a few hurried minutes.

All the things you cook sound very good. I agree with Dad in preferring your 'failures' to the shop cakes. Any failure of yours would be like a heavenly dish from the gods compared with what we generally get.

Towards the end of October we had been firing the tank guns on the ranges. It was, of course, stiflingly hot inside the tank and the air full of dust and cordite fumes. During an interval in the firing one of the crew in the turret passed me some cheese and bully beef wedged between two hunks of bread – this was 'lunch' – but the mere smell of it made me feel sick. Shortly afterwards I realized I had the usual symptom of jaundice (brown urine) and through the immediate efforts of Sergeant 'Taff' Poole was whisked to hospital in Ranchi. For a few days I could eat nothing and do nothing, but I was not too ill to appreciate the luxury of lying on clean sheets in a cool and clean ward (not to mention the attentions of the female nursing staff!).

(Sea mail) 1st November 1943

I am still in hospital, so I decided to use the time by writing another sea mail after rather a long interval. The jaundice is taking a little longer to clear off than I had expected. The cure seems to be chiefly in the diet. I am not allowed to eat fats, but must consume as much sugar as possible, to get the liver working properly again. Merely eating sugar was not enough apparently, so I am having injections of insulin twice a day as well. In myself I feel very well and want to get up. I have completely regained my appetite and am really ravenous for meals.

There have been quite a number of cases of jaundice (medical name 'infective hepatitis') in our regiment and round the camp district. I think bad diet was a contributory cause. We had been out on longish training schemes and had had to live on tinned food a great deal – bully beef mostly with potatoes and bread – great shortage of milk and sugar. I had not seen any green vegetables or eggs for months, impossible to get any fresh fruit. I told you that in camp we paid 2 rupees a month each towards the purchase of extra food, but eventually there was such an outcry against this that it was stopped. People complained that they were not getting anything for their money. It was extremely difficult for the people responsible to buy food, partly because of the scarcity and partly due to . . . (censored) . . . which . . . (censored) . . . in the local district and closed the market to us. For the last few months we have worked most Saturdays and Sundays.

(Sea mail) 3rd November 1943

I am glad to see that all my sea mail is getting through safely, although one or two AMLs seem to get lost sometimes. I have just received the three copies of the Beveridge Report. Thanks so much for sending them. I shall have a chance during the two or three days more I shall be in hospital to study the report. I know of several people who will like to have the other two copies.

I got up yesterday for four hours for the first time and am up for half-a-day today. I feel none the worse for it. I hope to be out of hospital in a few days.

I was surprised to hear that the Nursing Association nearly went bankrupt. It is extraordinary that it should be possible for an organization that does such necessary work to get into such a state.

The church out here is breaking away from its rut. The Bishop of Dornakal (the first and only Indian bishop so far) has a church built in the Indian style, where the services are entirely Indian (for instance, the Te Deum is sung to an Indian melody).

The Nursing Association was the charitable association which maintained the services of the District Nurse in those days. My mother used to collect subscriptions and donations. Due to the absence of so many people in the services and the shortage of money, she presumably found it extremely hard going.

* * *

In hospital the paper wallah used to come round the wards every morning. I took *The Hindu*, a 'quality' English language Indian newspaper. It was a large paper published for the educated Indian middle class and I had all day to read it and got a fair idea of Indian politics and political attitudes.

Every day a senior medical officer made the rounds and asked, 'How are you?' The scheduled answer was, 'Very well, sir' or similar. One day, not feeling too good, I said so. 'WHY, WHAT'S THE MATTER?!' was the explosive reaction. Ever afterwards I was always, 'Very well, Sir.'

One day an ENSA show was staged in the ward. The only turn that I actually remember was that of a well-known radio comedian. His act was to conjure up a group of small children by imitating their voices. The smallest one, Horace, was only just learning to talk and the noises he made were incomprehensible to everyone except his slightly older sister who had to translate for him, 'Horace says . . .' I think everyone who was not too ill enjoyed the show without any sophisticated inhibitions – a reminder of home in the otherwise deadly life of the British soldier in India.

It was a large ward in which all the patients had jaundice of one sort or another. Some had been there for a long time, some perhaps were never to come out alive. We all looked a bit like Dracula with our eye-balls turned an intense yellow. Until I was discharged I had insulin injections twice a day. These became rather irritating towards the end, partly because I was passed from the practised nurses to the less experienced medical orderlies, who tended to take pot-shot jabs which might or might not be successful.

I was lucky to have several books to fill in the time when I was feeling better. I remember Tolstoy's 'Resurrection' and some little-known plays of Bernard Shaw, including 'The Millionairess' and also a satiric novel by C.E. Montague about the Press.

About this time Cecil Beaton was in Delhi and afterwards wrote:

> I was allowed into the war-room of the SEAC. The Supreme Commander, Admiral Lord Louis Mountbatten, who had arrived in this theatre not long before seemed, as yet, unaffected by the climate. 'We mustn't let it be a damper on effort – we've got to galvanize everyone, got to teach 'em to hustle,' he said – and he appeared to have impregnated his immediate entourage with his own robust enthusiasm. In spite of all the difficulties he had encountered, no glaze of disappointment was visible in his eyes. They twinkled with the delight of a boy who has just been given a Meccano for Christmas – which incidentally was just about all he had been given.

One of the reasons for the appointment of Admiral Mountbatten to be the Supremo of SEAC was the intention to stage a landing on the Burma coast and to recapture the Andamen Islands. His naval training and his experience as Chief of Combined Operations in Europe made him the man for the job, quite apart from his other qualities. However, Churchill, Roosevelt and Stalin met in Teheran late in 1943. Stalin promised to enter the war against Japan if all Anglo American efforts were directed first to defeating Germany. Churchill and Roosevelt accepted this condition and as a result all the resources needed for sea operations in SE Asia were withdrawn.

Lt Gen William Slim, commanding XIVth Army, wrote afterwards:

> As our wider visions of amphibious operations on the Arakan coast faded, with the withdrawal of the resources necessary for them, we were thrown back on our original plans . . . a limited advance down the Mayu peninsular to secure, first, the tiny port of Maungdaw and then the road running from it, through the central spine of the Mayu Range, to Buthidaung in the valley of the Kalapanzin river. Having got there we could, by using the Naf river and Maungdaw, supply our forward formations in Arakan largely by sea, while the road would give us essential lateral communications to support forces on the east of the Range.
>
> The intention was to advance with two divisions (5th and 7th Indian Divisions), not only on both sides of the Mayu Range, but along its spine as well, while the 81st West African Division, moving down the Kaladan Valley well to the east, would provide a flank guard and would, I hoped, be in its turn a threat to the Japanese flank and their west-to-east communications.
>
> (Slim: Defeat into Victory)

* * *

(Sea mail) 9th November 1943

As I am still in hospital, I thought I would write you one more sea mail before I am discharged (which happens tomorrow morning). I have had no more mail from you for over a week. That is because they are holding it back at the Regiment, expecting me back anytime.

As you have probably realized by now, India is veiled in a mist of censorship, and whatever light is allowed to penetrate the gloom and reach the outer world has been carefully examined beforehand. For instance, practically all newspapers which do not express the orthodox government view may not be exported, neither may they be sold to the troops (unless of course you happen to be on leave, say in Calcutta and able to buy them in the streets). Even *The Statesman*, a most respectable paper, read by most European residents in the Bengal-Bihar area, was stopped coming to the Regiment. Similar restrictions, of course, apply to books.

Referring to the Bengal famine, the letter goes on:

Several months ago, I know, the men of the RAF were working with the local organizations in Chittagong to relieve some of the distress. Things were far worse in Chittagong than in Calcutta. Also in Madras the Army has been co-operating with the authorities in combating the floods. But the famine has got to such a colossal stage, and is bringing more and more disease in its train (malaria and cholera), that it will take a huge effort to conquer it. Medical supplies are needed almost as much as food.

My persistent references to the famine now seem to have been entirely justified. Mountbatten has a note in his diary for the 24th October that he went to see the Viceroy, Lord Wavell, for a long talk. He ends by saying:

'I am glad to hear from him that he intends to tackle the famine problem personally and is going to tour the famine areas at once.'

(Sea mail) 16th November 1943

My Dear Mother and Dad,

I have rejoined the Regiment now after my spell in hospital. I have a week excused of all duties followed by a week on light duties . . . This is instead of going to a Convalescent Depot which is the more usual procedure.

Up to the present I have been keeping all your letters to me but I have decided that I shall have to throw them away now as we have to cut down our kit to the minimum. I hope you will not mind.

On the last Sunday I was in hospital Mr Wilson, the chaplain, invited me to tea at his bungalow that afternoon and a 'friend'. So I asked another fellow who was in my ward (also in the Regiment) to come and we got permission from the MO who was most amused over it. As it happened, Mr Wilson was called away to take a funeral just as we arrived and we were entertained by a bishop for tea. He had been in Burma and was, I think, the Bishop of Rangoon. Later a Mr Smart arrived who had occupied a fairly important position in the Burmese Government and Mr Wilson (also from Burma) returned from the funeral. The Bishop had just returned from an extensive tour of America, so all round we had an interesting afternoon. Apart from the Padre at Risalpur, it is the first time a white civilian out here has asked me to his private house.

This incident of the Bishop gave rise to an amusing sequel. My mother, not averse to name-dropping, informed some friends, whose daughter had been sent on a 'passage to India' to acquire a suitable husband. The trip had been entirely successful and she had married a tea-planter in Burma and they knew the Bishop. However, they did not approve of him – much too friendly with the 'natives'.

I remember nothing of the conversation at the tea-party, only sitting under the trees in an Indian-English garden in our blue military hospital pyjamas, afternoon tea being brought out, the temperature warm and the dappled sunlight filtering through the branches. The war could not have been farther away.

1
Journey to the Jungle

Free from the chains that weigh the bows down,
Loose from the refuse that drags a blunted keel,
Clear decks for action! With steam and sail
Escape the dockside grasp.

Then we shall climb among the cliffs and breathe
Fresh winds fanned by the passing stars,
And chart new courses for the ships we've dreamed
To ride the sky-deep seas.

from 'Ships'
by Clive Branson
(25th Dragoons)

Lt Gen Slim had made his plans:

> I was determined that this time the *main* advance should have adequate armoured support. I gave Col 'Atte' Persse of the Indian Armoured Corps an assignment. I told him that, whatever else happened, he was to see that a complete regiment of Lee-Grant medium tanks, the 25th Dragoons from Ranchi with the necessary maintenance, was to be ready in November to go forward with the leading infantry. He had my permission to use my name, to send whatever signals he liked to whom he liked, and was to report to me only when the job was done.

During August, September and October, Col Persse with some 25th Dragoons officers made a reconnaissance of the forward areas in Arakan. A 'Hide Area', south of the Reju Khal river, was decided on and several square miles were declared a prohibited area and all villages were cleared.

On 23rd October, two days before I went into hospital, the commanding officer, Lt Col H.R.C. Frink (known as 'Frinkie'), had left Ranchi by road for Calcutta. He first spent four days between XIVth Army HQ and the docks. Loading trials were held in the Hooghly river in case the landing-craft coming from the Mediterranean did not arrive in time.

On 31st October Col Frink left by air for Chittagong and eventually reached Reju Khal in the evening. He inspected the proposed landing beach for the tanks and assembly area. He went forward to 7th Indian Division and met the KOSBs and the Gurkhas in the front line and spent a day climbing Point 1749 in the Mayu Range of hills which overlooked the whole area including the Japanese positions. He was able to see the difficulties of operating tanks in this area of hills and thick jungle. The post on the top of Point 1749 was raided by the enemy soon after he came down but it held out. He made detailed reconnaissance of the KOSB position and the Gurkha position, returning eventually to 7th Division HQ.

He ended with a visit to 5th Indian Division HQ, where the commander gave him a rough outline of his plan, but Col Frink added, 'Corps have yet to come up with theirs.' His general opinion was that, despite the far from ideal conditions, much of the area was workable for tanks and would allow us to give good fire support to the infantry. We had to accept the chance of anti-tank guns.

254 Indian Tank Brigade issued a Movement Order in October, providing for the movement of the tanks and 'soft' vehicles to Calcutta from Ranchi.

Late in October, 'A' Squadron tanks were transported by train to Calcutta and arrived on the 30th October to undergo trials for waterproofing in a special workshop in the docks area.

On 2nd November thirty-four tanks left Ratu on tank transporters for Barkhakana. These consisted of fifteen from 'B' Squadron, fifteen from 'C' Squadron and four from RHQ. At the same time Lt Vaughan also left for Barkhakana with ten men and ninety-five tons of ammunition. The following day Scout Troop, consisting of twelve carriers, left under Lt Somerville. The next day the 'soft' vehicle group, which included all echelon vehicles and 320 men, left by road for Asonol Staging Camp. By 8th November it was possible for the echelon vehicles to be loaded on the SS *Empire Ranee* at Calcutta docks. The rest of the 'soft' group embarked the following day on HMT *Nevasa* at No 4 Garden Reach Jetty, Calcutta and sailed the next day.

On 11th November the carriers of Scout Troop were loaded onto the SS *Jalavera* and the following day the personnel embarked on the SS *Ethiopia*.

Sgt Bill Nicholson of HQ Squadron describes the journey as follows:

> For this tedious two-day journey to Calcutta, my troop of scout cars was detailed to marshal and escort the long convoy of trucks. It was our practice to go ahead of the convoy to clear the way and on the second day, two of our cars had gone ahead and 'brewed-up' as usual. Unfortunately, the paraffin stove exploded and Eric Kershaw was badly burned, so I sent my driver, Taffy Reeves, with Eric back down the convoy as fast as possible to contact the MO. When Taffy returned the front of the vehicle was covered with skin and blood and it appeared that, when speeding down the convoy, a bullock-cart driver had pulled out between two of our trucks and collided with the scout car. There was the usual enquiry but the matter was 'settled out of court' by an arrangement to reimburse the bullock-cart driver with an amount of 70 rupees. The convoy eventually arrived at Calcutta and our 'soft' vehicles were parked in a sports field.

Having been discharged from hospital on the 10th November, I arrived back at the regiment in the middle of this packing-up. In view of the many hints we had previously received, some of which I had put in my letters, this was not surprising. The whole move was 'top secret'. The tanks were taken by transporter, camouflaged, to Calcutta for waterproofing. As the Royal Armoured Corps was the only corps in the British Army to wear black berets, these had to be put away and we were all issued with khaki forage caps. Our cap badges and all regimental insignia were hidden away and we became the 21st Advance Base Workshops of the Royal Electrical and Mechanical Engineers.

I remember very little of the move itself. After we arrived in Calcutta, twenty-seven Lee tanks were received from the 26th Hussars, thus giving us a reserve, together with twenty-six men, including five new officers, also from the Hussars as they were disbanded at that time.

Meanwhile the echelon vehicles, the Scout Troop and personnel had all landed at Chittagong and proceeded to the 'Deception Camp', five miles from the proposed 'Hide' at Reju Khal. They were in fact the advance party.

Bill Nicholson describes it:

The 'soft' vehicles and crews were now ordered to move from Calcutta so we took the vehicles down to the docks early one morning, only to find there was no dock labour in sight. The Jap airforce had made one of its infrequent raids on Calcutta the previous night frightening all the coolies and dockhands, who then disappeared from the city. It was then decided that we should attempt to load the vehicles on to the ships ourselves and our Tech Adjutant Capt, 'Pidgey' Winters, with some members of his staff, went aboard and operated the winches and we loaded the vehicles, in net-cages, and stacked them in the holds without any mishaps. The ships sailed across the Bay of Bengal and, when we landed at the dilapidated port of Chittagong, we then unloaded our vehicles and moved off in convoy across the Bawli Bridge towards Cox's Bazaar on the frontier of Burma by the coast. We pitched our scout cars and trucks at dead of night in the thick jungle and remained there with instructions not to show lights or to make any noise as we had Japs for neighbours. This was a very tricky operation to drive through tracks in the jungle on sidelights, but luckily there were no mishaps worth reporting.

The next day, after finding our bearings and checking all the vehicles, we settled in and cleared the undergrowth. Then we started to fell trees about a foot in diameter with which we made rough tracks through the jungle to the beach and made harbours under the trees for use by the tanks which were to arrive later in a sea-borne operation. Our few days here were very busy but we did manage to spend the odd hour lazing on the beach and swimming in the shark-infested sea. One fellow, Willesden, whose home was in Mapperley, Nottingham, had a stingray in his foot and had to be rushed in a jeep to the casualty clearing station. However, we were prepared for the landing of the tanks and had the support of some infantry units on our flanks.

The Japanese air-raid on Calcutta was remembered by H. Munro Watt of the RAF, stationed at the RAF Base Camp in Lower Circular Road, Calcutta 1942/43:

The Japs launched a Sunday morning raid on shipping in the Hooghly, swooping downstream in flights of four. The dock labourers panicked and thousands fled up-country in fear of invasion. The RAF quickly set up a fighter station with Hurricanes on the large ceremonial road known as Lal Road, which stretched across the maidan towards the Queen Victoria Memorial. It was quite thrilling to see the Hurries coming in to land, with flaps down, over Government House, steering well to starboard of the towering Ochterlony Monument.

(Airmail: Opened by Examiner)

21st Advance Base Workshops
REME India Command
19th November 1943

Since my last AML, I have received yours of the 19th and 29th October and the *Herts Mercury* which was very interesting. I noticed the item you marked that MacDonald was safe. I hope the rheumatism does not worry you much and has not come to stay.

You are right about the famine. It is part man-made, although Mr Amory tended to stress the more impersonal causes. There must be one colossal blackmarket carried on by hoarders and profiteers. There is no other way of explaining the fact that it has been possible always to enter any one of Calcutta's many excellent restaurants and have as sumptuous a meal as you could wish (provided you can pay for it).

I had a letter from Ralph Holgate the other day. He has been posted to the RAC Depot at Poona because of injury to his back, caused by a fall on the boat when we first got to Bombay. He ran his own business before the war, an outfitters in Lowestoft, and his wife is carrying it on until he comes back.

Love.

A sports field may have been all right for the 'soft'or non-fighting vehicles but the tanks had to be put away in a secret compound in the docks, to which entry could only be obtained by means of a pass. Calcutta was undoubtedly seething with Japanese agents and if news of the intended use of tanks on the Burma front reached the Jap secret service, a great deal of tactical advantage would be lost.

We ourselves stayed in some barracks to the south of the city centre and every day went to the tank park to work on the job of waterproofing the tanks. This was done by forcing what seemed like a mixture of wax and grease into all openings and crannies on the lower part of the tank and any other means which would ensure that the tank would be able to run in six foot or more of water. Middle Eastern experts were called in as some difficulties were encountered due to the heat and other causes. Col Frink says of this:

> The initial waterproofing went badly owing mainly to lack of co-operation, wrong materials, lack of experience and the fact that our workshops had gone ahead by mistake. However, after a fortnight of experimenting, they were turning out about nine per day and they should all be ready by the time 'C' Squadron sail.

However, the waterproofing eventually proved entirely satisfactory for what was required.

At the same time we were able to go into the city in the evenings, in our 'disguise', and have a final fling in its places of entertainment. Eat, drink and be merry for . . . This meant meals mainly at Chinese restaurants where Chinese food was very different from that served in England today at such restaurants. There were also cinemas, not to mention other 'places of resort'.

One evening, a few of us met some Indians in the Indian Coffee House at the north end of Chowringhee, the 'show' street of Calcutta. The conversation ranged over English literature, both modern and classic, and my lack of knowledge in this area became apparent despite a 'thorough secondary education'. It was, of course, tacitly understood that there could be no discussion of anything remotely relating to military matters. Being supporters of Congress and Home Rule they quoted Sir Walter Scott:

> Breathes there the man with soul so dead.
> Who never to himself hath said:
> 'this is my own, my native land . . .'

There was really no answer to this, except that the Japs had to be defeated first. However, it was a very memorable and civilised discussion.

At the same time Gandhi, Nehru and all the chief leaders of the Indian National Congress were locked up in prison and had been so since August 1942.

(Airmail) 8th December 1943

You must not expect regular mail nowadays, although I shall do my best to write whenever I can. I did not bother about celebrating my birthday and in fact just let it pass. I had rather a bad cough and cold at the time but it has almost left me. As I told you Ralph Holgate is at the depot so if you do not hear from me for a very long time, you could always write to him.

As regards famine statistics, it is becoming obvious that they are quite unreliable. Some villages are found deserted, in others the inhabitants are too ill to do anything – dead bodies here, dead bodies there – destitutes being collected from Calcutta and taken back to villages. How can any reliable record be kept?

Hope you have a very happy Christmas.

All my love.

Waterproofing had been completed. The tanks and crews were to proceed to Arakan by three 'flights' on LSTs (landing craft) supplied and sailed by the US Navy. The first 'flight' embarked on the night of 2nd/3rd December. Col Frink wrote:

I left Kiddapore Docks at 0700 hours this morning (3rd December) with the first flight of tanks – RHQ and 'A' Squadron in the LSTs 21 and 25. 'B' Squadron are due out tomorrow and 'C' Squadron on the 5th. The last month has been spent flying between Reju Khal and Calcutta.

It was with great relief that GHQ (I believe Lord Louis Mountbatten) managed to get the LSTs round from the Mediterranean in time. The combination of *Empire Ranee* and the RCLs might have been possible but there was far too large an element of risk for my liking. Having to off-load tanks in the open sea onto RCLs which were only just big enough to take them and certainly could not take any sort of surf, seemed very strange to me.

The LSTs we are using have come straight from the Italy landings and have plenty of experience. This is not such an easy operation owing to the flatness of the beach, about 1 in 150. They do not like working in less than 1 in 50. It looks as though they will have to beach, dry out and refloat on the next tide. It will mean rather a long trip for the tanks through the water and will be a test of the waterproofing. There should be about 8 hours of darkness for the operation. It will be an anxious time till the tanks are ashore.

Today will be spent going down the Hooghly and anchoring until we take to the open sea tomorrow. It is of the utmost importance to get the tanks to Arakan without letting the Jap become aware of it.

Dec 4th: Entered the Bay of Bengal at about 0800 hours and dropped the pilot. Picked up our escort of 2 motor launches and a Liberator aircraft at 1230 hours. Course appears to be S of E, I should think about 150. Very little swell but imagine this ship would roll in wet grass. They are about 2,000 tons unloaded.

LSTs are an American production on a British plan. They can carry up to 30 medium tanks as well as an enormous amount of motor transport as deck cargo. This particular group are crewed by Americans – different methods from RN but efficient. The group commander is Commander Blair and the ship's skipper, Lieut Brookfield.

Dec 5th: At 1100 hours a signal was received from one of our Liberator escort that a large enemy air attack was coming in from the SE. Luckily for us we were just off their course. They were making for Kiddapore Docks at Calcutta which our last flight of LSTs had left that morning.

The landing beach was sighted just before dark and we made a perfect beaching in about 5ft of water, shortly after 9pm. We allowed 2 hours to dry out and eventually off-loaded into 3ft 6ins of water without incident, all tanks reaching their 'hides' by 1.30am. The ships were afloat and off again by 2.30am.

The second flight was of 'B' Squadron tanks and the third of 'C' Squadron, embarking on successive nights, two LSTs for each squadron. Embarkation was at Kiddapore Dock.

The second flight embarked under their squadron leader, Major Johnstone, with twenty-six tanks, on the night of 3rd/4th December and sailed the following morning at 7am. No-one was allowed on deck until we were well out to sea in the Bay of Bengal.

It was the only occasion on which I have been a guest of the American Navy. The main novelty was the food which, at first, seemed truly wonderful compared to British Army food. However, after the first day the novelty somehow wore off and we had second thoughts about British Army grub! On this subject Col Frink was blunt:

It is impossible to compare our rations with those of the USA – ours are so infinitely inferior. It isn't that they have more but they have much better variety and everything is so much better turned out. There is no question that they take twice as much trouble to see that their fighting forces are properly equipped and looked after than we do. It is impossible to believe that it is all a matter of money and materials. I would like our QMG staff to spend a week in a USA camp and a week in one of ours living entirely on rations.

We were due to land on the beach at a spot south of Cox's Bazaar and just south of the mouth of the Reju Khal river, some two hours before midnight on the 6th/7th. Two white lights were to be shown on the beach one and a half hours before landing time, the lower one at the water's edge. However, both LSTs managed to get off-course and mistook the lights of Cox's Bazaar for the beach landing lights. They consequently sailed on Cox's Bazaar and beached there. The mistake was finally realized and they had to pull off. One was grounded to such an extent that it missed the tide and had to lie off and come in the following night with the third flight. The other LST was able to reach the correct beach by 2325 hours, some two hours late. The tide was wrong and there was a heavy swell so we had to land as quickly as possible.

The crews went down into the bowels of the craft and mounted the tanks. In order to be in position to drive forward straight off the craft, it had been necessary to load the tanks in reverse gear. Engines were started up and their throbbing reverberated threateningly round that confined space. In darkness the doors opened and one by one the tanks drove up to the mouth, balanced over the lip and plunged into the sea. It was deeper than planned, due to the delay, 5-6 feet, but our driver managed it okay. The next instant we were ploughing through the surf towards the shore, a run of some 200-300 yards. 'Against my expectations,' said Col Frink, 'They all got ashore without mishap' – a good test of the waterproofing.

Colonel Clare G. Vyner of the Royal Navy was Naval Beach Commander. He was a specialist in beach landing parties, having trained naval and army personnel for combined operations in Scotland, and may have been brought to India specially to ensure the success of these landings. Col Persse was there and Major H.M.H. Ley (second-in-command, 25th Dragoons) who was Military Landing Officer. Bill Nicholson and other members of the Advance party were also there and I leave Bill to tell his own story:

> Being a reasonably good swimmer, I was detailed to stand-by on the shore with six other men with some steel ropes, which were linked to static Don Rs (tractors), and I was to swim out to any tank which might get stuck in the water as it landed and fasten a hook to the tank to be towed ashore if necessary. The landing operation began early one morning at the precise moment arranged by the Army and Navy commanders. Signals appeared out at sea and, after a few minutes, we could see the dark outline of the tanks driving out of the landing craft into the water with their exhausts high above the vehicles as they drove through the waves to the shore, the drivers using their periscopes. All the vehicles (16 in all) landed safely and drove along the prepared tracks on the beach and into the jungle. One squadron of tanks landed on each of four successive nights and the whole operation was a success.
>
> While the landing took place, RAF planes were flying overhead to cover the noise of the tank engines. I remember on the second night of our mini 'D-Day'operation, a big American naval officer came ashore in

a small pinnace and had a drink of soup at the little improved kitchen we had put up, when we heard the sound of machine-gun fire. The American immediately asked who was doing all the firing and when we replied that it was probably the Japs he said, 'Oh, in that case I'll get the hell out of it' and disappeared into his boat!

We drove along the beach as directed and eventually turned inland along a track which led into the jungle. We progressed until we came to our allotted 'harbour' area, where a small clearing had been prepared for each troop. The advance party of HQ Squadron had done a great job. The place was Reju Khal and Regimental HQ was set up there pending orders to move further forward.

The other LST containing the remainder of 'B' Squadron tanks, which had beached herself firmly on the shoals, had come in on the following night with 'C' Squadron. Thus the landing party had to cope with three ships unloading forty tanks on that final night. They arrived on time about 11pm and, after one and a quarter hours wait for the tide to drop, all tanks were landed and in their 'hides' within two hours. This made a total of eighty tanks in all. Col Frink remarked that a very high standard of driving was shown throughout the whole of the beaching operations. It only remained to remove the waterproofing and make the tanks 100% battle-worthy.

(Airmail) 15th-25th December 1943

We are in the jungle at the moment, a long distance from civilization. To make up for the lack of fresh green stuff we are given Vitamin C tablets, one per day. We also have to take one yellow pill per day (except Sunday) called mepacrine. This is one of many devices to fight malaria. The mepacrine helps to keep the malaria in the veins and prevent it from affecting the body, so that one can carry on without feeling anything. When we stop taking the pills, we shall all immediately be given 'blanket treatment', that is, normal treatment for malaria. Incidentally, if we took the pills seven days a week instead of six we should turn yellow. This actually happened to one small unit without an MO!

In case this all suggests I'm getting hypochondriacal, I should say that I've never felt fitter since I've been in the Army. We get bathes in the sea every few days which are good exercise and keep us clean! Watch out for the activities of the 14th Army!

By now you will have received my airgraph Christmas card with the picture on it. It was designed and drawn by an artist in our squadron, Clive Branson.

The jungle met high above our heads and we were well hidden from enemy aircraft. The variety of vegetation was fantastic, as were the innumerable insects with their eye-deceiving camouflage. It was possible to look at a piece of lifeless bark, when suddenly legs or wings would appear and it would move swiftly away. Each insect had its own particular sound, usually rhythmical and, during daylight, they filled the air with a multitudinous hum. The most minute insects could produce sounds out of all proportion to their size. it was often impossible to locate the source of some very insistent sound. Across this lush scene flitted exotic butterflies with colours and patterns to equal those of any artist's imagination. And drenching everything with colour and light and shadow was the relentless sun.

Snakes there may have been, wild elephants, bears even, but for the most part these kept out of our way. This was just as well – dealing with the Japs was enough for the time being. For us the jungle, in addition to being a spectacular and beautiful back-drop for our acts of destruction, was both friend and foe. It gave thick cover from aircraft and the enemy in general, but made the enemy very difficult to find and destroy, as well as being impenetrable to tanks in its natural state.

(Airgraph) 29th December 1943

Since my AML of the 15th December I have received yours of the 28th November and airgraph Christmas card. Many thanks for these. I do hope you had a happy Christmas. Although we are in the jungle and supplies have to come a long distance, I can say that we had a really excellent Christmas. In fact, it was the best I've had since I've been in the Army. We had duck, tinned Christmas pudding, nuts and sultanas for dinner which were very satisfying. There was plenty of singing on Christmas Eve and Christmas Night, from carols to the most bawdy ditties. A Christmas service, held in a clearing which made a grand church, was very well attended and entirely voluntary. Then down to the beach for a bathe, by which time I had a good appetite for dinner.

What I did not say in the above letter was that the packets of nuts and sultanas were crawling with tiny insects which were all eaten up just the same.

Col Frink wrote:

To complete my Xmas, mails and a cable arrived from home which made me feel much better about things. Some snaps of my family arrived – over two years since I saw them. The children have grown enormously and look fit and attractive. How much longer will it be before I get home to Jean and the family? I hate missing all these years.

Such thoughts must have been in many minds at that time. Col Frink had a daughter and son, Elisabeth and Timothy, aged about fourteen and nine respectively.

Major Oliver C. Horne, 'C' Squadron, writing of this period, said:

On one occasion there was the sound of drunken hilarity in 'C' Squadron lines and the Sergeant Major was asked to find out how, as only one bottle of beer per man had been issued. Apparently it was achieved by mixing the emergency ration pack of raisins with sugar until it fermented.

(Airmail) 1st January 1944

It has been published that much of the Christmas mail has been lost at sea, but I hope the gifts that people have sent will arrive. I have had airgraphs from Assheton and David Gilling, and a Christmas card from Sister Churchill, also an airmail letter from Joyce MacDonald giving her husband's address in Germany and a photo of the two of them after their marriage.

Sometime ago I was able to go to an orchestral concert, the first since I've been in the Army. Needless to say it was a great treat, although the playing did not come up to the standard of a professional English orchestra. However, I am grateful for any music. The programme included Grieg's Piano Concerto and Beethoven's 7th Symphony.

We stayed up till 12 o'clock last night and saw in the New Year, singing 'Auld Lang Syne' round the log fire. So here's a happy New Year to you, which will see the end of the European war at any rate.

The concert was held in a cinema in Chowringhee and the players were a miscellaneous collection of Europeans, Indians and service men who happened to be in Calcutta at the time. The pianist had a long Greek name and a spectacular manner at the piano. I had not heard the concerto before in full and was not worried whether the performance was good or bad, just grateful to her for giving it to me at that moment.

(Airgraph) 9th January 1944

I have just received a long and interesting letter from Ron Chartres, Ron Assheton's brother-in-law, whom I used to meet at the Hoddesdon office. He is in the Persia and Iraq Force and having 'interesting experiences'.

I have written to MacDonald (POW) and had to give my home address. I think much of the sea-mail has been lost but I'm not giving up hope yet.

On the 10th January the first edition of *SEAC* (pronounced See-ack) was published, a newspaper for all forces in South East Asia Command, set up by Mountbatten. Afterwards he wrote:

> I decided that the man to solve the problem was Frank Owen (former editor of the *Evening Standard*). When I managed to trace him he had just blossomed from a trooper in the RAC into a fully-fledged cadet and was, with difficulty, persuaded to abandon his ambition to be a 2nd Lieutenant in a tank in order to come out here as a desk-wallah and run a daily newspaper.

Mountbatten made this appointment in face of strong protests from James Grigg, the Secretary of State for War.

The paper was printed in the offices of *The Statesman* in Calcutta and was flown daily to all troops in the Command, so far as this was possible. It consisted of four pages printed on one sheet and was priced one anna. In the first issue Frank Owen wrote an article on the folks at home, in the course of which he said, 'All Britain today believes in the absolute certainty of victory in 1944.' This was a reasonable thing to say in the optimistic climate of the time, but it was not to be.

News items came from all over the world: the Russian front, the Italian front, the Pacific. It reported the production of a propeller-less aircraft which flew at 500-600 mph at a great altitude, the invention of Group Capt Whittle.

On 2nd January the Regiment received orders from Corps 'to take over protection of the Teknaf Peninsular'. This peninsular consisted of a piece of land running north to south with the sea to the west and the estuary of the Naf river to the east. Reju Khal formed part of this land. In pursuance of these orders the Regimental Scout Troop was sent to Taknaf and 'A' Company of the 3/4 Bombay Grenadiers to Nila on the following day.

The Bombay Grenadiers (affectionately known as 'the Grinders') were an Indian regiment attached to us, partly to 'look after' us and partly for the purpose of co-operation in battle. A tank regiment in the jungle is peculiarly vulnerable to surprise enemy attacks and the presence of an infantry regiment to occupy its immediate surroundings was both necessary and a great relief to the tank personnel. We had every cause to be grateful to them. They were commanded by Major 'Junior' Dunlop, described by Major Ley as 'a great character but a bit of a rascal'.

Before we could get into the battle area, which was in the vicinity of Maungdaw, it was necessary to cross the Naf river. On the 4th January orders arrived to carry out this operation (called 'Operation Mills'). We were to move to Tumbru Jetty, then up river to Bawli Bazaar and south to Chamba. However, man proposes, God disposes. In the middle of the night it began to pour with rain and continued for nearly forty-eight hours. The personal consequences of this downpour are mentioned in my letter of the 15th January. The military consequences were that all roads were closed for two days and Operation Mills was to be postponed for four days. On the 8th January Col Persse, commander of the Armoured Group at Corps HQ, ordered the operation to proceed. A few hours of sun could go a long way to drying out many hours of rain. It was essential to avoid the tanks and other vehicles getting bogged-down in the mud.

On 9th January the echelon vehicles moved across the river to Chamba. For the tanks, it was not an easy operation as there were no bridges that could bear them, only two barges with two 'Z' crafts nostalgically called the *Folkestone* and the *Fowey*. The Regiment was to move in six 'flights', the first of which departed on the 10th January. Further orders were received that the move was to be speeded up, as we were urgently required in the forward areas. The moves were to proceed by day as well as night, despite the lack of security.

The loading of the tanks on the metal barges was a hazardous operation as the barges had sloping decks and the rubber tank tracks had difficulty gripping the wet decks. The co-operation between commanders and tank drivers, at night without lights, was exceptional and, due to the good driving and confidence between crews, no vehicle was lost.

SKETCH MAP OF OPERATIONAL AREA, ARAKAN, JAN–JUNE 1944

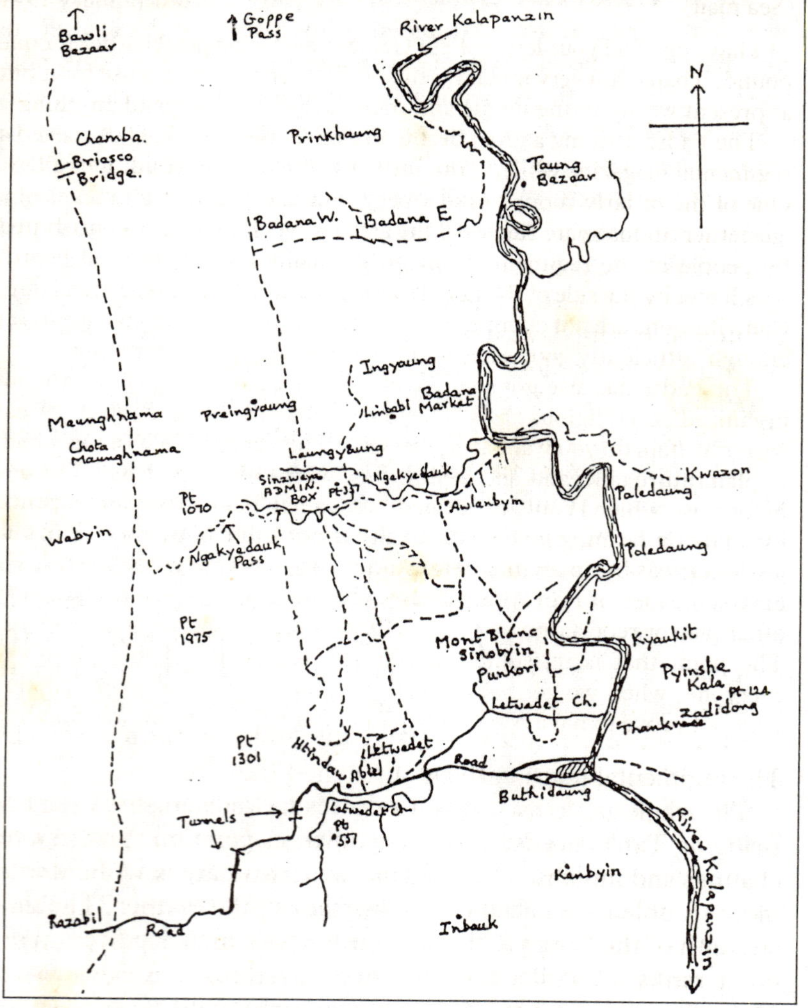

'B' Squadron was on the second flight which left on 11th January. We harboured at 'Agra' that night and were loaded onto the barge at 7am the next morning. This took us to Bawli South Jetty and we stayed in Bawli South Keep for the night, moving to Chamba at 5am the next morning. As far as I remember we got across without mishap. In addition to the tanks and soft vehicles, there were six Valentine bridging tanks, two D8 tractors and two Ward la Frances deck-loaded onto the 'Z' craft.

(Sea mail) 6th January 1944

I have just had your letter of 8th October enclosing postal order for one pound. Thank you very much for this. I shall certainly find a use for it but at present we are in the jungle and there is nowhere to spend anything!

The Padre is doing a great deal to organize 'welfare'. He has started a regimental magazine which is produced weekly as far as conditions allow. One of the orderly room clerks types it out and prints it by means of a 'gestetner' in his spare time. All the articles, verses, etc, are contributed by people in the regiment. I am provisionally on the editorial board, which met by the side of the tank last night lighted by an inspection lamp. Contributions are not coming in too fast, of course, but we manage to get enough sufficiently good ones to fill four foolscap pages per week.

The Padre has also got some weekly discussions going. They are not organized on a religious basis. The first one had the broad subject: 'What sort of Britain do you want after the war?' This served as a basis on which to plan future talks and decide how they were to be conducted. The one before last, which I could not attend, was called 'Back to the land' opened by a talk on farming given by a small farmer from Worcester. The talk last week was by an architectural student on 'replanning the towns'. He gave some idea of Prof Abercomby's plan for London which, like every other plan or report drawn up since the war broke out, has been shelved. The point that is insistently coming up is that it will be the job of everyone, when we get back, to see that all this talk of reconstruction does not prove to have been mere windy phrases to get the war fought.

The regimental magazine was christened *Bully-tin*.

The whole group had arrived by now, the last being the Valentine Bridging Tanks needed for laying down instant tank bridges over chaungs and nullahs. They had had a precarious journey and were more trouble to land than all eighty tanks put together. The total strength of the Corps Armoured Group was now 61 officers, 1975 other ranks, 89 tanks and 361 wheeled vehicles. All these were under the command of Col Frink who says wryly:

No extra regimental staff has, as yet, been allowed to run it, neither am I getting any extra pay for a command as big as an infantry brigade – who cares as long as we get cracking and finish the job.

In another vein he continues:

I suppose there is some good reason for wasting precious moments in the none-too-long dry season – only another four months before the rains start when the country becomes impassable to everything except mules and feet.

2

Blooding the Hounds

> So the 25th Dragoons are to be the first of the newly-formed (armoured) regiments to be employed in active operations after all. It hardly seemed possible a year ago. The problem they have set us is a difficult one – a difficult landing and a difficult country to operate in. At any rate I have confidence that the troops will do their best and are keen to have a crack.
>
> *Lt Col H.R.C. Frink*
> *3rd December 1943*

Imperial General Headquarters, Tokyo.
Army Order No. 1776

For the defence of Burma, the Commander-in-Chief Southern Army shall destroy the enemy on that front at the appropriate juncture, and occupy and secure a strategic zone in North East India in the area of Imphal.

7th January 1944

Whatever the Japanese High Command may have intended by this order, it was taken by their generals in the Burma front to mean 'The Invasion of India'. The possibility of such an invasion had been argued up-and-down the chain of Japanese command for the previous ten months and had now crystallized in this order from the Imperial Government itself.

Imphal, on the central Burma front, was defended by IV Corps of the 14th Army. We (XV Corps) were on the southern front (Arakan), and American General Joe Stilwell was in the north aided and abetted by Gen Orde Wingate and his Chindits. All were under the command of Gen 'Bill' Slim.

Needless to say we were quite ignorant of the Japanese plans and they appeared to be equally ignorant of us, hidden as we were in the dense jungle.

(Airgraph)

'B' Squadron, 25th Dragoons
RAC India Command
15th January 1944

I know another fellow from Cuffley so we are able to exchange local papers. Will you give Trevor my congratulations through Mrs Vivian. Sorry to hear it was tanks he knocked out!! Your description of the garden all frosty sounds lovely. It's so long since I've seen anything like it.

By the way, recently we had a visit from a 'Very Important Personage', Lord Louis Mountbatten himself in fact. His speech was quite interesting, in one way definitely disappointing, but anyway things are happening.

A week ago we had two days of rain which caught us unawares as few of us expected it. Everything got soaked but we were able to dry things out when it stopped and the 'old currant bun' came out again.

I hope you are both keeping clear of the 'flu epidemic.

Mountbatten visited all the troops under his command and made a similar speech on each occasion: 'I hear you call this the Forgotten Army. Well, let me tell you this is not the Forgotten Front, and you are not the Forgotten Army. In fact, nobody has ever heard of you – but they will!' It was basically a morale boosting pep-talk. Col Frink says of this visit:

Lord Louis Mountbatten came down to visit the Regiment. I had not seen him since the Cowdray polo days before the war when his one ambition was to command the new 'K' Class Destroyer Flotilla, which he duly did. At the age of 43 to become Supreme Commander of the South East Asia Command is nothing less than brilliant. He has more personality than any man I have ever met. He talked to the men of the Regiment and put them in the picture as regards the war – an excellent short talk, put over like the great man he is. Before going away he commented on the great spirits of the men and his last words were, 'Good luck. The Regiment has a great chance and I know they will take it.'

An entry in Mountbatten's diary for Thursday, 13th January 1944 reads:

During these four days I had given the following number of talks: Monday – 7; Tuesday – 10; Wednesday – 16; Thursday – 10. A total of 43 talks in four days, equivalent of 14 hours talking!

He visited all types of regiments and units under his command – Indian, Gurkha, West African, American and British – and, no doubt, had to adjust his style accordingly. The West Africans gave the most vociferous reception, cheering and waving their knives and rifles in the air. He says:

> I have arranged that I always shake hands with all the officers, British and Indian first, then I go over and talk individually to one or two dozen selected English-speaking NCOs and men. If the unit is British, I have all the soldiers or airmen gathered round me and stand on a soapbox and talk to them for 20 minutes about the war.

By 13th January the whole Regiment was in its 'hide' at Chamba near Briasco Bridge, some 14 miles north of Maungdaw, a port at the mouth of the Naf river which had recently been taken by the allied troops.

During the next few days reconnaissance of the area was carried out. The first shot was fired at the enemy by Lt P.C. Somerville's troop near Keinchakata on 17th January. They had been sent to accompany a patrol of 4/7th Rajputs to 'recce' the bridge south of Razabil. They went to Keinchakata to join the Rajput Company and were attacked by the Japs from high ground to the east of Razabil Bridge. The attack was repulsed and the troop joined the Rajputs and moved south to the bridge. The Japs again opened fire causing two Rajput casualties. Lt Somerville observed the bridge as unfit for tanks but located a possible crossing south of the bridge and the patrol withdrew.

On the following day one poor lad was shot dead by accident with a Thompson submachine-gun. Tension had been accumulating over the past weeks of waiting and this was to continue for another week or so.

(Airgraph) 19th January 1944

As the BBC might put it, 'This news bulletin comes to you from Burma, from the heart of the jungle.' You will have heard all about the 14th Army on the wireless and you will almost certainly hear about it when we start moving, so I don't have to tell you what's happening.

Many thanks for sending on the November Law Notes, which I have just received. My last airgraph was dated 15th January.

Yesterday afternoon we had some spare time and took the opportunity to climb a neighbouring ridge of hills (nearly 1,800 feet). It proved to be an extremely steep climb but we reached the top and came down with our skins still intact, except for a few scratches. There was a good path but this faded out half-way up. It was just as well the undergrowth was thick as this was all we had to grasp to pull ourselves up. The view from the top was magnificent.

I am feeling extremely fit, fitter than I've ever felt since I've been in the Army.

It was announced recently that a large amount of surface mail was lost between 30th September and 20th October. I am wondering whether the books that Cooper sent were among this batch. I hope not.

All my love,

The ridge of hills that we climbed was part of the Mayu Range which extends north to south through Arakan, we being on the western side. 'We' in this context meant a friend and myself.

Clad in our boots, puttees, shorts and berets, with loaded pistols and a map, we set out on what appeared to be a good path up the hill. We reached the top of the ridge with, behind us, a magnificent view over Teknaf Peninsular and the sea. Before us however were yet more hills and the jungle with no distant view. There was clearly no point in going further so we turned back down the slope, the sun now getting low in the sky.

Somehow we lost the path and found ourselves climbing down a steep chaung or dried bed of a stream. This chaung tended to proceed by deep steps, which would have been waterfalls in the rainy season. As we got lower the walls became steeper and higher and it became clear that we could get trapped on one of the 'steps' with unclimbable walls on three sides and a steep precipice on the fourth. We saw the prospect of a night or more in the hills with virtually no clothes, not to mention small bands of Japanese operating on their own in the jungle. Just in time we managed to find a way of scrambling out of the chaung and, by a fluke, picked up the path again. It was much later than we had expected and the sun was setting, to be followed quickly by darkness.

We reached a guard post of the Bombay Grenadiers and felt very foolish on realizing that we did not know the password, not having expected to be out after dark. However, there was just enough light for the guard commander to see that we were not Japanese and he allowed us to pass into our own lines.

That was not the end. We realized that, in our haste, we had dropped the map which could not be allowed to fall into Japanese hands, though it contained no markings of any sort. There was nothing for it but to go back the following morning and look for it (fortunately we were still off duty). Luck was on our side and we found it on the path without having to go far up the hill. Another chap in the Regiment had done a similar thing and had actually got stuck in a chaung and had to be searched for and rescued. However, I wouldn't have missed it – a memory of the Burmese jungle without war.

Cecil Beaton, war photographer, was in Arakan at that time and wrote:

The tablelands on the Arakan front are unlike anything one has ever seen except, perhaps, in the background of idylls and fantasies painted on Chinese fans, screens and porcelain. Around Maungdaw it is as if the compact mountain ranges have erupted and dotted the earth with hundreds of rugged hillocks. These hillocks are covered by peepul trees, spreading their huge dark leaves, and by bamboos, while the feathery undergrowth is pierced by long white shafts of pampas. The landscape is pastoral; so lush, sylvan and peaceful is the general aspect in the brilliant sun or moonlight that, in spite of the intermittent thuds of gunfire, one cannot quite believe that deadly warfare is being carried on nearby.

(Sea mail) 22nd January 1944

We are fairly near the Japs here but have not started operations yet. Everyone is in very good spirits. I went through the lines of an Indian regiment the other day and they seemed very cheerful and friendly. There is no chance of them deserting to Subhas Bose's 'JIFS'. I understand JIF stands for 'Japanese Indian Forces'.

Subhas Chandra Bose was a one-time President of the Indian National Congress. After a visit to Germany in 1936 he showed distinct fascist tendencies so, because of this, he was thrown out of Congress and in 1939 organized the Forward Bloc in opposition to Congress. Its members are largely dissident congressmen and it has little influence outside Bengal, Bose's home province. In 1940 he disappeared mysteriously from Calcutta and went first, I think, to Berlin but is now known to be in Japan.

He broadcasts from Tokyo and was, of course, able to make much propaganda out of the Bengal famine. 'Let the Japanese in and we will bring you Burma rice,' was his line, but apparently it was not allowed to have any effect. He has managed to persuade a number of Indian prisoners-of-war in Japan to join the enemy, working chiefly on their dislike of British rule I imagine.

These Jifs make appearances on several fronts and shout to Indians to desert and join them. So far I think they have not been very successful but no information has been published on this subject.

(Airmail) 22nd January 1944

I have just received Dad's letter of the 12th November enclosing postal orders to the value of two pounds. Thanks very much.

Thanks also for your sea mail of the 4th November. As always I was very glad of the socks. Reports reaching us say that Britain has never been healthier than she is now. I hope this is true in your case.

I have borrowed a book which I am reading in odd moments – 'The Film Sense' by Sergei Eisenstein, Russian film director – about the putting together of sound, colour and photographic image – fascinating.

During the last week or two the Regiment had acquired a mascot. A wounded baby elephant had been found, its mother having been killed. It was three to four feet tall. His or her origins were unknown (though the Burmese police are said to have expressed an interest). After a certain amount of informal adoption procedure, 'it' was taken on the Regimental strength and introduced to Capt Ernie Manners, the Quartermaster, who would be responsible for its rations, kit and quarters. A keeper with a truck was appointed to look after it and they developed such a rapport that the elephant tried to get under his mosquito net at night!

An elephant made an appropriate mascot. There was a certain affinity between an elephant lurching through the jungle and an M3 medium tank doing the same. Over two thousand years ago Hannibal had frightened the Romans out of their lives by suddenly descending from an Alpine pass with thirty-seven fighting elephants!

In the meantime plans had been laid for the 25th Dragoons to join the action. On the western side of the Mayu Range the 5th Indian Division was spread across the Japanese positions at Razabil and the 'tunnels' area. These two tunnels passed through the Mayu hills and took the metalled road from Maungdaw (now in our hands) past Razabil (heavily fortified by the Japs) to Buthi-

SKETCH MAP OF THE RAZABIL FORTRESS AND ITS ENVIRONMENT

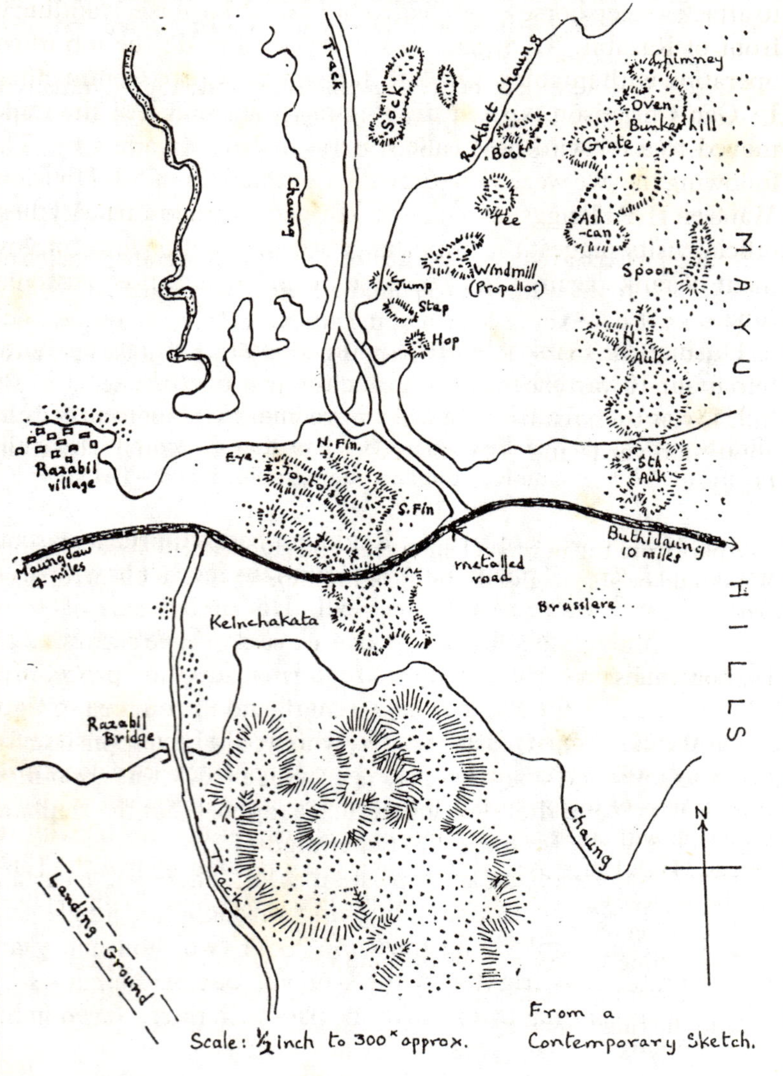

daung on the east side, a distance of some 14 miles. On the other side of the hills was the 7th Indian Division facing the remainder of the road and Buthidaung. The capture of the whole of this road was the main objective.

The tunnels area was very heavily fortified by the Japs. We were to attack a steep horse-shoe shaped hill called Tortoise, standing in front of Razabil. 'C' Squadron was selected to do the job in co-operation with infantry. On 24th January the Corps Commander, Lt Gen Christison, visited the Regiment at noon. All the tanks moved to a forward hide called 'Ezra' in 161 Brigade area. The following day we were visited by the Commander of 5th Division, Maj Gen H.R. Briggs, of which 161 Brigade formed part. All these official visits suggest the importance attached to this first employment of tanks against the Japanese in this area at this particular time.

During Col Frink's 'recce' for this operation, a mortar-bomb fell about 10 yards behind him, luckily just over the crest of the hill. It was then realized that they were in full view of the enemy at about 600 yards and they moved to a more 'congenial' situation. He says:

> Apart from the normal chaungs the going appears to be satisfactory. We should be able to give useful close fire support (to the infantry) at any rate.

He continues:

> On the 21st January the Strategic Air Force are going to bomb the battle area with Fortresses and Liberators. I only hope they don't make such a mess of the ground that we can't get across. Personally I would rather do without them. They have made me set up my HQ with 161 Brigade HQ. I suppose it is reasonable but it is damn annoying as I shall not be as close up as I had intended and find it much more difficult to see what is going on.
>
> Everything is very peaceful behind the line and it is hard to realize there is a war on. There's a feeling in the Regiment rather like waiting to go into the ring but no sign of nerves that I have noticed.

That night 'C' Squadron moved to the assembly area.

(Sea mail) 25th January 1944

Our artillery are putting down a barrage and the shells whistle overhead on their way to destroy the Japs. Apart from this it is like a glorious summer's day. We are well hidden in the thick jungle undergrowth, mostly tall pampas grass, their feathery plumes waving against the sky. I think this war will prove to be one of the turning points in the development of civilization.

Everyone is very optimistic about the operations tomorrow and we are glad to be getting down to it at last. For myself I have always been sure that I'm coming back; there will be so much to do afterwards. So don't worry about things.

Au revoir for now. I may not be able to write for some days but will always send an airgraph when I get the opportunity.

This letter was premature, so far as 'B' Squadron was concerned, as we did not go into action until 28th January. Perhaps that is why I had time to write it. In fact an attack had been made by the infantry, the same day I wrote the letter, on North Bunker Hill. They failed to gain the objective and this necessitated a change in plan to avoid our attack going in with an exposed flank. However, 'C' Squadron's attack on the hill feature Tortoise was to go ahead and Major Oliver Horne, squadron leader of 'C' Squadron, and his second-in-command, Captain Alexander, made very careful preparations to ensure that this, the very first occasion when the Lee tank had been used in Burma, should be a successful one. Liaison with 161 Brigade (of 5th Division) was tied up in great detail after joint reconnaissance and rehearsals were conducted on the sand table.

Says Major Horne:

Eventually the force moved up to its assembly area where a mixed group of spectators had arrived to witness this historic occasion of heavy tank-infantry co-operation. There was the Padre, who wanted to bless us, the Court photographer, Cecil Beaton, who wanted to snap us, various senior officers to give us last-minute advice and, finally, local girls to offer us bananas (on payment) but we could not be late over the start-line.

The action began at 1000 hours on 26th January. The first phase in the attack on Tortoise was aerial bombardment from Liberators followed by Mitchell B25s. Whilst the Liberators' bombing was accurate, the Mitchells were late arriving on the battlefield, having lost their way. In the meantime the dust from the first bombing moved back over the tanks. This confused the Mitchells and a stick of bombs fell alongside a troop of tanks, putting one out of action and damaging two others. Trooper John Swinburn was killed, and two tank commanders and four men from the Support Group were wounded. Col Frink said he never liked the thought of the bombing and, in his opinion, the results were not worth it.

After this setback, 'C' Squadron was in action by 1045 hours firing HE (high explosive) and AP (armour piercing) from their 75mm guns as well as using their Browning machine-guns. The 4/7th Rajputs' attack went in about 1130 hours. They got almost to the top of the hill without incident but were held up there by a Jap strong point and were bombed and machine-gunned off the position.

A further fire plan was made and 'C' Squadron blasted all around the strong point, except the back which they could not reach. The final assault went in and this time held within 10 yards of the top but could not be taken further. Col Frink comments:

> The Jap positions are all circular, following the ring contours on the map, and they hang on like grim death and fight like men. May be wrong, but I feel a bit more dash would have got us in. The men behaved splendidly in their first action. The shooting was first-class and they completed every task they were given. The 75mm gun on the tanks is a great gun and opened up every target.

As nightfall approached the battle for Tortoise was seen to be a stalemate. The Japs had honeycombed the hill with tunnels leading to numerous bunkers from which they could cover every approach. The attack had been made from the west and controlled by Col Frink and Brig Warren of 161 Brigade at the Rajputs' HQ. Col Frink said that a lot of enemy shelling scored several very near-misses in the HQ area. Apart from the casualties caused by the bombing, the Regiment sustained only one man wounded.

Next day 'C' Squadron continued in action with much the same result. The trouble was that the Japs retreated down the back of the hill and came up again with grenades when the bombardment stopped. Thus the top of the hill was never taken. That day two tanks were bogged down, one losing its tracks. It took one hour for two D8 tractors under Lt Evans to recover these tanks under fire.

'B' Squadron was ordered to stand by and on 28th January took over the attack from 'C' Squadron. An attack was made in support of the Rajputs from the west. Two 37mm guns were silenced or destroyed but the Japs remained in position. Somewhat unexpectedly some British mines Mark II were found in the area which blew off the bogeys and tracks of one tank. The Japs fired mortars, 37mm and 75mm guns, our only casualty being a man concussed by shell-fire in the Scout Troop.

On 29th January four tanks of 'B' Squadron destroyed two Jap bunkers on 'Fin' and 'Eye', two features of Tortoise. The infantry were pointing out the bunkers which had to be systematically destroyed. The same work was continued on 30th January but on 31st January 'B' Squadron was ordered back because of rain.

In the meantime, 'A' Squadron (under Maj Charles Sloane) had sent out three patrols on foot under Capt Munro and Lts Gray and Spooner respectively, who carried out night reconnaissance to find crossings over the Rekhat chaung, in order to attack the hills to the south and east of the chaung. One of the crossings was found to be mined and when lifted by the sappers the mines turned out to be British, laid the year before.

On 28th January 'A' Squadron joined the 4th Royal West Kents, also of 161 Brigade, in an attack on 'Hop', a small hill to the north of Tortoise. One troop of 'B' Squadron gave fire support from the west of the Rekhat chaung area. Casualties were inflicted on the enemy and anti-tank guns knocked out. The tanks were in action from daybreak to nightfall but progress was slow and the Japs were being reinforced. Our tanks were sometimes inhibited by soft ground and by chaungs whose banks could be 20ft high. However, the West Kents gained their objective with only three casualties – a tremendous decrease from the normal and due almost entirely to the tanks.

During this time two troops, one from 'A' and one from HQ Squadrons, were assisting the Dogras and the Suffolks of 123 Brigade on Wrencat and Bamboo with the same result as on other high positions. Though the bunkers were blown up, enough Japs still remained to beat off the assault. During these operations of 28th January, one sapper was killed and two wounded. Later one of the wounded in Support Group died. Col Frink commented on the casualties very fairly, 'I hope we continue to get away so lightly.'

Major Horne wrote:

Although Tortoise remained an impregnable Japanese fortress, covering the much needed tunnels route through the Mayu Range, some valuable lessons were learnt.

The first was that the accurate flat trajectory of the tank 75mm gun was much more effective than aerial bombardment or artillery fire against the Japanese, who were well dug-in and occupying steep hill positions. The second was the 'bunker-busting' technique developed by Major Hugh Ley which set out to plaster the hillside with HE in timed lifts, followed by AP directed at the bunkers and finally Besa (machine-gun) along the top of the hill and above it. This method, together with mortar fire put down on the reverse slopes, enabled the infantry to advance closer up to the tank support fire and kept the Japanese underground at all times.

So we had our baptism of fire. We were probably glad to get it over after some six weeks of waiting in the jungle. All I remember now is the tracer and incendiary bullets flying around, the trees catching fire and blazing away, and a general feeling of organized confusion. It was interesting to find the differing attitudes of ourselves and the infantry. We greatly admired the infantry for their courageous determination in carrying through their attacks, exposed as they were to every bullet and shell coming their way. They on the other hand, when shown the interior of a tank, were appalled at going into action in such a small cramped space and had no wish to take our places.

Col Frink received a very complimentary letter from the Army Command congratulating him and the regiment on the support carried out by the tanks 'of a standard beyond compare'. 'No more than our job,' he commented. At any rate, like a true cavalry man, he had 'blooded his hounds'.

3

Panic in the Parlour

Japanese Objective:

> Now we are going into battle and you will conquer and overrun the British as you have always done. You will smash them and you will drive them into the sea. Now the sea will run red with your blood as well as theirs and you must take pride in it.
>
> *Col. Tanahashi: Order of the Day*
> *before the start of Operation 'Ha-Go'*
> *Arakan, 3rd February 1944*

With one exception, all roads in the locality fit for motor transport had been built by the Army. They were not metalled and the sun had turned the surface into a dry cake which rose in a thick dust every time a vehicle passed over it. All the drivers wore goggles as this dust entered the eyes, ears, mouth and every other orifice of the body.

Cecil Beaton remarks:

> We drove in a jeep over rough roads which were being sprinkled with water by native women wearing dark gloomy-coloured draperies. This spraying from gourd-like vases seems futile for it succeeds in laying the dust for only a few hours but, I am told, it helps to keep the roads from rapid and total deterioration.
>
> The rates of pay for this job are small yet the women are like princesses doing their humble job with dignity and heart-rending poise. Some of their features are wonderful. Their children help too and throw water from old cigarette tins, jam jars or other little receptacles.

The one exception was, of course, the old road that stretched from the port of Maungdaw, through two tunnels in the Mayu Range, and on to Buthidaung, mainly in Japanese hands.

* * *

I climbed a hillock to an observation post and there, between the British and Japanese outposts, was a wonderfully peaceful scene. Water buffaloes were browsing in the paddy fields, the herd guarded by cheerful brown children. White paddy birds were unconcernedly taking ticks off the backs of the buffaloes. It was sunset and the villagers, who had been working on the roads on our side of the line, were passing over into enemy territory for the night as their homes were in Japanese occupation.

Two batteries of field artillery opened up on the Japanese positions. We heard the shells screaming overhead and saw the bursts, but the interesting part was that the children, the work people and the cattle took not the least bit of notice.

I am told that the Japanese do not fire on the Burmese unless they wander too close to one of their bunkers or strong points and then they machine-gun them, whether there are women and children among them or not, so that by now the local inhabitants have learnt to avoid the strong points.

Mountbatten: Diary 1943–46

(Airgraph)

'B' Squadron, 25th Dragoons
RAC India Command
31st January 1944

My dear Auntie Gwen,

Thank you for your airgraph of the 1st January. Do not worry about not being able to send a gift. We are definitely on active service at last. During the last few days we have been pounding the Japs and made them very uncomfortable, I hope. Naturally, what spare time we have is taken up with eating, sleeping and having a wash when the opportunity occurs.

I hope you and Auntie Lillian are keeping very well and cheerful. The war in Europe will be over soon enough but it will take a bit longer to finish the Japs off. Evidently the Allies full resources will not be brought to bear on this front until Germany is beaten.

I am very well myself despite the mosquitoes and the jungle.

This letter was written at the start of four days 'rest', that is maintenance and general checking out of tanks and equipment and preparation for the next assignment. We were in our old 'digs' at Chamba. On the 1st February the CO held a conference at Regimental HQ to discuss the forthcoming operation, which was to be in support of the 7th Indian Division in an attack on Buthidaung, on the *east* side of the Mayu Range. This would involve getting the bulk of the Regiment over the hills and into the valley of the

Kalapanzin river which could only be done by proceeding south and then taking the road east leading over the Ngakyedauk Pass, in no time at all re-christened the 'Okydoke Pass'. Less than three months before, this pass road had been little more than a steep winding narrow track through the jungle, but Gen Messervy's sappers had spotted it as suitable for development into a fair-weather road to carry vehicles, including our tanks. The Indian sappers had worked fast, blasting out the hillside, constructing bridges and creating a reliable surface. It was the main, indeed the only, line of communication between Corps HQ, reinforcements, supplies and the 5th Indian Division on the west of the range and the 7th Division on the east. It was about five miles long and was a magnificent piece of military engineering for that time.

The tanks were to move on the night of 4th/5th February and were to concentrate in an area code-named 'Delhi', not far from the bottom of the Pass road on the eastern side of the hills, which had already been selected in January. In making this move we would come under the command of Major General Frank Messervy, commanding the 7th Indian Division.

This division had been formed in Attock on the border of the Punjab and North West Frontier province in October 1940. Attock was some twenty miles south-east of Risalpur. After various changes they had moved to Ranchi in May 1943 and had done joint training with ourselves in the months of May–July that year. They had, however, moved into Arakan rather ahead of us, towards the end of August. Each of the three brigades, numbered 33, 89 and 114, consisted of one British regiment, one Punjab and one Gurkha.

On 2nd February reconnaissance parties under Major Ley went across the Pass to 'Delhi'. On the night of 3rd/4th February 'soft vehicles' moved over the Pass and the POL (petrol, oil, lubrication) vehicles dumped their loads at 'Delhi' and returned. For this operation we were to take only the minimum of kit. Everything else was left behind at Chamba. Since we had arrived in the jungle we had been living with and on our respective tanks, which had become our 'mobile homes' but, except when on operations, had been eating in mess. Now each crew was to draw rations and feed itself, using the primus stove on each tank. This was officially known as 'vehicle cooking', an unfortunate phrase which, for tank crew, is more likely to describe what happens when the tank catches fire.

(Airgraph) 3rd February 1944

My dear Mother and Dad,

I have received your AML of Jan 4th, seamail of November 20th enclosing the 'The Lighter Side' (very popular with the crew).

Apparently a question was asked in parliament about the cost of *SEAC*, the newspaper of the South East Asia Command. This is an excellent paper and well appreciated by everybody. It is far better than *Contact*.

At present we have a few days' rest from action but shall be having another shot shortly at blowing the Japs out of the area. More details when I have time.

* * *

At 11am on Friday 4th February, Regimental HQ received an urgent message that the Japanese had infiltrated in force along the east bank of the Kalapanzin river, moving north and advancing on and through Taung Bazaar in the rear of 7th Division. The 89th Brigade (part of that division) had been turned northwards to deal with the situation and the 4/8th Gurkhas were in contact. In fact 89th Brigade had recently been withdrawn from 'the front' in the south for a rest and also to enable them to rehearse with us for the breakthrough to Buthidaung. Its place was being taken by two battalions from the 9th Brigade of the 5th Indian Division. They crossed the Ngakyedauk Pass that day and took up a position on the right flank (facing south) of 7th Division. A crowd of Burmese refugees passed them in the opposite direction on the Pass, fleeing from the battle to come.

To meet this dire emergency, one squadron was to go over the Pass as quickly as possible and that squadron turned out to be 'B'. We moved off at 4pm in the late afternoon sun. Wireless silence was observed in the interests of secrecy and in any event communication was not necessary as it was a case of following the tank in front.

The drivers had a tough time. At the foot of the Pass was a picture showing a jeep falling over a precipice with the words 'A Jeep can go anywhere'. There were hairpin bends which could not be taken in one turn and involved reversing on the edge of a drop of anything from 200 feet or more. The tanks weighed twenty-six tons. Only a small error of judgement could bring disaster. No such mishap occurred and we arrived at 'Delhi', as the 'Diary' says, 'without incident' at about 6.30pm.

I was able to ride on the outside of the tank and remember how the Naf river, the Teknaf peninsular, the jungle and the sea all rose up behind us as we also moved upwards, a magificent panorama dominated by the setting sun. The thick forest came down to the edges of the road.

When we reached the summit and began to descend, it was as though we passed through a dim gauze. It was now dusk. Deprived of sunlight, the jungle looked menacing and eerie. We seemed to have left the real world behind and moved into a dimension where anything might happen.

When we harboured that night it was confirmed that a 'large fighting patrol' of the enemy had passed through Taung Bazaar and was probably moving southwards towards our area and Division HQ. We were ordered to be ready to move at first light.

'A' and 'C' Squadrons and Regimental HQ moved over the Pass to join us at 'Delhi' during the night. To deceive the enemy, the Reserve Squadron was left on the west side of the range and was able to take part with the 5th Division in further action in the Razabil area, thus suggesting that the whole regiment was still there. Liaison officers were sent for attachment to 7th Division HQ and 33 Brigade.

No one really knew what was happening, neither ourselves nor the Japanese, as it turned out. It was one of the most eerie nights that I have ever spent. Further south, Capt Wilson Stephens RA of 33 Brigade describes 'night' in the Kalapanzin valley:

> The moonlight falling on the mepacrine-coloured faces of the men gave everybody a leaden, almost corpse-like appearance. The silence got on one's nerves but was often broken by a kind of tree-climbing lizard, known locally as a Tucktoo, which would occasionally call in a feminine almost human voice. Squirrels and ant-eaters kicked up the leaves, but it could be something much more dangerous. There were not many jackals but enough to mask the howling noises by which the Japanese signalled to each other. There were some large monkeys which often laughed in a demented kind of way in the middle of the night. They were far more frightening than hyenas. Towards dawn a heavy dew always formed and the drops falling off the leaves of the bamboos made a sound like snapping twigs.

Due to the tense and uncertain situation, two men of each crew were to remain on guard on each tank, all ranks taking turns throughout the night. Sleep did not come easily and I am not sure that I ever dozed off. The recurring rattle of small arms fire echoed distantly round the jungle hills.

The 89th Brigade consisted of the 2nd Battalion King's Own Scottish Border Regiment, the 7th Battalion 2nd Punjab Regiment and the 4th Battalion 8th Gurkha Rifles. This brigade was in the area north of our harbour that night, in the vicinity but to the north of 7th Division HQ.

The Punjabis had met the enemy the previous evening at Ingyaung and had spent the night in that area. They were now, the 5th February, at Badana East. The KOSBs were at Linbabi behind them, with Brigade HQ 139 Jungle Field Regiment RA providing close artillery support.

The enemy was thought to be advancing south and therefore a threat to Division HQ. A visit by Col Frink to Messervy's HQ at dawn on 5th February produced an order to fight north with the 4th/8th Gurkhas to intercept them. 'B' Squadron took on this task and accordingly moved off northwards with two Valentine bridging tanks to an area east of 7th Division HQ which was about 4 miles from our harbour. Movement further north was not possible until the sappers had prepared four nullahs for tank crossing, one of them by bridging tank. This had to be done under fire by the Armoured Group's own small handful of sappers under Lt Briggs. The crossings were ready by midday but by this time the Japs had got a strong footing in the hills. Only limited numbers of tanks were able to cross, so the Squadron Leader and two troops went forward. Our troop was held in reserve, which entailed a listening watch on the wireless for the rest of the day waiting for orders.

The Squadron Leader contacted the Gurkhas in the valley of Laungyaung in which 7th Division HQ was situated. Contact with the enemy had been made at Preinyaung and they were in the hills on both sides of the valley. The rear column of the Gurkhas came under heavy fire from a jungle-clad ridge on the east of the valley, an area through which the company had only just passed. An immediate counter-attack with the tanks drove the enemy off but held up any advance until the evening. By this time it was clear that the enemy force was much greater than first estimated – perhaps 7,000 strong. By nightfall they were even further to the south and into the hills to the west. In the meantime the Gurkhas had lost wireless communication with 89 Brigade HQ.

One Bren-gun carrier of Scout Troop had to be abandoned. It had been doing a forward ground 'recce' with an officer of 401 Field Squadron, Indian Engineers and its track had come off. Lt Briggs and his sappers performed a very valuable and courageous task in preparing the tank crossings under fire and in keeping them fit for the return of our tanks southwards. Col Frink later recommended him for the MC.

Col Frink had been with 'B' Squadron that day and remarked on the very unpleasant trip back to harbour when they were sniped and shot at incessantly. He dined that night at Div HQ and the atmosphere of unrest and doubt in the camp was borne in upon him. It was now blatantly clear that not only were the Japanese getting close to Div HQ but the HQ itself lay directly in their line of advance. Capt HG (Mick) Ablett was Divisional Intelligence Officer and attended a meeting that evening with the General and staff. The question was: should they attempt to move the HQ during the night or wait for the morning? In the event it was decided to wait for the morning in view of the difficulties of a night move through the jungle. Nevertheless, it must have been evident to all that an attack might come at any time.

That night 'B' Squadron harboured just south of Div HQ and the 4th/8th Gurkhas on the chaung to the north. Two men with Tommy-guns and grenades were on guard on every tank during the night. Trucks kept passing through our harbour very noisily throughout the night, moving south from Div HQ which was apparently being evacuated. The sound of heavy fighting reached us from the north and east of Div HQ, being from fierce attacks made by the Japs on the Gurkhas, Punjabis and KOSBs.

Between the bottom of the road leading up to the east side of Ngakyedauk Pass and our regimental harbour 'Delhi', there was a large flat clearing about 1,200 yards square. It was surrounded by steep hills, rising abruptly from the padi and covered with dense jungle. In the centre was a small scrub-covered hill, 200 yards long and 150 feet high. This whole clearing was the Corps Administrative area at Sinzweya and tucked into the surrounding hillsides were petrol dumps, rations, equipment, clothing, barbed wire, vehicles, an Officers' shop, main dressing station and, all round the hill in the centre, quantities of ammunition. These were the forward supplies of 7th Division and the supply echelons for the three brigades were quartered there, as also was a mule company. Defence was in the hands of the 24th Light Anti-Aircraft and Anti-Tank Regiment commanded by Lt Col R.B. Cole (inevitably 'King Cole'), in civilian life an Oxford solicitor.

The trucks passing through 'B' Squadron's harbour that night had been making for that area.

* * *

Early on the morning of 6th February, a Sunday, small arms fire could be heard quite close to our harbour. Numbers of men, apparently unarmed and presumably administrative personnel from Div HQ, rushed through our area. We were mounted and ready to move, whilst the squadron leader, 'Bumper' Johnstone, had gone forward on foot to make a reconnaissance. When he returned we moved off and our troop took up positions with our guns covering hills which, we were told, were occupied by the Japs.

Major Johnstone on his 'recce' had found about 150 Japanese in position with mortars in the Div HQ area. It was clear that the Japs had attacked Div HQ that morning.

Major Horne of 'C' Squadron wrote afterwards:

> Major Tony Johnstone arrived just in time to find the HQ in disarray and the Japs ready to massacre all personnel and capture secret documents scattered on the ground. Quick action dispersed the surprised Japanese and General Frank Messervy escaped, still in his pyjamas, on the back of Major Johnstone's tank to the Admin Box from where he continued to command his division.

This is, in fact, roughly the story that passed round the Regiment at the time and was indeed a good story – so good that it has been repeated in large glossy war-books for the coffee tables of the world, but the truth is not nearly so neat and tidy. The one detail on which everyone agrees is that the General slept in his pyjamas that night, as did many other officers in the Div HQ. When he was awakened by the attack, he got up and walked around the area trying to find out what was happening, still in his pyjamas.

John Leyin, who was Major Johnstone's personal driver (not his tank driver), and who had a 15cwt truck for the purpose, remembers driving his truck, probably in the vicinity of Div HQ behind a tank. Suddenly he saw General Messervy emerge from the jungle and wave down the tank. The General climbed up onto the tank and as he did so his hat blew off and came to ground in front of John's truck. John can remember nothing further, either before or after, or even if the hat was retrieved. Obviously the General was not wearing pyjamas. If he had been, his appearance at that moment in a wavy-brimmed bush hat on top of a pair of (striped?) pyjamas would have embedded itself in John's memory ever after. It seems probable that Messervy told the tank commander to take him to his squadron leader and this he appears to have done.

Sergeant Philip Gabriel, Major Johnstone's wireless operator and Control Station on the squadron wireless net says:

> As far as I remember, the General was wandering about on his own somewhere until he came upon 'B' Squadron tanks and was then taken to Major Johnstone. What he had been doing before that I have no idea. The General and 'Bumper' consulted out of my hearing.

The regimental diary reads:

> 'B' Squadron attempted to organize the scattered infantry and services personnel in the area to form a secure base. At 7.30am 'C' Squadron was ordered to contact 'B' Squadron to patrol the road between the Corps Administrative area and 7th Div HQ. The officers commanding 'B' and 'C' Squadrons did make contact and the road was patrolled throughout the day. At about 8am it started to rain heavily and the road out of 'Delhi' became very difficult.
>
> 'C' Squadron was ordered to put two troops in the Admin area as protection immediately, for this was becoming a collecting area for all divisional and corps troops and there were large numbers of vehicles and guns in a very small harbour.

7th Division headquarters had been set up at Laungyaung, a narrow steep valley some three to four miles north of the Admin area running west and east. It was established in a hollow near the top of an abrupt 300 foot hillock in thick jungle. A stream ran through the area. A single track had been hacked up the hillside and the camouflaged tents very well concealed. The rear HQ was in an adjacent natural bowl rimmed with thick wooded slopes.

Messervy had ordered the battalion assigned to HQ defence, the 1/11th Sikh Regiment, to fight the on-coming Japs in the Kwazon area across the river to the east. In consequence any defence of the HQ fell on the HQ personnel themselves, especially the Divisional Signals under Lt Col Patrick Hobson, and a company of the 24th Indian Engineers Battalion.

Col Hobson afterwards wrote of his experiences:

> During the 4th and 5th February considerable fighting took place in our rear and on the afternoon of the 5th noise of battle began to draw near Div HQ. Our HQ defence company had been withdrawn for another purpose and it was clear that any attack on Div HQ would fall heavily on us. I was therefore very busy on the 5th checking up on our defence lay-out, made up of a series of strong dug-in positions supported by LMGs (light machine-guns) sited to give flanking and covering fire.
>
> Basically the lay-out consisted of the Signal Office on the right, a main strong point in the centre, and a position on top of the ridge on the left facing towards open ground on our front. Both the Signal Office and the ridge on the left had dug-in LMG positions manned respectively by Major Piddington and Capt Gittall, both of whom were later awarded the MC for the part they played in the defence.
>
> There was also a stop position in the rear to guard against possible infiltration from this area. By the time night had set in, all defensive positions were fully manned and sentries were on the alert.

Before going to sleep that night the General had asked Col Hobson to move the signals motor transport, in laager about a mile from HQ, down to the Admin area together with 24 wireless sets. These must have been the trucks that passed noisily through our harbour that night.

Lt Col Hobson continues:

> An eerie night ensued. Strange rustlings in the jungle were interspersed with odd rifle shots – some quite close. There was an inescapable feeling of impending crisis. The question was, when would the storm break? For break it must. At about 0530 hours it looked as if the unit was going to get through the night without being attacked, but this thought

was shattered by a sudden and dramatic outburst of shouts and screams from the Divisional headquarters jeep car park, about 300 yards away. The officer commanding No 1 Company, who had spent the night in the signal-office area, rang up to say that an NCO had just come from the car park to report that there were a number of strange figures there and he thought they were Japanese. Shortly after this, very loud shouting was heard on the immediate front coupled with a stentorian voice yelling orders. This was quite astonishing as one associates a Japanese attack with a silent crawling approach rather than with the uproar that was now going on. Suddenly, out of the dark misty night, a long line of figures could be discerned approaching the main defences. There was no doubt who they were and fire was opened. The LMG on the left flank was particularly well sited to bring enfilading fire to bear and this weapon took its toll, causing a number of casualties who were seen to fall. The advance wavered, came to a halt and then swiftly withdrew – the wounded and the dead being dragged away.

⋆ ⋆ ⋆

General Frank Messervy had been educated at Eton – as also had Major Johnstone, though of a later generation. He then joined the Indian Army – Hodson's Horse – and became involved in the First World War, though not to any great extent because the Cavalry could hardly find a place in trench warfare. In 1921 he met Mountbatten. He was Aide-de-camp to the Viceroy and Mountbatten was ADC to HRH The Prince of Wales (later Edward VIII) on the latter's official visit to India. Mountbatten admired Messervy's polo playing and said afterwards, 'He told me the proper way to mount a polo pony was to run at it from behind, take a flying leap and vault up into the saddle. It was a lesson I quickly learnt. I always mount a horse that way today.' Messervy, in fact, possessed a very well-schooled pony which *could* be mounted in this way, using its tail as a handhold!

In the 1930s he became Brigade Major of the 1st (Risalpur) Cavalry Brigade. Later he went as an instructor to the Staff College at Quetta as Brevet Lt Colonel. Another instructor was an infantry Lt Col, Bernard Montgomery. Despite Messervy's over-developed sense of humour and Monty's entire lack of same, they and their families became friends. One day Messervy insisted on taking both families to the cinema to see 'The Lives of a Bengal Lancer'. I, with all other schoolboys of the period, had seen this film at the age of about 10. It was Hollywood's version of the British Empire and bore no relation to the book of the same name by Major F. Yeats-Brown. There was a spectacular cavalry charge in the middle which in fact had been made by Hodson's Horse and some of the production team had stayed at Messervy's house in Risalpur. Monty's verdict was 'No infantry, no tanks, no GOOD'.

After this he became CO of the 13th Lancers. In 1937 the Cavalry regiments were at last 'mechanised' and the lancers exchanged their horses for tanks and armoured cars. At the outbreak of war he was sent to help train 5th Indian Division at Secunderabad and went with them to the Sudan and Eritrea. There they fought the Italians in mountainous country. He made his name as Commander of Force Gazelle. From there he went on to command the 4th Division fighting the Germans in the desert, then ultimately commanding 7th Armoured Division (the Desert Rats), although he had not previously commanded armoured vehicles. In this position Rommel managed to catch him out. The Desert Rats had previously reconnoitred defensive positions but the division was caught by Rommel's attack and thrown into complete confusion. Divisional HQ was overrun and Messervy and many of his staff were captured (fortunately he managed to escape, by pretending to be a batman, and re-joined the residue of the HQ behind British lines forty-eight hours later). He was criticised for having his HQ too far forward (thus leaving his division without a commander during some vital hours) and lost his command.

In September 1942 he was sent to Delhi to create 43rd Indian Armoured Division. No sooner was this done than it was disbanded. He was then (March 1943) appointed Director of Armoured Fighting Vehicles at GHQ Delhi, where he set about changing the policy that light Stuart tanks were the only tanks for the jungle. He believed that a big gun and reasonably thick armour were both needed against the deeply-dug Japanese gun-bunkers, and in the central plains of Burma. He was successful in getting his opinions accepted.

In July 1943 Messervy was at last given an active command again, that of the 7th Indian Division. In a speech to his officers in the Rupa Sri cinema in Ranchi he said, 'I foresee that our brigades and the Japanese regiments will become interposed with one another, like the layers of a Neapolitan sandwich.' On 19th September 1943 he took up command of the division in Arakan.

* * *

All of which led to his beleaguered situation at Laungyaung at dawn on the 6th February 1944 and his conversation with another old Etonian in the damp morning mist. The position was all too reminiscent of North Africa. General Messervy wrote:

> I was awakened by an outburst of yells and groans, though oddly enough I heard few shots. I jumped out of bed and walked about in pyjamas for an hour or so, trying to find out what was going on. The whole camp was aroused but there was confusion all around us. It was very dark. Suddenly the Japanese, with a cheer you hear when Arsenal scores a goal at home, charged the signals quarters. The signal men, with a company of Indian Engineers, were acting as Divisional Headquarters Defence Force.
>
> The Japanese came on in waist-high mist which partly concealed them. They pierced only the outer fringe of the position in force however. No Japanese actually came my way, though some who approached were shot by the liaison officer's batman; the others ran back.

A signalman informed the General that all telephone wires seemed to have been cut. Communication with the signals position, some 300 yards below, had therefore been lost. Messervy is said to have 'walked back to his tent, methodically dressed, armed himself with his favourite light carbine and awaited the Japanese next move'. His last wireless message was 'Div HQ is being attacked. 89 Brigade less 4/8 Gurkhas to pull back on 17th Indian Field Regt' (near Awlanbyin).

Meanwhile Col Hobson and the signals continued with their valiant defence of the position:

> Leading Japanese elements had penetrated as close as a few feet from the signals forward positions and a wounded Japanese was pulled in by some soldiers. 7th Divisional Signals had taken its first Japanese prisoner; an unusual feat as the taking of Japanese prisoners was very rare. Meanwhile a further thrust was made where the stream intervened between the main position and the signal office area. Here a number of enemy managed to infiltrate into the Divisional headquarters area. This caused the GOC and other members of the staff to vacate their normal positions and to withdraw to the high ground on the south of Divisional headquarters. This infiltration also cut off the signal office from the rest

of the signals defence area. A number of the enemy were now milling about in the rear of the main strong point. It was quite light by this time but the thickness of the jungle and the well-dug-in positions concealed signals from the Japanese, whom they were able to dispose of, almost at their leisure, with grenades and rifle fire. An astonishing sight was that of a group of Japanese setting-up an MMG ten yards in rear of a signals' dug-in position. They appeared blissfully unconscious of any danger and were shot down, one by one, at practically point-blank range, without appearing to comprehend where their peril lay. This was typical of the attack, which was conspicuous throughout for lack of any subtlety on the part of the enemy. A distinct impression lingered afterwards that the Japanese were under the influence of some sort of drug, so unaccountable were their actions at times.

Meanwhile it had become apparent to Messervy that nothing could save Divisional HQ. An attack had been made on the Engineers' HQ which had been 'bloodily repulsed', but the whole position now seemed surrounded. The General ordered all secret documents and wireless sets to be destroyed and all survivors to slip away in small parties and make for the Admin area. As all communications in HQ were severed, he sent out runners with the message but none returned, so only those immediately around him knew of this order.

He gathered together a party of some thirty men. They went down the hillside to the chaung below, which at this time of year was largely dried-up, with a small stream running down the middle. They followed it in a south-westerly direction towards the Corps Admin area, a gloomy green tunnel, knowing that the whole area might be infested with the enemy. Once Messervy slipped and fell into the stream. Despite this he pushed on with his carbine on one shoulder and a Mills bomb in the other hand. All the rest carried a grenade each. The going was slow, partly because there were a number of wounded in the party. Lt Bullock, a new ADC, was, at one point, found to be missing. They could only trudge on and hope he would follow, but Lt Bullock was not seen or heard of again.

After several miles they found a path on the left bank leading into the jungle which they took. This path soon led into a clearing which was occupied by an Indian Infantry Mobile Workshop of 89 Brigade, commanded by Capt Smith who remembers the occasion very vividly and describes it as follows:

We were sitting about after breakfast, in the sunshine, our lorries hidden in the trees, when a straggle of men came through the bushes. They were in various stages of undress, most were hatless, few had weapons and were strained and exhausted. Some five or six were badly wounded and were supported by others. One was using a rifle as a crutch, its muzzle in the ground. They fell or sat down among us while we hurried to help them. There was an urgency, a nervousness about them. They looked at us with relief and gratitude, finding us here.

In all, twenty to twenty-five British men appeared. They were followed by five Indian soldiers, acting as though they were a rear guard. These men were all uniformed, wore steel helmets and carried rifles with fixed bayonets. Two of them went back through the bushes to keep a watch behind them.

Among the refugee British was the General himself. I had not seen him before but I recognized his badges of rank. He was fully uniformed but without a hat. He went to stand on one side by himself.

There was confusion in the scene that followed but a sense of order also from our men. Although we had slept in the open the night before, we were washed, shaved and uniformed. On their own initiative the men of the unit set about giving whatever help they could. Fetching water was easy because we had goatskin bags of it hung in the open to keep cool.

They told us that our Divisional headquarters, some five miles to the north-east, had been overrun in complete surprise, during the night, by a strong force of Japanese. Many of the staff officers there had been killed or captured. They believed that large numbers of Japanese would now be encircling us from the north and then would come down south towards us to attack the Division itself. Those who had escaped in the confusion of the night had come from the headquarters position. They had followed a dried-out river course, west and south, and had come out of it completely by chance into our position. It had been slow travelling with the wounded during the night.

Most of the British were staff officers of high rank. Since their work was sedentary and many were no longer young, the shock of unreality could be seen on their faces. It was by an ironical chance that the wounded man I dealt with was the officer who had been in charge of the divisional medical services, for I had no medical training. He was in great pain and partly unconscious. He was a thin, grey-haired, balding man, dressed in green uniform shirt with red tabs and medical insignia on his collar and the rank of colonel on his shoulder. He wore pyjama trousers and had a brown boot on one foot. The other foot was bare, with the flesh of his heel hanging loose as if it had been struck open by a sword. He had been walking on the toe-pad of that bare foot along a rocky riverbed, at his best speed, during the night, supported by another man. He was too far gone in suffering to notice the way I attended to him. Someone brought him tea from the dixie still warm by our cookhouse fire, but he scarcely had the strength to sip it.

While I had been working, the general had 'let it be known' that he wanted three of our lorries taken out of cover and got ready to drive his men away. In a short while the lorries were loaded with those who were not badly hurt and they were driven off at speed.

Six men were left behind with us, four of them seriously wounded. We had three jeeps in the trees so we put two sick men in each, with much pain and hardship to them, and sent them off with some of our men in attendance. Our warrant officer went in charge of the party and to see that the jeeps were driven slowly. They were to go to our Divisional Field hospital, which was south and west from where we were.

From *The Turning Point*

Capt Smith said that the whole incident occurred at 8am and that the sun was shining. Messervy's party later arrived at the Admin area and he described the journey as 'uneventful' which in the context it probably was!

Col Hobson knew nothing of all this, as can be seen from the following:

No further attacks were made. Instead heavy LMG fire from the neighbouring airstrip became the order of the day. As things were quieter I made my way to the divisional command post area to report on the situation. This I found deserted but I ran into a sergeant from 'I' branch who said the GOC and the 'G' staff had decided to move to the Divisional Admin area (some two and a half miles away) with a view to re-establishing command from there. I was wondering what to do next when I came upon the CRA and his staff in a dug-in position ready to sell their lives dearly. After some discussion it was decided to hold on and see how things developed.

At this juncture, a squadron of 'friendly' tanks suddenly appeared on the open ground to the front and all felt considerable relief at seeing this powerful reinforcement, but hopes were dashed. They passed several times in front of the headquarter area and, believing it to be evacuated, subjected the defence to an intense and terrifying concentration of all the fire power they could muster. This was much worse than anything the Japanese had produced and it was with relief when they were seen to disappear in the direction of the Divisional Admin area.

These tanks were clearly 25th Dragoons, probably part of 'B' Squadron. It may be that the troop commander, seeing the Japanese LMG posts in the HQ area, thought to silence them and some of the defenders were caught in the two lines of fire. Or he may have been told, or assumed from his observation, that the HQ had been abandoned, as indeed might have been the case if the general's orders had reached all personnel and been carried out. The rain, mist and jungle could only add to the confusion and poor visibility. Col Hobson refers to 'a squadron' but it is unlikely to have been as much as that.

Colonel Hobson continues:

> At about 1030 hours things started to liven up and it was clear that the Japanese were endeavouring to gain a tighter grip on the headquarters position. LMGs had been worked forward and a dangerous threat was developing from the high ground, which overlooked signals from the north. The small detachment in this area reported that they were being badly harrassed by Japanese infiltrators and that an LMG had been moved up very close to them. It became apparent that if the Japanese succeeded in occupying this high ground, the defence would be in an awkward position. The enemy would then look down into the dug-in positions and signals would be at the mercy of their fire, to say nothing of the unpleasant prospect of having grenades rolled down into their midst. In view of this, I went across to consult with the CRA. The CRA told me that he had decided the time had come to evacuate Divisional headquarters as we were serving no useful purpose in staying on, divorced from the remainder of the headquarters staff. After some discussion, it was decided to move out to the south and make our way through the jungle to the Divisional Admin area, situated at Ngakyedauk Pass.

Their only communication with the outside world was a wireless link with the Admin area. The last message on this link reached the area about 11.20am and, as it finished, the words 'Put a pick through that set' were heard and no more. Col Hobson continues:

> The evacuation started and this proved to be a long-drawn-out nerve-racking and dangerous operation as there were no longer the safety of well-dug positions to give protection. However, the thickness of the jungle afforded help in concealing movements and saved many casualties during this critical period. This time rain had started to fall and the going became very slippery and difficult. Furthermore, the line of withdrawal

to the south was denied by a Japanese LMG position sited astride it and so, perforce, a detour had to be made to the west where the jungle was even thicker and the hillsides almost vertical. Divisional Signals became split up into a number of small parties and it was a question of each party finding its own route through the jungle, as best it could, to the Admin area. This was far from easy as apart from the very thick jungle, which often had to be cut, steep hillsides and narrow winding streams made progress very slow and sense of direction soon became very confused. It was during this evacuation that a number of the unit got lost – never to be seen again.

There was another party in 7th Div HQ which had to take its own decision to evacuate and was led to the Admin area by Capt Wood, the Camp Commandant. Brig Roberts gives the following account, said to have been written at the time:

Soon after this 'blitz' (about 11.50am) a wounded havildar (sergeant) of Signals and a BOR clerk from 'G' branch appeared, coming along the path at the north end of the area. From them it was learnt that 'G' branch and the CRA's headquarters had withdrawn to the Admin area. The BOR had lost contact about half-an-hour earlier with the CRA's party and had found the wounded signaller in his wanderings.

It appeared that the hill to the north of Rear Division HQ was unoccupied and it was decided to try and withdraw by that route to the Admin area. Orders were issued to destroy documents and a small party sent to 'A' branch office to pass on the orders.

The party found the Sergeants' Mess occupied by a Japanese Light Machine Gun post and, as it was within some 20 or 30 yards of 'A' office, the only thing the party could do was to collect what they could and quietly withdraw. This they managed to do without being seen.

At 12.35pm the withdrawal started led by Capt Wood, who had reconnoitred a route, and headed by a small party of armed officers and clerks. Behind them was a group of non-combatants, then another armed party, more non-combatants, and in rear an armed party of officers and their orderlies. This column moved off in single file up the hill to the north and then straight down the other side on a very steep and seldom-used track. As the rear party crossed the top of the ridge, enemy could be heard talking not far away.

The column broke up into three parties owing to the non-combatants failing to keep in touch in the dense jungle and steep hills, but the three armed groups moved on independently, each with its quota of non-combatants, picking up stragglers as they progressed, including a party of 15 signallers, of whom many were wounded, which had lost its way.

Only the rearmost party was molested. They were seen crossing an open space and fired on but escaped without loss and finally reached the Admin area at 5pm that evening.

Yet another person who did not get the general's orders was Capt Mick Ablett of 'I' branch of the HQ. He had attended the meeting the previous evening and was under no illusions as to the dangers that might steal up in the night. He decided to get what sleep he could. Towards dawn he had a dream in which he was doing something he had never done in his life – attending a Cup Final at Wembley. The crowd was cheering madly but, after a time, a voice gradually imposed itself above the cheering, 'Wake up, wake up Mick. It's the Japs.' It was Capt Raymond Scaramanga. Mick jumped up and into his split trench which formed part of what was the main dormitory area for the staff of Div HQ. He felt as though he was on the edge of this area and seemed to be taking on the whole Japanese Imperial Army on his own.

At one point he was joined in the trench by an Indian soldier (sepoy) with rifle. This was a comfort because, until then, he had had only his revolver. They faced in opposite directions and suddenly the bushes about five yards in front of him parted, disclosing a Japanese soldier with rifle and bayonet. He was able to fire straight at him – but his revolver went 'click'. He pressed the trigger again and this time it fired. At the same moment the sepoy turned round and fired his rifle and between them the Jap soldier was rendered harmless. Capt Ablett continues the story in his own words:

> We had a flying visit from a padre who could give us no real news, but eventually we were joined by Major Pakenham's batman. We spotted three Japs approaching cautiously up the path from the main Div HQ and the batman fired three times and three Japs fell dead. It was a fantastic piece of shooting.
>
> However, it became obvious that a mere handful of us had become virtually isolated and I decided to try to get down the slope to the old 'G' area with the vague notion of destroying documents. However, on a rain-soaked path, I ran into a stream of our own people withdrawing from the area I was making for and was told that the Japs were already in occupation of the 'G' area. It was a very mixed bunch that struggled single file up

that muddy path while being mortared by the enemy – I imagine they were mainly signallers, cooks, orderlies and so on, survivors from the worst part of the battle in the northern part of Div HQ. It was at this point that a British corporal and I hit the ground together with his elbow in my stomach. When we got up his elbow had been shattered by a shell fragment, my stomach was intact!

Although the order to withdraw from Div HQ never reached me, I knew, of course, where we were supposed to rendezvous in the event. The simplest way was to walk in the shallow waters of one of the tributaries of the chaung running south towards the Admin area. Typical of meandering streams the mileage was greater but progress was easier.

At first I thought I was bringing up the rear of about 60 or 70 of our men, and I picked up a sten-gun as a more effective weapon than my revolver for a rearguard action. However, because the stream meandered so much it was impossible to keep the party in view all the time and I suddenly found I was guarding the rear of a motley crew of six or seven – one BOR, the rest non-combatants including wounded. I took over the lead.

As I stepped cautiously from a smaller tributary into a larger one I saw a Jap marching in the stream for all the world as if he were on guard outside the Imperial Palace. I darted back under cover but he must have been almost blind not to have seen me. The chatter in Japanese indicated a patrol of some strength, perhaps part of a larger group, and our only hope was to find a way round them. I managed to do this but, unfortunately, it meant crossing an area of open ground covered in pampas type grass. Even if you crouched the movement of the grass would give you away. Sure enough, we had not got very far when that very movement indicated that someone was approaching! I motioned the men behind to keep down and keep quiet. I knelt down on one knee and took careful aim at the waving grass. Suddenly a head popped up, said, 'Oh, my God!' and popped down again. It was a lieutenant from Signals leading another motley but slightly larger crew. I turned them round and soon afterwards we met up with an even larger group which, as the senior officer present, I then led into the Admin area without further incident.

Major Ablett says that even today he cannot watch a Cup Final on television without feeling that at any moment he may be awoken with 'Wake up, Mick. It's the Japs.'

4

Rendezvous for Battle

Wandering and fortuitous the paths
We followed to this rendezvous today
Out of the mines and offices and dives,
The side-streets of anxiety and want,
Huge cities known and distant as the stars,
Wheeling beyond our destiny and hope.

Some things we cleaned like knives in earth,
Kept from the dew and rust of Time,
Instinctive truths and elemental love,
Knowing the force that brings the teal and quail
From Turkestan across the Himalayan snows
To Kashmir and the South alone can guide
That winging wildness home again.

From *The Jungle*
Alun Lewis
(died Arakan 5 March 1944)

At about 11.30am one brigadier, Geoffrey Evans, arrived in the Admin area. He had been Brigadier, General Staff of IV Corps, operating in central Burma. At short notice he had been ordered to join the 5th Indian Division (under Maj Gen H.R. Briggs) and take over 9 Brigade.

On arrival at 5th Div HQ on 4th February he reports the following conversation:

'Hello, Geoff.'

'Hello, Briggo!'

'What brings you here, Geoff?'

'I've come to join you, Briggo.'

'I'm very glad to have you, but what are you going to do?'

'I have been sent to command 9 Brigade.'

'Oh, really. I have already got a temporary commander for that – Sally (Brig Salomans), but never mind, you take over and he can remain with you for the time being.'

Such were the ways of the High Command!

9 Brigade was east of the Mayu Range. Only two battalions, 2nd West Yorkshire Regt and 3/14th Punjab Regt were there; the remaining one, 3/9th Jats, being still with 5th Division on the west side of the Range. To reach them Brig Evans had to cross the Ngakyedauk Pass. He found Brig Salomans in his HQ and explained what had happened.

Capt Anthony Brett-James was in charge of 9 Brigade Signals and that evening walked into the mess tent where he met the new brigadier. The latter wasted no time in making his acquaintance. 'Are you my signals officer? . . . Good. I want perfect communications, understand?' Though taken aback by the abruptness, B-J did understand. He describes Evans as blunt, downright, brusque, hard, unrelaxing, an energizing force, who set a high standard of industry and swift decision which others were expected to equal. He had fought through the North African campaign and had been awarded the DSO twice. He had been presented with a staff by the officers of the 1st Battalion of the Royal Sussex Regiment whom he had commanded in Africa, in commemoration of the battles they had shared. He now had the staff with him and used it through the often steep and sometimes muddy jungle paths.

Brig Evans settled down for the night which was disturbed by some shells and mortar bombs but otherwise quiet.

In the morning, the 5th February, news reached him that enemy forces were at Taung Bazaar and enemy aircraft were more than usually evident. He was ordered to send a company of the West Yorkshires to the Admin area (the position of which was unknown to him). Apart from that the day was quiet.

Next morning, the 6th February, Briggo came on the line:

> This morning the Japs overran Frank Messervy's HQ at Laung Chaung. Nobody knows whether he or anybody else got away . . . the corps commander wants you to take command of the Corps Admin area. Go back there with the West Yorkshires, less one company. Put it into a state of defence and hold it at all costs.

As he himself says, Brig Evans was somewhat staggered, not even knowing where the Corps Admin area was. He told Brig Salomans to follow him with the West Yorkshires and set off in a jeep. It had been raining for the past two or three hours and the jeep slipped all over the place. Nearing the end of his journey he almost ran into another jeep being driven fast in the opposite direction which turned out to contain Major Hugh Ley. Evans had been Commandant at the Staff College at Quetta where Ley had been an instructor. Obviously they knew each other well, though they had not met for about a year.

In answer to Evans' enquiry, Ley explained that he was second-in-command of the 25th Dragoons and, following a visit to 7 Div HQ the previous day, he was on his way to make a 'recce' for a tank harbour in the forward area. Evans told him he had better forget it. Obviously he had not heard the latest news. 'The Japs are around the back of us and are threatening 7 Div HQ. I have been ordered to go to the Admin area and organize a defensive position with any troops I can get hold of. Now how many tanks have you got?' 'Well, actually the whole Regiment.' 'Right. You come along with me. I need someone I know in these circumstances.' So Major Ley radioed back to RHQ as to where he was going, turned round and followed Brig Evans to the Admin area.

* * *

The 2nd Battalion, the West Yorkshire Regiment, had a bad time moving themselves, their supplies and equipment from the south of the Admin area in the pouring rain. Mules had to be pushed and pulled uphill, even when all loads had been dumped in the mud. Bren-carriers, ambulances, trucks, all found it near impossible to make progress and everyone was soaked to the skin. Capt Brett-James and his men had been out trying to repair the telephone lines to 7 Div HQ but, needless to say, could get no reply. They finally received orders to congregate at the eastern entrance to the Ngakyedauk Pass, in fact the Admin area. After half an hour in a jeep, they arrived.

The atmosphere in that place was one of confusion and uncertainty. Men were lurching about in the mud, as were tanks; people were straggling in from all directions but particularly from Div HQ and military police were trying to make some sort of order out of the chaos. Nobody seemed to know what had happened but something had gone badly wrong. No one knew what to expect.

Where were the Japs and where would they strike next? Regular army officers began to wonder about their careers. People who had been in bad situations before began to make comparisons and feared the worst.

In truth, the enemy could be anywhere, sheltered as its movements were by the jungle. Two of Brett-James' Indian signallers were sent out to repair a cable in the jungle. Only one returned. He shakily described how they had been kneeling to test the cable and a party of soldiers approached whom they took to be Gurkhas. When these soldiers asked whether the two signallers wished to live, it flashed through his mind that they were Japanese. He darted into the jungle pursued by a hail of bullets. His companion, however, was seized by the Japanese and not seen again.

Brett-James eventually found Brig Evans outside a tent by a group of trees near the centre of the Admin area. He made his presence known by a smart salute. 'What the devil have you come up here for?', said the Brigadier turning towards him abruptly. 'To produce you some communications, Sir'. He managed to beg some cable from the sole active signal centre nearby and was soon able to fix up a telephone for the Brigadier.

Sometime before this, Gen Messervy had arrived at 'Delhi' Harbour with his party from Capt Smith's enclave. It could hardly have taken him more than an hour by truck but the going may have been made difficult by the rain. Major Ley saw him on arrival and remembers he was wearing battle-dress but no hat. He had nothing but what he stood up in which included a Mills bomb in each pocket. He went to the Dragoons RHQ saying 'Frinkie, I've lost my Division.'

After being revived with char and whisky, his first anxiety was to re-establish communication with his brigades and Corps HQ. The 25th Dragoons were happy to arrange this and in fact the general and his staff moved into our regimental HQ (the historian of the 3rd Carabiniers makes the nice historical parallel of the Duke of Wellington riding into the nearest British square at Waterloo, a battle also fought on a Sunday and also in heavy mud!). The Regimental Signals Officer, Capt Robertson, set up a forward divisional control set and this was used by Div HQ for the next fortnight as their command link. A telephone back to Corps was also in operation all day. 25th Dragoons supplied the General with a light armoured car and wireless. As cyphers had been compromised in the Japanese capture of 7 Div HQ, guarded language had to be used over the air. Some officers (including the General) talked in schoolboy French, which the brigadier admitted 'would have stumped the French, let alone the Japanese'. For sometime the only communication line to the west of the Pass was 'Q Link', between 9 Brigade HQ and 5 Div HQ.

Lt McVicker took the General in his tank to the Admin area and during the rest of the day various small parties from Div HQ at Laungyaung continued to arrive at 'Delhi' or the Admin area.

Col Hobson says:

> Parties of the Divisional Signals started arriving in the Admin area from 1400 hours onwards but by evening, when a check was made, there was still a considerable number missing. Many came in during the next few days as stragglers but some were taken prisoner by the Japanese and a few perished in the jungle. Later, when a final check was made, signallers' casualties were found to be five officers killed and two missing, three British ranks killed and four missing, eight Indian ranks killed and fifteen missing. However, the Japanese had suffered very considerably in their attacks and while it is difficult to be precise, a fair estimate would be about forty killed and a considerable number wounded.
>
> During the fighting the signal office had been in the thick of the battle. It had been rushed four times and also had been subjected to a number of infiltration attacks. All efforts to break through their defence area had failed. The GOC therefore had some cause for making a special telephone call to the CSO XVth Corps later that day saying he was proud of his Divisional Signals!

Col Hobson may have underestimated the Indian casualties. Louis Allen gave these as *ninety* Indian ranks killed or missing, a vast number considering the scale of the battle and it does not take into account the wounded. This battle was an heroic stand lasting over five hours and has not been given the attention it deserves. However, many years later, the Royal Corps of Signals commissioned a painting of the episode and this can be seen at the Depot of the Corps at Blandford Camp, Blandford Forum, Dorset.

One of the last persons to leave the Div HQ must have been Lt Col R (Dick) McCaig, Brigade Major Royal Artillery. He remembers being woken by 'a hell of a din' and soon discovered that the general and 'G' branch had all gone – unknown. He was present when Col Hobson and Brig Tim Hely, Commander Royal Artillery, took the decision to pull out. This was about 10.30am. He was determined that there should be a rearguard and stayed behind to form it with a dozen or so picked men. After having seen off Tim Hely and the bulk of the HQ RA together with Pat Hobson's party of signallers, he decided it was time to go about noon. He moved his party on to the ridge above the HQ offices, collecting one or two on the way through. He had the satisfaction of shooting a Japanese with his .303 at 15-20 yards and dispersing the encircling party he was leading.

Shortly after, Col McCaig's party was bombarded with explosive missiles. They did not hear them coming and assumed they were Jap mortar bombs. One 'grievously tore apart a fine young clerk of ours.' Col McCaig now, however, thinks these were fired by tanks into the HQ area, assuming it was evacuated. It seems unlikely that the Japanese would fire blind into an area which their forward troops were already penetrating. Col McCaig adds, however, 'I would not hold that against the magnificent 25th Dragoons on whom we were to rely so much in this battle and later ones. A hard core of steel, I always felt, could never be penetrated.'

One other escapee from Div HQ must be mentioned. Capt Raymond Scaramanga had, with others, been in a 'G' branch office from which they had all moved out. He went back to try and destroy secret papers but this was probably not possible owing to Jap infiltration. So he went out the 'front' entrance of the HQ and was picked up by a tank and taken to the Admin area. This was probably one of 'C' Squadron tanks who were patrolling the track between Div HQ and the Admin area. No one inside the HQ knew of this patrol, so they all escaped through the 'back' entrance which was thought to be safer.

* * *

139 Jungle Field Regiment of the Royal Artillery was in the area and caught up in the general confusion. The Regimental Quartermaster Sergeant describes the 6th February:

Whilst en route to Div HQ to collect W/T (wireless) sets, we were informed that the HQ had been attacked and had evacuated its positions. On returning to the dump (near the Admin area), we were informed by V Force that the Japs were practically all round us and firing was heard at the rear of the dump. Bren-gun posts were sited and defence lines made. At 1230 hours RQMS Butcher and his wagon-line party (503 Battery) and Sergeant Mainwaring and his party (364 Battery) arrived with information that they had had to evacuate their position in view of superior enemy forces coming in their direction.

Capt (QM) Wallace went to see the CRA who gave orders to abandon the dump and endeavour to obtain protection with the tanks until the following day when we could perhaps return to collect the stores. The dump was left at 1745 hours, too late to fire any documents because of approaching darkness. The tanks gave us protection and we defended approximately 100 yards of ridge overlooking a Jap position until 1030 hours next morning. We took with us all the vehicles in the dump, with the exception of one Chevrolet 15cwt, and all stores which could be loaded in the time at our disposal. A party under BSM Reid (362 Battery) arrived at 1600 hours and took shelter with the 'Q' staff at the opposite end of the tank lines. This party eventually joined the main body of the 362 Battery near the Base area.

(RQMS Murgatroyd, RA)

362 Battery had had an unpleasant experience that day:

362 Battery in Wet Valley was attacked by a large force of Japs as the men were queuing up for breakfast. Being taken completely by surprise and forced to abandon their jeeps, mortars and some 3,000 mortar bombs, the majority of the Battery managed to withdraw westward to a hill called Ngakyeindauk Taung. It had suffered many casualties including eighteen men killed. Making their way to the Admin area some scattered survivors passed through the wagon-lines, a mile or so from the Battery's original position. On being informed of the situation and the enemy threat, the wagon-lines personnel abandoned the 3-tonners and ammunition quads and withdrew to the Admin area with the party from 362 Battery. Later Capt Hill of 364 Battery, with a party of drivers, managed to recover 503 Battery's vehicles but was unable to move 364 Battery's trucks owing to heavy enemy fire. The main body of 362 Battery eventually moved back into the Admin area.

Six days later at night a party from 362 went with 'C' Company of 4/8th Gurkhas to Wet Valley and recovered thirteen mortars and a 21 set. It was found that the Japs had removed the rotor arms from the jeeps.

(Bill Harding, 139 Jungle Field Regiment)

In his *Defeat into Victory*, Field-Marshal Slim writes:

> Yet when the Japanese struck I am ashamed to say it was a great surprise. On the morning of the 4th February,a motorcycle despatch rider roared up with a message. It told me that the Japanese had suddenly swept down out of the blue and rushed Taung Bazaar, five or six miles in rear of 7 Divison. The situation was obscure said the signal, but it was clear that the enemy was in considerable strength.
>
> I had expected ample warning of the Japanese move but this meant that they had passed right round the 7th Division unobserved and were within two or three miles of the Ngakyedauk Pass and the Administrative Box which I knew was prepared for nothing more than raids.

At some point after we crossed the Ngakyedauk Pass on the 4th February the higher command, perhaps appalled at the thought of losing a complete regiment of tanks, brought into Arakan at immense trouble and expense (and the only Allied tanks there at the time), and issued an order to Col Frink to withdraw the Regiment back over the Pass. As the officer commanding in the field, he refused to do so. This order was probably given by Col S.H. Persse of Corps HQ whose responsibility was the Corps Armoured Group. Normally Col Frink would have felt he 'had to go along with him' but on this occasion he clearly did not.

This decision was in accord with the procedure agreed by Mountbatten and Slim, that where a unit was cut off it was to stand its ground and would be supplied by air. To withdraw the tanks at this stage would have meant abandoning 7 Division, probably to be broken up by the Japanese, and to struggle back over the Mayu Range as best it could. The Japanese would have commandeered much of their equipment, swarmed over the Pass, cut off the 5th Division from its land supplies and pushed on to India. In any event with the Japanese advancing in unknown numbers through the jungle with the obvious intention of capturing the Pass, it would have been a high risk to move any tanks over the Pass, let alone a whole regiment.

Whatever the outcome it would have been yet another British defeat in Burma. Neither the Government nor the Army could afford that. Col Frink's supreme confidence in his regiment was amply justified by events.

* * *

In the meantime Brig Evans had had time to meet Gen Messervy and some of his officers and Lt Col Cole, commanding officer of the Anti-Aircraft and Anti-Tank Regt, and generally to sum up the situation. He was to remain 'Box' Commander and with Major Ley and Col Cole toured the Admin area, allotting a part of the perimeter to each small unit. There was not enough units to man the whole perimeter and the eastern and north eastern edges were left open and covered by fire power alone.

The units on the perimeter were inside the jungle and dug themselves in. Two companies of 2nd Battalion of the West Yorkshire Regiment, commanded by Lt Col 'Munshi' Cree, were kept as a mobile reserve – 'A' Company under Maj Chris O'Hara and 'B' Company under Lt Alec Dunlop. These were, like the tanks, to be used wherever it seemed most necessary during an enemy attack. 'C' Company was placed on a hill to the north of the Pass road which became known as 'C Company Hill'.

The Corps Administrative area had now become a defensive 'Box' and was therefore so called. Brig Evans established his command post in the western side of the Box near the exit into the Ngakyedauk Pass. Nearby were the 7th Division's new HQ, 9 Brigade HQ, RHQ 2nd Battalion West Yorkshire Regt, RHQ 24th AA and AT Regt RA and RHQ 24th Mountain Regiment, Royal Indian Artillery.

Brig Evans at 5pm called the unit commanders to his HQ and gave them a forceful talk:

> Your job is to stay put and keep the Japs out. Hold your fire and conserve your ammunition. Wait till you see the yellow of their eyes before your shoot. Make sure that one round means one dead Jap. The tanks and the West Yorks are there to back you up.

There was to be no withdrawal: the best chance of survival was to fight and to kill as many of the enemy as possible. He had put a road block across the Pass road to stop any vehicles trying to get out (a few had already done so). He added that he wanted reports every morning on the number of dead Japanese in front of each section, so introducing a spirit of competition.

The men who were to carry out these instructions were mainly Indian corps and division administrative personnel, commanded by British or Indian officers and NCOs. They had been trained to fire rifles out of trenches but not a lot more. Col Cole visited all these small units with a view to assisting the officers in making their defensive positions in the jungle, they being somewhat unaccustomed to these activities. All were put in telephone communication with Box HQ. To quote Col Frink, 'scarcely the troops that would be selected in a Staff College paper for the job'.

Major Ley reported his conversation with Brig Evans to Col Frink. The tanks were still in the 'Delhi' harbour but Evans wanted two squadrons brought into the Box. They were to take up a porcupine-like formation on the open ground, well away from the edge of the jungle and with their guns pointing outwards. 'B' Squadron was deployed west of Ammunition Hill and 'C' Squadron east of it. Regimental HQ was placed to the rear of 'C' Squadron.

Evans attached such importance to the tanks that he wanted a senior liaison officer from the Regiment to be permanently attached to his HQ. This created a delicate situation in that Evans and Frink had met and decidedly did not get on. Normally Frink himself might have gone to the HQ. Ley however had Brig Evans at the Staff College and was familiar with his manner and methods (and, as a younger man, was able to admire him as a soldier). So, Ley moved to Box HQ and shared a slit trench with Evans. Though he and Evans got on well, Evans seems to have taken some offence so far as Frink was concerned. It has been said that Evans was a bully; it was certainly not the time to fall out with the commander of the Corps Armoured Group.

Evans insisted that Ley brought his tank with him, partly as a guard tank and partly as an armoured run-about, ready to hand for Evans himself. Major Ley's tank carried on the back not only the crew's kit-bags but some non-regulation items peculiar to the tank commander – a suitcase with a second suit of jungle green battledress, a folding wicker chair and a lavatory seat. The extra suit of jungle green provided Gen Messervy with a change of clothes, being of a similar build to Ley. The folding chair was used for sleeping in the slit trench at night, and as for the lavatory seat . . . a use was quickly found for that.

* * *

If there was an over-reaction at corps level to the report of Japanese forces at Taung Bazaar, there may have been the opposite at divisional level. The report was first made by the Gwalior State Cavalry on the morning of the 4th February. It may well be that some British officers thought this was mere panic on the part of the Indian State troops who were more used to guarding the Maharajah's Palace. The reports were confirmed by V Force, the secret service which operated amongst the Arakanese people, but then again V Force had often reported the imminent happening of events which never materialized. Officers who took the reports too seriously were considered 'nervy'.

It has often been stated that the Japanese attack on 7 Div HQ was a surprise. It was not. From the morning of the 4th February it was always a possibility and by the evening of the 5th it was a certainty. Yet when it happened Col Hobson and the signals personnel appear to have been the only ones in the HQ who knew what they should do and did it. The rest was left to flounder as best they could. No arrangements had been made for the destruction of secret papers and cyphers and all fell into Japanese hands. Not all the brave efforts of the signals and engineers could save the office and dormitory area of the HQ which was ransacked by the Japanese. The result was indeed a shambles. Only in one respect did everyone know what to do; they all rallied on the Admin area; those that is, who were not killed or taken prisoner on the way. There was nowhere else to go.

The Signals' defence of their position was of great value in that it held up the Japanese force for some vital hours during which Brig Evans was able to organize the Box. It also was effective in inflicting a considerable number of casualties on the enemy but was almost equally costly to ourselves. Indeed our casualties in this whole affair do not appear to have been calculated but must have been of a very high order.

* * *

In the north, for the 4/8th Gurkhas, the enemy seemed to be on every side. A liaison officer was sent by carrier to contact 89 Brigade HQ, as wireless communication had been lost. On entering the valley north of Brigade HQ he saw a squadron of tanks deployed and engaging an invisible enemy on both sides of the 1,000 yard wide valley. He made contact with the Squadron Leader from whom he learnt that the Division HQ had been overrun in the early hours of the morning and the hills on both sides of the valley were full of enemy who appeared to have come in through the foothills of the Mayu Range.

The Gurkhas had also lost contact with their other two companies and these were not seen again for eight days. At 4pm they were able to pick up an uncoded message from Messervy, sent from the Admin Box, ordering the Battalion to withdraw to the eastern entrance to the Box and report to 9 Brigade for orders.

In the meantime the rain stopped and the sun had come out. 'B' Squadron with 'C' Squadron and a section of the Scout Troop had been operating in the jungle to the north-east, both fighting off the enemy and rescuing men and wounded, artillery, jeeps, motorcycles, trucks and ambulances which had been abandoned at Div HQ or were struggling through the jungle. In particular Lt Banerjee of the 3/4th Bombay Grenadiers and his platoon, who were operating with us, did a great job evacuating about a dozen wounded from the Div HQ area under fire.

In the early morning Major Johnstone estimated that his tank guns had killed between one and two hundred Japanese whom they had caught in the open. Later in the morning he reported to Col Frink that a patrol had been inside Div HQ and had seen some fairly horrible sights. The Japanese had gone from office to office systematically killing everyone they came across.

At 6pm 'B' Squadron was ordered to return to the Admin Box for the night. However, this could not be done at once. First, we had to help a battery of the 6th Medium Artillery pull out their guns from the mud, caused by heavy rain, and give cover while doing so. Second, we escorted a mule train of the 4/8th Gurkhas back to the Box. Eventually we made a pretence of harbouring in the same area as the previous night and then, on a given signal, remounted the tanks and made full speed back to the Box. Both the 6th Medium and a company of the 4/8th Gurkhas also entered the Box. It was pretty well 10.30pm before we were settled in harbour, having been operating since before light. There had only been three casualties: three men wounded by mortar fire.

Just to keep people on their toes the Japs at 7pm started a raid on the north-east corner of the Box which was defended by a mule company of the RIASC. There was a lot of noise and tracer bullets flying about but the attack was not pressed home. Earlier in the day Japanese Zeros had strafed the Box killing a number of troops and two small mules close to Evans' HQ.

That night the Punjabis and the KOSBs withdrew on Messervy's orders south and took up a position astride the Ngakyedauk Chaung, covering the position of the 7th Indian Field Regiment of Artillery. They were back to back with 33 Brigade and covered the track leading from the Admin Box to 33 Brigade. One company of 7/2nd Punjab remained at Awlanbyin throughout the battle that was to follow, dominating the east and west tracks along the chaung.

So the 6th February 1944, which seemed like the longest day ever to those taking part, came to an end in relative calm, though the night silence was peppered with much small arms fire from 'itchy fingers'. As with the horses of old, the needs of the tanks had to be satisfied before our own wants. They had to be checked over and made ready for use during the night or next morning before we could settle down to bully and biscuits (or bully stew if we were lucky). As before, there were two guards on each tank throughout the night, the crew taking turns. Sleep did not come easy, even when it was possible.

Tokyo radio summed it all up as follows, 'General Messervy was surprised in his pyjamas. His Division was routed and he fled, leaving his troops behind.'

What had actually happened to cause this chaos? At 2300 hours on the night of 3rd/4th February, a large force of some 9,000 or more men had left the Japanese lines near Buthidaung, infiltrated north up the Kalapanzin valley and passed by or through 114 Brigade of 7 Div. They arrived at Taung Bazaar on the morning of the 4th February and it was the report of the Gwalior Lancers (Horsed Wing) at 9am that gave the alarm. (The Gwalior Lancers were a partly mechanized cavalry regiment of the Gwalior State Force placed at the disposal of His Majesty George VI, 'King Emperor', by the Maharajah.) The enemy crossed the river and moved south-west. Shortly thereafter a battalion under Col Kubo had left the main force and moved north-west towards the Goppe Pass. The remainder under Col Tanahashi moved south and west

SKETCH MAP OF THE ADMIN BOX AT SINZWEYA, FEBRUARY 1944.
(FROM A CONTEMPORARY SKETCH)

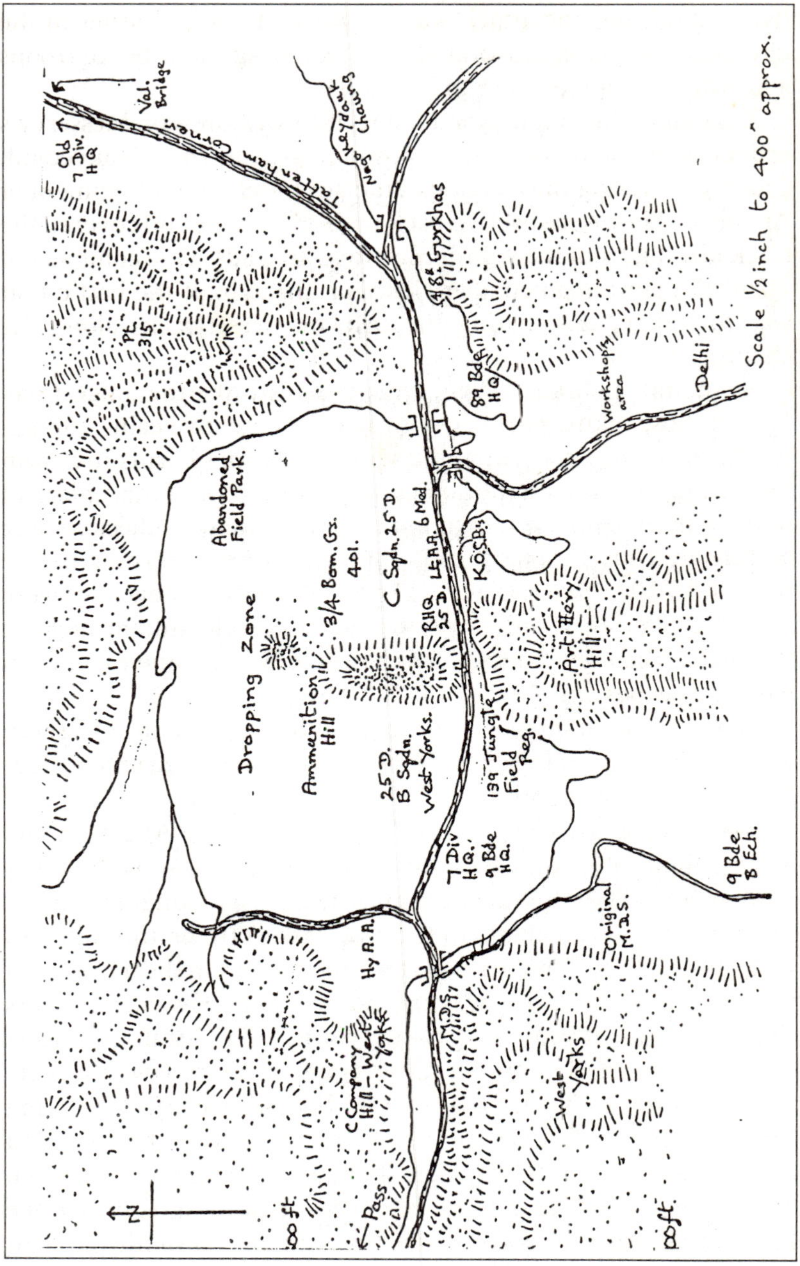

with the intention of occupying the heights of the Mayu Range and blocking the Ngakyedauk Pass.

Meanwhile in the south the Japanese remained in their established positions along the tunnels–Buthidaung road and even launched attacks, thus pinning down 114 and 33 Brigades (7 Div). Another force under Col Doi moved from here northwards along the Mayu Range with the intention of meeting Col Tanahashi's force and completing the encirclement of 7 Div 25th Dragoons, et al.

With supreme confidence the Japanese radio announced: 'The march on Delhi has begun. Tanahashi, Victor of Arakan, will be at Chittagong within a week. New British 14th Army destroyed in one thrust.'

Tokyo Rose crooned to the Allied Forces in the Pacific: 'Why not go home? It's all over in Burma.'

The Japanese force had brought along with them members of the Indian National Army. On reaching Chittagong and Calcutta they would call on the population to rise up and throw out the British. Nothing would then bar the way to Delhi.

5
Besieged

The night had been long and tense and we were glad to see daylight. There had been a great deal of rifle and machine-gun fire by our troops with nothing to show for it. In the luminous yet murky Burmese darkness, it was only too easy to 'see' all sorts of figures moving silently amongst the bushes and tall grass – only a light breeze was needed to activate the illusion. However, as we had no idea when or how fresh ammunition would reach us, nor indeed how long we should be trapped in this jungle basin, it was essential to conserve supplies. So an order went out from Brig Evans to the whole Box in no uncertain terms.

On the morning of the 7th February the Brigades of 7 Indian Division were standing on a rectangle roughly 7 miles by 4 miles. 33 Brigade with the 3rd Battalion 14th Punjab Regiment (9 Brigade) were in the south and facing south, their original position for the proposed attack on the Maungdaw road and Buthidaung. 114 Brigade was across the Kalapanzin river in the east and 89 Brigade (less the Gurkhas) was in the positions mentioned at the end of the previous chapter. Two companies of Gurkhas were lost and remained out of contact for a week. The third company with Regimental HQ was escorted back to the Box by a troop of 'B' Squadron tanks. To the north and west of these groups, at the foot of the Ngakyedauk Pass road, was the Admin Box itself. Beyond the Pass to the west were the remaining brigades of the 5th Indian Division and the Reserve Squadron of 25th Dragoons.

In addition there was the small enclave or island to the north-east of the Box where Gen Messervy and his party had first made their appearance after escaping from Division HQ. Consisting of an Indian Infantry Mobile Workshop of 89 Brigade of seventy-five men, it was commanded by Capt Smith. Like the Admin Box it was dominated by higher ground and Brig Evans sent a party of some forty men and a captain from the KOSBs to defend the position.

'B' Squadron had been almost continuously in action for the past two days during daylight, so it was a change to have a wash, shave and breakfast, however primitive, without having to rush off immediately on some new assignment.

For some reason No 1 Troop of 'B' Squadron was ordered to move towards Buthidaung at full speed, perhaps to contact 33 Brigade. However, they were recalled before they got there and on the way back the Troop Sergeant's tank got bogged down. Whilst putting on the tow-cable he got the fright of his life – a gentle tap on the back, 'Sahib', said a voice. It was an Indian soldier separated from his unit and alone in the jungle and 'scared out of his wits' (who can blame him?). They took him back with them and then came across an artillery unit who had been left with their guns stuck in the mud. They hauled them out and escorted them back to the Box.

From now onwards each squadron had a wireless net at 10am daily, assuming they were in harbour. The radio frequency changed each day and all operators had to be at their sets to tune in to Control Station's netting call.

In view of the gaps in the eastern perimeter of the Box, Brig Evans ordered the company of 4/8th Gurkhas to take over the eastern entrance to the Box and Point 315, a small densely-wooded hill dominating the Box in the east. However, a Japanese force attacked before the Gurkhas could reach the positions and forced them back beyond the actual perimeter. An immediate counter-attack made no headway. The tanks were accordingly brought in and 'C' Squadron shelled the enemy whilst a second counterattack was organized by 'D' Company of the West Yorks. The latter attacked, supported by 'C' Squadron's guns and this time was able to drive the enemy out. By nightfall the Gurkhas had dug-in and were firmly established in their positions. They had lost the equivalent of a platoon in the morning's action. This clearly showed the difficulties of the infantry when attacking these hills without tank support.

During the morning a shell dropped very near No 1 Troop Sergeant's tank. It killed the wireless operator, L/Cpl Walter Heesom, and wounded two other members of the crew. The driver was very shocked and, says the Sergeant, was a nervous wreck by the time the Box was relieved.

Trooper William H. Williams of 'C' Squadron showed great courage and presence of mind in driving a tank to safety which had caught fire whilst refuelling in the Box. The fire was extinguished and very little damage was done, though two men were slightly burned.

The Diary recalls 'all surplus had been ordered to return over the Pass during the afternoon and two of our vehicles were shelled and hit on the road. The corporal in charge of the vehicles transferred the loads and returned to the Box on his own initiative, leaving only one vehicle on the Pass'. Presumably this refers to non-combatant personnel and equipment which was not needed in the Box. It seems to imply that after the shelling the 'loads' were transferred to the vehicles that were still roadworthy and, all except one, then returned to the Box. This experience certainly makes it clear that the Japanese had now gained control of the Pass. We were cut off from our source of supplies with rather more than a whole division to feed and keep battleworthy.

About noon Col Frink decided to clear the 'Delhi' area and half 'A' Squadron was ordered to cover this and it was cleared by 4.30pm. The other half of 'A' Squadron took rations to 33 Brigade in the south and brought back their wounded to the main dressing station in the Box. Normally the rations would have been taken by mule trains moving through the jungle at night (known as 'ghost trains') but this was now out of the question. 'A' Squadron now moved into the box alongside 'C' Squadron and Col Frink set up his HQ in their rear and to the south, on the east side of Ammunition Hill.

The Box Command Post, somewhere to the rear of 'B' Squadron consisted of Brig Evans and a telephone operator with Major Ley in a slit trench, while Gen Messervy insisted on sleeping in a tent above ground – come hell or high water. In moments of emergency he was persuaded to join the others in the slit trench. The remaining HQ staff were in a complex of slit trenches around them, with wireless sets in touch with XV Corps and 5 Division. Gen Messervy had moved into his 'new' HQ at 12.30pm.

Brett-James of 9 Brigade Signals had set up a signals office close to the Command Post which had a telephone exchange. It was excavated out of the ground and covered with old blankets and tarpaulins and was, of course, in operation night and day. As the Japanese infiltration extended over the west of the Mayu Range, Corps HQ under Gen Christison decided to move north of the chaung at Bawli but, says Brett-James, indecision in selection of a new location led to a collapse of communications. The Division was out of touch with Corps for two days and made direct contact with XIV Army HQ instead.

Major Ley had, from time to time, to use the telephone in Brett-James' office and the latter described him as 'the burly, swiftly padding tank adviser to the Brigadier', sound, vigorous, aggressive, reassuring, full of ideas and so fitting with Brig Evans. 'He wore', he said, 'an independent expression that was almost arrogant when not lit by a charming smile'. Well, no-one likes to be thought arrogant, even almost. Nor did Major Ley!

Gen Messervy made it his practice to speak to his brigades morning and evening, during which other wireless sets were asked to remain silent. He ignored security for the most part. All his codes had fallen into Japanese hands at Div HQ.

All tanks were back by dark, including one of 'C' Squadron which had been ditched for the last twenty-four hours at Tattenham Corner. At 1800 hours the Box was machine-gunned and mortared by the Japs from the hills in the area of Point 315 and one 4/8th Gurkha was killed.

Each evening at dusk there was 'Stand-to' when all crew had to be with their tanks and guard was mounted on each tank until dawn. Each tank had a canister of shot placed in its 37mm barrel and a guard remained in the turret all night ready to fire. The rest of the crew were in slit trenches at the side of the tank with one on guard. There was a further 'Stand-to' at dawn.

For some the night of the 7th February was a night of terror.

Not long after dark, about 8pm, an attack started, from the south-west. It was preceded by shouts in Urdu from the Jifs . . . in the hope that they could persuade Indian soldiers to desert. In this they were entirely unsuccessful.

Bursts of rifle and automatic fire broke out about 300 yards from Box HQ. These were accompanied by more shouting and then screams and cries for help.

A voice in the darkness said, 'Good God, they've got into the hospital.'

Brig Evans got on the telephone to Lt Col Cree, CO of the West Yorkshires, to send in a patrol to try and find out what was happening but the carrier that was sent was driven off by grenades. Clearly the enemy were in greater strength than he expected.

He could only wait for the day to come and take what comfort he might from the fact that the ward, theatres and resuscitation installations were dug down. In the darkness the Japanese might miss them otherwise, when they discovered they had entered a hospital, they might take what prisoners they could and leave the remainder. For sometime the shooting and agonized cries went on and then silence reigned only to be broken now and again by one or two shots. Had the Japanese withdrawn?

A little later the commander of the 66th Field Ambulance (Lt Col Brunet) arrived at Box Command Post. He knew little of what was happening but thought that only a small enemy party had forced their way into the hospital. He had been in the Officers' ward attending a patient when his Staff Sergeant appeared to tell him that the Japanese had entered the hospital. He doubted this could be the case but, when the Sergeant pointed out where he had seen the enemy, he was shot dead.

The hospital or main dressing station (MDS) was sited on the south-eastern slopes of a small hill named, naturally enough, MDS Hill. This feature was on the southern side of the road which led up the hills to the west and over the Okeydoke Pass. It was separated from the main Mayu hills by a nullah running north and north-west of it. The site was chosen for the cover it gave from air-bombing and long-distance shelling. By widening and deepening three dry nullahs it was possible to place wards, theatres, resuscitation etc, underground, leaving only the office, guard-room, reception tent, officers' mess and quarters above ground. The whole area was hidden from observation from the air by thick jungle. Brig Evans says, rather amazingly, that until the alarm was given he did not even know where the MDS was.

It was thought an attack would come from the north-west. 'C' Company of the 2nd West Yorks was posted on the hill immediately to the north of the Pass road – soon known as 'C Company Hill'; a section of that Company guarded the approaches to the rear HQ of 7 Division on a feature north-west of MDS Hill with fields of fire to the west and north-west. Infiltration of the MDS area by the enemy in small numbers was however very possible and measures were taken to deal with such a thing.

Despite these plans the Japanese did succeed in overrunning

the position with appalling consequences for both doctors and patients. The one precaution which was entirely successful was the transfer earlier in the day of all walking wounded and others that could be moved to a nullah north of MDS Hill.

Lt Basu of the Indian Army Medical Corps was on orderly medical officer's duty that evening in the dark MI room. He heard some men rushing from the direction of the dispensary. One of them caught hold of his arm and said, 'Aiyo' ('Come along'). He saw another man pointing a bayonet at him. They took hold of him and the other men lying in the MI room and dragged them towards the officers' ward, where was a man whom they described as their 'general'. They were told to sit together on the ground. The Japs saw Lt Basu's 'pips' and their interpreter began to question him. The 'general' was asking questions which were being translated into broken English and Hindi.

They asked Lt Basu many questions about himself, the patients, the officers, Indian and British, the units and the place. To all these questions he replied that he had been there for three days only and knew little about military organisation, that he was a doctor and interested only in medicine. He was threatened with a bayonet.

Then they asked to see the operating theatre and the laboratory. He took them to the small minor operating theatre. They examined the things there and took a mackintosh, some cotton and bandages. Three medical officers were sleeping there and were made prisoner at once.

Next they took all the prisoners back again to their 'general' for further questioning. They were very inquisitive about the supply depot and about the various roads in those parts. Lt Basu maintained his ignorance of these matters.

Their hands were tied together behind their backs. They made no difference between officers and other ranks. Their hands were set free after about eight hours but the British soldiers were kept tied up till the end. Then the 'general' solemnly drew his sword from the sheath, waved it over them, sheathed it again and went away.

Soon after an Indian came near and told them not to worry; they would be taken to Rangoon to join the Indian Independence League. Asked about his native country, he said that he came from

Maungdaw in Burma. He spoke fluent Urdu and Japanese.

All the medical officers (Capt Paul, Lieutenant Khadilka, Lt Basu, Subadar Mazumda and Subadar Choudhury) were taken to the dispensary and were ordered to pack up things for them. They were very keen regarding quinine, morphine, anti-tetanus and anti-gas-gangrene serum, tincture of iodine and other articles for emergency surgery. They examined even the smallest phial and discarded those which they did not want.

Then they were taken back to the nullah and ordered to sit there. Most were in acute pain due to the tight ligature at their wrists and some were crying for water. The sentry was jabbing them with a heavy stick.

In the morning one tank came near the MI room. The Japs immediately took shelter in the trenches made by themselves. One Jap dragged the British soldiers in front, so that they received the first shots. The tank began machine-gunning. Most people had their hands tied up; there was no shelter for them. They tried to crawl back to take advantage of the bend in the nullah. Eight were wounded. The Japs were watching them with smiling faces and with cigarettes in their mouths. The wounded received no attention.

During the two days they lived with the Japs, they gave them only a handful of small biscuits and two water-bottles for all of them.

At about 3pm they were mortared. One of these fell right in the place they were occupying, injuring about ten, including Lt Basu.

They lay in the nullah, some dying and some crying piteously for a sip of water. The Japs shot one wounded man and bayoneted another because they were crying too much for water. Lt Basu had two field dressings with him with which he dressed his wound and that of another man, bleeding profusely from the thigh.

In the evening the Japs stood before them with their rifles. When they actually shot the BORs they all knew they were going to be shot. Most of them had their Red Cross badges on their arms, Captain Paul and Lt Basu had their stethoscopes on their shoulders. They shot every one, most being killed then and there. They shot Lt Basu twice in his left ear. He was stunned. He put his fingers in his ears, but could not feel any blood coming out. His faculties of sight and thinking were still retained. He stealthily took some blood from the wounds of one of his friends and applied it over his face, ears and shirt, groaning all the time. He slipped into a trench and passed the night there. The Japs left in early morning in two parties and later he saw two BORs coming towards him with tommy guns. He thanked God and came out of his trench.

An Indian ambulance driver of the Royal Indian Army Service Corps had perhaps the most horrific experience of all but nevertheless survived to return to British lines after some twelve days. This driver was with his unit at the MDS.

At about 10pm they were fired at and some got hit. They scattered into the bushes. Three of them were captured by the Japs but two escaped. The third tried to do so, but was caught. The driver was hit with a rifle butt and kicked and dragged to the MI Room. He told them he was an ambulance driver. There were about twenty Jap soldiers and one officer. Questions were put to him and in reply he said he was an Indian and there were more Indians than British in his unit.

By this time they had captured several men and patients (BORs) and were gathering them in the nullah by the side of the officers' ward. All prisoners' hands were tied and they were left for the night under the charge of a sentry.

Next morning (8th February) there was firing from tanks. The Japs hid themselves in their trenches, leaving the prisoners tied as before in the nullah. There was LMG fire and later aerial bombardment, as a result of which some men were killed, and most of them were wounded.

When this was over the Japs went round all the men and selected six of them – the Ambulance Driver, himself, Naik Verghese, Driver Hasim, labourer Rulia, and two men of the sappers and miners. They were unhurt so far.

At about 10am they were ordered to carry three wounded Japs on stretchers; they travelled southwards the whole day till they reached the other side of the hill, where they stopped for the night and rested.

In the morning they walked up to a nullah where the Japs cooked and ate their food. They were not given anything.

The wounded were left with some Japs there. The six had to carry the kit loads of Jap soldiers accompanying them, up to one of the tunnels, where they arrived in the early hours of 11th February.

There they were handed over to two sentries who were armed with LMGs. There were about 1,000 Japs living in the tunnel. They had their store of arms, ammunition, vehicles and guns, rations and wounded.

That day six Indians – two Punjabis, two Sikhs, one Madrassi and one Bengali – came to them and said they need not worry, they would have trouble for a few days, after which they might be sent to Rangoon to work. They also said that their major (Indian) had gone towards Goppe Pass and that, after his return, everything would be settled in their favour and they would have no torturing from the Japs.

They also told him that there were about 400,000 Indian followers of Subhas Bose and that in two months' time they proposed to reach Chittagong via Dohazari road.

The next day (12th February), after starving for four days, they were given a little rice with salt on plates by these six Indians, with some water and biries (country cigarettes).

On 15th February, after three more days in the tunnel, they were taken out with hands tied, across a bridge on the side of the tunnel to a road overlooking a nullah about sixty feet deep. Their hands were untied and all six were made to stand in a row at the edge of the road. They were told to remove their clothes, then their paybooks and money were taken away. There were six Japs – one officer and five men. They started shooting the prisoners one by one. Two men (sappers and miners) were shot down first with rifles and their bodies kicked down the nullah. The ambulance driver was picked on by the Jap officer to be shot with a pistol. He misfired twice, got irritated at his weapon and, after examining and putting it right, began to fire again. The shot was also a misfire. The fourth one hit him through the right arm and left shoulder. He fired again and hit him through the right hand. Instantly he fell, called out 'Amman', and managed to tumble down the nullah without being kicked down. By this time all the others had been also shot by the Japs and thrown into the nullah where there were already more than twenty dead bodies decomposing. All were dead except Rulia, who was conscious and could whisper.

After about half an hour the driver cautiously looked up towards the road to see if the Japs were still there. It was all clear so he walked across the nullah. Rulia was still conscious but bleeding profusely from a wound over the temple. He dressed the wound with his vest and helped Rulia to move, but he dropped unconscious after only about 100 yards.

The driver crawled slowly and carefully up the hill where he passed the night.

Next day he walked over to the other side of the hill from where he saw our planes dropping parachutes a few miles away. He was too exhausted to move further and stayed where he was the second night.

Next day he tried to walk towards the area of dropping parachutes but could hardly stand up. He was living on leaves and water and getting desperate. For two days he walked short distances till, on 19th February, he recognized some of our men and shouted for help. They helped him to the RAP of the 3rd Bn 14th Punjab Regiment.

A wounded British lieutenant had been admitted to 66 MDS about 6pm, 7th February. He was given treatment and put into a shelter in which, at that time, were Major Harrington, 4/8th Gurkha Rifles, Captain Robinson, RAMC, and one Signal Sergeant.

At about 7.30pm he heard sounds of firing in the area. They gathered that the Japs were attacking the MDS and considered it inadvisable to move. Four BORs, whose defence had been overrun by the Japs, joined them. They heard considerable movement around them, but no one disturbed them.

At about 7am on the 8th they saw three or four Japs walking about; they lay still and remained so all day. At 9.15pm they heard a voice shouting something like, 'You go.' Captain Robinson rose up and said 'What do you want?' Once again, 'You go.' Captain Robinson shook his head in a negative manner and lay down again. Then a Jap shot him through the right thigh. Captain Robinson shouted 'I am a doctor, Red Cross, I am a medical officer.' In spite of this, the Japs fired two magazines into the shelter, killing Captain Robinson, Major Harrington, one mess servant and two BORs. The rest of them lay perfectly still all day and at 7am they managed to get out of the MDS to the West Yorkshires' nearest post.

A British private of the RAMC was taken prisoner in the MDS

by four Japs at about 3am on the night of the 7th/8th February. He was interrogated and taken with others to a quiet corner by some Japs who relieved them of all valuables, then tied their hands behind their backs, made them face an earth wall, and kicked them to the ground. They were taken to another place and tied in pairs by their necks. At daylight, some Japs came back and cracked them on the heads with the butts of their rifles. Afterwards they used him as a shield when the tanks came to blast out the Japs. They refused to give water or medical treatment. Eventually, after a lot of persuasion, the prisoners managed to get two bottles of water between twenty of them at about 5.20pm. It was getting dark when an officer told them to 'come and get treatment'. They took them far down a nullah to a clearing where a stream was running. They then opened fire with their rifles, killing seventeen of them. They left them all for dead and evacuated the place. Next morning an officer from the Queen's came that way and saw that the British private was still alive and got him out.

These stories are told here because they reveal the brutality and perhaps desperation of the Japanese Army at this stage when their bold plan had been dislocated after less than four days. Also they speak for all those who did not survive the ordeal. The majority were unarmed and entirely non-combatant. The random acts of cruelty, the delight in humiliating the prisoners, the callous barbarity of it all, were a lesson to all Allied troops fighting in Burma.

The only pattern of behaviour that might be drawn from these murderous acts is that the Japanese were mainly concerned in killing all British and Indian commissioned officers and British other ranks, but had a somewhat ambivalent attitude to Indian other ranks. Whilst they treated the latter with cruelty and contempt, they may have had some half-hearted orders to placate them with a view to recruiting them to the Indian National Army (INA).

The main Japanese attack had now come up against unexpectedly difficult resistance and their whole timetable had been upset. Their commanders were losing face and the feeling was passed downwards to the lowest ranks.

Two days later the West Yorkshires, supported by one troop of 'B' Squadron, cleared the Japs out of the hospital. The task was made all the more difficult because the enemy had cunningly camouflaged their machine-gun posts with stretchers in the wards and theatres. The West Yorks found the dead bodies of thirty-one patients and four doctors, as well as seventy Japanese.

It seems unbelievable that these events occurred within a few hundred yards of 'B' Squadron's position at night in the Box. We could not have known what was going on and anyway could not have moved from our allotted positions. The commission of such acts by one side soon arouses revengeful feelings in the other.

It is not surprising that Mrs Pat Messervy, wife of the General, said after the war:

> All the time he was fighting against the Italians and the Germans, his letters were mostly about family matters, particularly the children. He never wrote anything bitter about the enemy until he was fighting the Japs. Then he wrote such things as 'What a brute the Jap is. I hate him as I have never hated him before.' For Frank to feel like that, they must have been bad.

On the morning of the 8th February the general positions were still very confused and 7th Div HQ were still not in touch with their sub-units. However, a message was dropped by air with instructions to open up wireless communications with XV Corps HQ and saying that petrol, oil and ammo were going to be dropped by air. This at least was good news. Whilst the Admin Box was very well stocked to begin with, these stocks would soon be used up when supplying a whole division or more.

During these early days the tanks spent a good deal of time giving covering fire while many abandoned jeeps, carriers and other vehicles were rescued from under the Japs' noses. We ourselves towed back a carrier packed with rations (tinned milk, fruit, biscuits etc). I must admit we dug into them. We also managed to acquire a large container of rum, which would not otherwise have come our way. There was a 'surplus' of biscuits and one member of the crew, Brewer, was expert in devising recipes for making biscuit pudding, biscuit soufflé and biscuit porridge. At the slightest sign of a pause in operations, he'd be pumping up the primus and restoring morale with mugs of char. Major Ley admits that his crew drove his tank over to a supply depot in No-man's Land to top up with rum and fruit juice. This was raided every night by the Japanese for rice and meat but they soon gave way to the tank crew at dawn! These practices were soon stamped out.

Inside the Box there were numbers of water-carriers, staff cars, 3-ton and 15cwt trucks, an 'Ascot car-park' Messervy called it, standing in full view of the enemy throughout the fighting.

Outside the Box and at the foot of hills held by the Japanese, there stood another hundred vehicles, large lorries laden with pontoons.

'When I discovered that the Japs were not destroying them but were using them to sleep in,' said Messervy, 'I decided to thin out the Ascot car-park and stick some more of my motor transport in No-man's Land, an even more completely safe zone! The Japs stuck rigidly to their orders that these trucks were to be preserved to carry them to Calcutta when the British had been annihilated or driven into the sea. They never fired on them to the end.'

This was one of the reasons why the capture of the Box was so vital to the success of the Japanese plan. They were relying on *our* supplies for *their* advance into India. Various officers appropriated vehicles for themselves and even the padre increased his status with a staff car. There were ration dumps, petrol dumps, stores and MT offices.

Major Ley's batman was Trooper Evans, a 'gentleman's gentleman'. Whatever might have passed during the night, he always brought the officers a mug of hot char first thing in the morning. He was, however, allergic to digging and always enquired, with Jeeves-like calm, 'You *won't* be requiring a new slit trench today, will you, Sir?' Trooper Evans' view on digging changed somewhat after we were attacked by Japanese Zeros. He dug himself a veritable catacomb and told Major Ley he would be welcome to join him in times of danger. The latter, however, regarded the possibility of burial alive with Trooper Evans as a fate worse than death and politely declined.

Every morning Ley would leave Box HQ and go over to the Dragoons Regimental HQ for the daily conference and orders group with Col Frink. He trundled along the track in his tank which ran east over the shallow saddle between Ammunition Hill and Artillery Hill. This saddle was in the sight of an enemy anti-tank gun and, after one or two near misses, Ley solved the problem by deception. The tank would gather speed approaching the saddle, followed by the usual cloud of dust and then stop dead. The dust cloud would roll over the vehicle onto the saddle, the

Japanese would fire into it and, before they could re-load, the tank was over the saddle and into dead ground. The Japanese never worked out what was happening and the ritual continued throughout the siege. The return journey was less complicated as the tank was screened throughout the journey by dust.

As soon as 'the balloon' was known to have gone up on the 4th February Gen Slim, at XIVth Army HQ, at Comilla, had ordered the 26th Indian Division (under Maj Gen Lomax), then at Chittagong, to move forward to Bawli Bazaar (HQ of XV Corps) and likewise the 36th British Division (under Maj Gen Festing), then at Calcutta, to move forward and take its place at Chittagong as Army Reserve.

The 26th Division consisted of a number of Indian regiments plus two British, the 1st Battalion of the Lincolns and the 1st Battalion of the Wiltshires. Lt Col Jack Houghton Brown was 2nd-in-command of the Wiltshires and afterwards wrote of his experiences:

On 5th February our CO suddenly got a warning order to be prepared to move in eight hours. No one could believe that at last the day had come and it was some time before much action was taken. However, a few hours later I was ordered to proceed to Chittagong with the intelligence officer and one representative per company. We hurriedly packed essentials and jammed ourselves into a jeep. We bumped over very rough tracks and eventually found ourselves by midday at the crossroads near the centre of the town. The BI was there munching sandwiches. He told us a little of the picture and informed us that the battalion was following in our wake by train. As we drove south to Dohazari there was a lot of transport on the eastern road but all seemed orderly and fairly peaceful. Dicky Canning, the IO, kept us amused by producing strings of anecdotes. We laughed as if we were off to a race meeting – instead of to battle and to his death.

We arrived at Dohazari rest-house about dark. We were told at the station that one brigade and our division had already moved through. We had orders to drive on through the night till we met the Brigadier on the main road about 100 miles south. We snatched some supper, then drove on. The road was only dried mud but it was well cared for and, for the first part, had a fair surface. It carried on over innumerable bridges and seemed endless in its length. I realized then, for the first time, the enormous lengths of the lines of communication of the 15th Corps. There was no railway and all supplies for the forward division had to be carried south from Dohazari by MT for about 150 miles. It was a ghostly night – the thick jungle hugging the road in a sinister embrace. Some time after midnight we bumped the tail of a long convoy moving the same way as we were – great lorries packed with mules, their large heads poking out inquisitively as we drove by. From then on we drove amidst a solid stream of traffic. Towards morning we met the Brigadier standing by the side of the road smoking a cigarette. He looked cheerful and happy and seemed pleased that we were again about to invade his old battle ground. We followed him down the road, twisting in and out amongst the long line of vehicles. When daylight came we crossed the big bridges over the Pruma Chaung and landed up in south Bawli. Here we found the fore part of the other brigade already de-bussing. A chaos of troops, mules, vehicles and guns. We shaved, in turn, in the mirror of the jeep and then looked round for some breakfast. We found a basha laid out for a large mess and, boldly going in, ordered a meal. To our amazement, porridge, eggs and bacon, and steaming tea were immediately produced. Where it all came from I do not know to this day.

At the same time Gen Slim arranged for Troop Carrier Command and Third Tactical Air Force 'to put 7th Division on air supply'. Arrangements had long been made for such an emergency, although this particular emergency seemed to have taken both Corps and Army HQ by surprise. It had been agreed that if the Japanese tried their outflanking movements, then the allied units were to stay put and would, if necessary, be supplied by air.

The implementation of the plan to drop supplies by air involved a great deal of paperwork. It was not a simple matter to get all the information required by the Air Forces for the boxes and their needs, and many people were engaged 24 hours per day setting it up and keeping it going.

During the morning Mitchells and Vengeances came over and bombed Taung Bazaar and Badana. Our own fighter cover (Hurricanes and/or Spitfires) was overhead for most of the day. Until recently the most modern allied fighter on the front had been the Hurricane but now we had Spitfires and these were able to chase the Zeros out of the sky. During those early days Jap aircraft had been much in evidence and they were said to have had some 100 planes on this front.

A week or so before, a dog-fight had occurred overhead between two Zeros and a Spitfire. Bill Harding of 139 Field Regt relates:

The enemy fighters clamped onto the tail of the Spitfire which soon began trailing black smoke. The pilot bailed out over Hambone South but the Japs, not content with this, continued machine-gunning the poor fellow as he floated down into the trees. A patrol from F Troop found the dead sergeant-pilot's body in the jungle and took it to the ADS. Four machine-guns and some instruments were salvaged from the wreckage of the plane.

Nevertheless the Allies, consisting of RAF, IAF and USAAF, were able to assert their superiority whenever necessary and it was in no small measure to them that we owed our eventual survival. I only remember being strafed once by Jap aircraft and that was at an awkward moment when we were in the open and having a bit of lunch beside the tanks – not a pleasant experience but they did little harm. These 'Zero' fighter-bombers were only an embarrassment to Major Ley when they attacked him in the nude whilst washing in a stream.

The battery of 6th Medium Artillery, whose position in the Box was initially between 'A' and 'C' Squadrons, let off a considerable amount of harrassing fire during the day. As shrapnel came back from the firing as far as the tanks and guns, the gunners informed the tank crews when they were firing over open sites at Point 315. At about 2.15pm three or four Jap planes shallow dive-bombed the area and a bomb landed near Regimental HQ and set light to the ammunition dump on Ammunition Hill. Shells in the dump started to explode and continued to do so well into the night. The fire was eventually put out by the heavy dew at about 2am the following morning. The effect was that pieces of hot smoking metal rained from the sky on and off for the rest of the day over the immediate area, which included 'B' and 'C' Squadrons. There were several minor casualties from the bursting shells and the Regimental Signals officer's carrier and several corps and sapper vehicles were completely burnt out. One bomb fell within a few feet of Col Frink's slit trench burying a lot of his kit but not himself fortunately, although he did suffer delayed concussion. A shell sent his camp bed 'for six' the next day.

Earlier in the day 'A' Squadron had been ordered to put out a troop in defence of the north-east approaches to the Box and one troop of 'C' Squadron supported 4/8th Gurkhas in their attempt to consolidate certain features in their position on the perimeter to the east. At 11.40am 'C' opened fire on the hills to the north of Point 315 and continued firing throughout the day, which kept the enemy fairly quiet. It was from this ridge that the majority of sniping, mortaring and shelling had been coming. They were finished off by a company of West Yorks who swarmed up the hill and used bayonets.

Our own medical officer, 'Doc' Gaunt had managed to fix up an underground regimental aid post which could take some of the casualties and so avoid pressure in the overcrowded MDS.

Trenches by the tanks and round the perimeter were always being improved and wire was put down all round. As usual the tanks gathered in their allotted positions for the night in close harbour from 'Stand-to' to 'Stand-down' in the morning. It may have been on this evening that I received and took down the following messages on the wireless and read them to the crew. They were relayed by Squadron Control Station:

Order of the Day. From the Supreme Commander. Re-inforcements are coming up. If we hold them off tonight we have made history. Mountbatten.

Order of the Night. Please convey to the men that I think and I know that they have done magnificently. Stick it out tonight and give the bastards hell. The Colonel.

On the morning of the 9th February the counter-attack on the MDS was resumed by 'A' Company of the West Yorks. They were supported by one troop of 'B' Squadron. The operation was very difficult because the ground was broken and the undergrowth dense, and some of our wounded were believed to be still alive. The fighting had to be close, with rifles, machine-guns, grenades and bayonets. What they eventually found, when the Japs had been cleared, has already been described. Gen Messervy's hat was found on a dead Jap in MDS area and was ceremoniously returned to him.

At about 10am Zeros and Spitfires appeared overhead in battle. Our light anti-aircraft-guns opened up from time to time to keep the Zeros away from the harbour area. On the ground the 'Diary' reports that during the morning there was 'no mortaring and very little sniping', a negative statement indicating that the opposite was usually the case, as indeed it was, in one or another part of the Box.

Very early that morning a company of Japs had attacked the B Echelon area of 9 Brigade. This was on the southern fringe of the Box where a road out of the Box crossed a dried-up nullah. It was defended by men of the West Yorks under RSM Maloney and also of 24 Animal Transport Company. They neatly caught and killed some fifty Japs including one officer. However, the Jap company continued to hold the area for some days and used it as a rendez-vous. One troop of 'B' Squadron was sent in to support the West Yorks in clearing this area. The infantry indicated the targets on both sides of the roads and some good targets were engaged. Clearing the area continued until dusk. The place became known as 'Blood Nullah'. Eventually the stench of dead bodies was so bad that a bulldozer was called in to clear them.

The dead officer turned out to have on him a map showing the complete plan for the Jap 'Ha-Go' offensive and its follow-up. This was eventually sent to Corps and then Army HQ. Other dead men were found to have on them rations looted from the MDS.

Major Ley suggested to Brig Evans that there were far too many tanks in the Box and indeed the Box had become a highly congested place. Brig Evans did not agree but Gen Messervy happened to pass at the time and agreed with Ley.

It was decided that the presence of Regimental HQ and 'B' and 'C' Squadrons in the Box were sufficient for its defence. Ten tanks of 'A' Squadron were accordingly sent to join 33 Brigade in the south-east. Of this brigade, its HQ and the 4/1st Gurkha Rifles were on the hill called Abel, adjoining and to the north of the Maungdaw-Buthidaung road, the 4/15th Punjab were on another hill called 'Mont Blanc', and Brigade HQ, the 1st Queens Royal Regiment, one company of 1/11th Sikhs, one company of 4/1st Gurkhas, with 136 Field Regiment RA and Brigade Admin, were all in the area of Point 182. The 24th Engineer Battalion was in Tatmingaungwa. Nos 364 and 503 Batteries of 139 Jungle Field Regiment were also in this area, 364 in support of the 1st Queens overlooking Letwedet Chaung, and also 503 in support of 4/15th Punjab on Mont Blanc. Both these positions were in 'Gun Valley'.

'A' Squadron, led by Major Charles Sloan (known as 'Tod Sloan', presumably after the American jockey), was involved in a number of attacks with the regiments of this Brigade, which was commanded by Brig F.J. Loftus-Tottenham.

Towards evening a big calibre Japanese gun, 'Whizz Bang Willie' opened up. It may have been during this shelling that John Leyin had a narrow escape. As Major Johnstone's driver with a 15cwt truck, he was posted with Corporal Hodgson and the orderly room clerk (all of 'B' Squadron) in a slit trench on Ammunition Hill during daylight. His truck, which had an uncertain starter, was parked on the slope so that it could run down to get going. Also sharing the trench was Sergeant Cameron, an Anglo-Burmese who had got separated from his unit. He was utterly contemptuous of the Japanese. They had killed his mother and father. He was in his early twenties and so full of contempt that he would walk around during a bombardment and refuse to take cover. This was his way of expressing his contempt.

When the shelling started, Leyin and his two mates got in the trench. Gradually they realized that the shells were falling closer and closer. A deluge of earth poured down on them so they decided to run for it. They rushed to the truck, got it started and were about to move off, when they noticed Sgt Cameron shouting amid the smoke and the dust. Was he ordering them back into the trench? No, he had been hit, one leg blown off and the thigh bone sticking out. Forgetting the shells, they jumped down, picked him up and got him into the truck and drove off. He did not live and Johnny visited his grave in the Box cemetery a week or so later.

On another occasion a corporal fitter made a big mistake. He dived into a latrine trench to escape the shells. 'Covered all over with shit, I was!'

During the night two patrols of the 3/4th Bombay Grenadiers, who were out in a nullah forward of our harbour area, came into contact with large enemy fighting patrols. One section of seven men, with support fire from the perimeter, accounted for twelve Japanese casualties for the loss of one man. Sixteen Japanese were recovered but a larger number must have been wounded and taken away. Amongst documents found was some Indian money, prepared and printed in Japan, seen for the first time. This confirmed that their objective was India and no less.

With sunset and 'Stand-to' we wondered what would happen next and hoped to get at least some sleep.

6

ODTAA

Col Kubo's battalion had detached itself from Tanahashi's force after passing Taung Bazaar on 4th February and had moved north-west with the intention of crossing the Goppe Pass. At the approach to this Pass they ran into one of our mule companies who frightened them into thinking that the Pass was strongly held – which it certainly was not. They therefore moved directly west, hauled their machine-guns and mortars up and over the steep sides of the Mayu Range at a place called Chota Maunghnama (a feat in itself) and occupied the foothills on the western slopes. Their objective was to break the coastal road running from Bawli Bazaar in the north to Maungdaw in the south. This would sever the line of communications and supplies to the 5th Indian Division and so complete the first part of the Ha-Go plan.

Bill Nicholson of HQ Squadron writes:

> Just prior to this action the 25th Dragoons had moved forward as a unit leaving behind at Chamba, Briasco Bridge, such personnel as storemen, clerks and so on, at our vacant tank site at the foot of the Mayu Range. A fifth squadron was formed as a reserve squadron with Major Youens in charge and I was made Squadron Quartermaster Sergeant!! 'R' Squadron remained at the foot of the Pass with the 5th Division. Early one morning there was a signal from rear echelon reporting that the Japanese had overrun our rear base at Briasco Bridge during the night and that there had been some casualties. Major Youens ordered me to take some men to Briasco Bridge and ascertain the position, which I did, and found that the Japs had made a lightening raid on our base. They had apparently rushed screaming down the 'cud' side and killed several of our men with their bayonets as they were sleeping.
>
> However, Sergeant Munday had taken over and reorganized the remainder of the men and formed a smaller perimeter. I returned to 'R' Squadron only to learn that our other three squadrons were actively engaged with the enemy on the other side of the Pass. At first we were unable to establish radio contact with them owing to the height of the intervening mountains but, after certain modifications with aerials, the signallers eventually picked up the units over the Pass.
>
> Life became quite hectic and we were subjected to occasional gunfire and some too-accurate mortar fire.

In addition to the non-combatant personnel and Reserve Squadron mentioned by Bill Nicholson, there was also the 4th Indian Light Aid Detachment (LAD) which was attached to the 25th Dragoons and formed part of the Corps Armoured Group. It was commanded by Capt Allison and consisted of a warrant officer, two British other ranks, a viceroy's commissioned officer, fifty-seven Indian other ranks and two followers.

This attack had in fact taken place at about 2am on the night of 5/6th February in the old 'B' Squadron area at Chamba. It was made by both Japs and Jifs using small arms, mortars and grenades. They had attacked only a few hours before Tanahashi's men overran 7th Division HQ.

Keith Fox (usually known as Freddie) was the first to awake in the 'A' Squadron area and realize what was happening. He attempted to wake Cpl Charlie Fairweather who was in charge of the small 'A' Squadron party of 'B' Echelon (non-combatants) and who was slumbering peacefully.

'I say, old boy, a man has been shot in 'B' Squadron and there are men walking about.'

'Don't be a bloody fool, Fred. It's those bears they've been talking about.'

'It's the Japs, Charlie.'

'Oh, pull the other one, Fred.'

Keith persisted and suddenly Charlie was bolt upright and everyone else as well. Grenades and machine-guns could be heard close at hand and the whole camp was awake. Cliff Reeves, a member of the party, always said that Keith was foremost in enthusiasm for attacking the Japs, but Cpl Fairweather got his men into a nullah with their rifles, 'If anyone comes this way, shoot the hell out of them!'

However, things quietened down and they made their way to Group HQ, as did the parties of 'B' and 'C' Squadrons. It was a 'B' Squadron man who had originally given the alarm as it was 'B' Squadron that was first attacked. Cpl Brock, the cook, had been killed in that area and Chalky White had been wounded.

At Group HQ, Capt Pain collected the office staff and signals personnel and went into a nullah nearby. Most of the squadron personnel had withdrawn further to the workshop area, followed by the attacking party who overran the place and set fire to the field ambulance. They then proceeded onto the main Bawli-Maungdaw road, demolished one bridge and laid a mine on another. On their return the workshops were attacked again.

Coming into this area shortly after, Cpl Fairweather and party armed themselves to the teeth with the weapons lying all over the place. Charlie arrayed himself like Errol Flynn in all his glory – a Gurkha kukri in his belt, a revolver, a Lee Enfield rifle and a bayonet.

Capt Allison of the Royal Electrical and Mechanical Engineers and three BORs were killed, and one BOR died later from wounds. Two IORs were also wounded (IEME). One BOR of 'A' Section 14 Light Field Ambulance received two bayonet wounds in the legs. In the recovery section, two Macks, one Ward La-France and one 15cwt truck were burnt.

Before dawn the attackers withdrew in the direction from which they came, destroying a certain amount of kit on the way. They occupied positions on the hills above 'A' and 'B' Squadron areas and they continued to engage targets as they presented themselves. The orderly room, Group HQ and signals were fired on. Sergeant Rayfield, Signals Sergeant, was killed. Patrols were organized by SQMSs Robson and Munday and, at about 7.30am a detachment of the West African Recce Squadron arrived. It was very difficult to pinpoint the enemy who fired at specific targets only. At 8.30am the West Africans withdrew. They had insufficient men and the destruction of the enemy required a strong force of infantry.

'A' Company and one platoon of the 2/1st Punjab (5th Division) arrived soon afterwards and put in an attack which continued most of the day with little success. The Punjabis had four men killed and some wounded. In the late afternoon they received permission to withdraw.

During the day all vehicles possible and all personnel were concentrated in the area east of Brasco Bridge. The small hills surrounding this area were piquetted, thus forming a defensive perimeter.

One naik (corporal) of LAD, who was taken prisoner and escaped, reported on his return that he had been invited to join the Jifs. On saying that he did not particularly wish to, he was told that if he ever changed his mind he would be made most welcome (!). Seven other IORs were missing but later returned.

During the evening and the night following, the Japanese patrolled all round the perimeter. The telephone lines were cut again on the main road.

The company of Rajputs in the area opened up the road but it was by no means safe. In fact this was not such a serious matter as the bulk of 5th Division supplies were now coming by boat through Maungdaw. When General Slim had first entered Maungdaw after its capture in early January, he thought the docks were incapable of restoration. Within a week or two the engineers had the wharves ready for unloading.

We in the Box knew nothing of all this.

* * *

In the meantime the Japanese force under Col Doi had been making its way up the Mayu Range and on the 10th February they reached the Okeydoke Pass and met Tanahashi's force from the north. The encirclement of 7th Division was now complete.

Kubo's force, Tanahashi's force and Doi's had all now achieved their initial objectives and by rights 5th and 7th Divisions should have been annihilated. The army had been given until 10th February to do this but these divisions were an all-too-material presence and, apparently, in good fighting order. The Japs did not know but they had already missed their chance. The 36th British Division had left Calcutta and was well on its way to Arakan. The 26th Indian Division had left Chittagong and had come into Arakan itself. Its leading battalion, the 1st Lincolnshires, had already crossed the Goppe Pass and retaken Taung Bazaar and was now moving south in the rear of Tanahashi's force. These were the reinforcements Mountbatten had spoken of in his message.

36 Brigade of the 26th Division was kept on the west side of the Mayu Range and its task was to clear the area from Briasco Bridge northwards. Japanese troops were still much in evidence in the Chamba-Briasco Bridge area. On 7th, 8th, 9th and 10th February, salvage parties from our 'B' Echelon group made sorties into the old tank harbour area to recover personal kit and immobilized vehicles. Many of these parties were fired on, machine-gunned and mortared. There were a number of casualties and it was clear that the Japanese in the area were in much greater strength than had at first been thought – one battalion in fact.

On the 8th February 1,000 gallons of petrol was lost due to the perforation of the containers. On the 9th a party escorted by two Bren-carriers was shot up by three machine-guns in the hills and had to withdraw, one man being wounded. At 1pm the main road (Bawli to Maungdaw) was mortared at a point a mile north of the camp. Two vehicles on the road were destroyed and there were a number of casualties. 'A' Company of the Wiltshire Regiment arrived and made plans for attacks on the Jap positions. Lt Col Houghton Brown says:

That day, the 8th February, we saw the first of the Japanese aircraft. Their Zeros dive-bombed the bridges over the river. Every time they just missed but on one occasion our general had a narrow escape. A bomb dropped within a few yards of him. That afternoon the Battalion marched over the bridge and took over from the 5/1st Punjabis who had been defending Div HQ. We dug hard most of the night and by morning had a fairly strong perimeter defence.

The next day (9th Feb.) we had to send two platoons of 'A' Company (which was all that company consisted of) to mop up some Japs who were interfering with the main Bawli-Maungdaw road, near Briasco Bridge. Major Christopher Green, who was company commander, packed his men into trucks and moved off. We heard no more of him that evening so next day I set off with an escort in a jeep to see how he was getting on. As I drove down the road I soon sensed trouble as there were already some recently burnt out trucks on the verge, still smouldering. Suddenly an MMG opened up on us from the hills to our east. Bullets spluttered around but magically missed us. Around the corner I met one of the AFVs of our 25th Dragoons. They told me our company was, even then, engaging one of the enemy positions that was dug-in on the hillside in the jungle. I went back and found Chris Green had wisely run out a telephone line to the road. The signallers explained the situation and I got through to Chris on the 'phone. He said he was up against a Jap MG but he could not manoeuvre because the enemy was dug-in on a razor-back ridge. (How often later we were to find ourselves in similar difficulties!) Protected by my escort I walked across the padi stubble to the foot of the hills. Here I saw four of our wounded who had been carried down the hill by our stretcher-bearers. I walked up the one narrow steep path and then, nearly at the top, bumped into the company. They were digging frantically each side of the path where I found Chris who was slightly wounded. The situation was unpleasant as the Jap was well dug-in above us and was only about 30 yards from the leading platoon. Both sides of the jungle sloped away precipitously and it was thus impossible to swing out a platoon to a flank. I went up to have a look at the leading sections and was met by a shower of bullets from the Jap position. It was obvious the company was doing no good where it was so I ordered Chris to withdraw his company 100 yards onto the other ridge and then to return and have his wounds attended. With some difficulty we pulled out, the enemy firing at us every time we moved on the path. We withdrew and then dug-in on the other slope. By this time we could hear other enemy MMG firing onto the road from various positions along the hills nearby. It was apparent that our opposition had been badly under-estimated – there must be at least a company of enemy dug-in on the hills.

The CO, Lt Col Bevan (known as 'The Bear'), arrived and I explained the situation. I told him I thought it would need at least a battalion to shift the enemy. (I heard afterwards it took a brigade.) He agreed and went back to report to the general. That night, after dark, we were relieved by 8/13th FF Rifles. Our battalion had bigger things ahead and the company had to return to the fold.

On 10th February the company of the Wiltshires, the 5/1st Punjab less two companies and some two companies of Sikhs, were all engaged to clear the Japs from the area. Initially their attacks were not very successful. Reserve Squadron tanks supported the attacks in the usual way.

During the morning another salvage party was heavily attacked and forced to withdraw, luckily though without casualties. Orders were received to evacuate 'B' Echelon and the LAD workshop to an area north of Bawli Bazaar as it was considered unwise to store so much ammunition and petrol in the Chamba area. Most of the vehicles, including some non-runners, were in the new area by 8pm. The task was completed the following day with all the stores, petrol and ammunition being evacuated. No further casualties were sustained.

So ended this unexpected episode for the 'non-combatants' of 'B' Echelon who obviously put up a high-spirited resistance to this surprise attack. It was a party of Jifs who occupied the old harbour area and the former 'B' Squadron cookhouse was used as an HQ. No difficulty was found in getting volunteers to take part in the raids to recover kit, vehicles etc. In this 'Battle of the Box' everyone, in the chaos and confusion that reigned in the early stages, whether cook, clerk, batman, 'admin' or fighting man, found themselves in the thick of battle.

A lot of personal kit was destroyed including a kit-bag of mine which was never seen again. It contained my 'civilian clothes', khaki-drill trousers, shirts etc, and one or two books – other things were further back. Most people in the Box did not know of these happenings but it made little difference because the Pass was still blocked by Tanahashi's men.

On 10th February outside the Box, as on the previous day, a troop of 'B' Squadron carried out support tasks in the area of 9 Brigade 'B' Echelon. The West Yorks gave good indication of targets by telephone and wireless which made it possible to give efficient fire support.

A troop of 'A' Squadron took supplies to the 4/5th Punjabs of 33 Brigade and were fired on by a 37mm anti-tank gun on the road running east from the Box, but there were no casualties or damage. The gun was sited in a bunker on the side of Hill 315 and was to cause more trouble later.

At about 4.30pm a mortar bomb fell on RHQ killing Trooper Reginald Widger and wounding three others. It landed next to the control wireless set in a jeep and some senior officers were lucky to escape injury. Col Frink remarked of the shelling:

> The Jap has OPs (Observation Posts) on all the hills. There are two guns of particular nuisance value – Big Willie, a 105mm, who lets fly without warning from the south and Little Willie plus a few friends who open up without warning from the north. It is difficult to stop the chaps from becoming too careless and they are apt not to go to ground till the shelling is under way; in some cases it has been too late.

* * *

11th February:

During the day the tanks fired on surrounding hills at targets indicated by the artillery officers. 'C' Squadron brought down a heavy barrage on Artillery Hill as snipers had become active in that area. Our troop ('B' Squadron) was directing its fire into a feature to the north-east of the Box. The three tanks were drawn up so that Corporal Howden's tank was in front, the troop leader's behind and to the right, and ours behind and to the left. We were on open ground when suddenly a flash occurred over Howden's tank and the vibrant Welsh tones of Taffy Poole were heard on the intercom. 'Howden's *hit*. By God, *he's hit*.' The flash was shortly followed by a whiff of dirty yellow smoke rising from the hatch above the 75mm loader, sinister in its implication. What was happening inside the tank? The tank did not move and it seemed certain that the crew had been put out of action. The troop leader's driver, John Monger, volunteered to go and investigate. He walked coolly across the padi and climbed onto the tank. He managed to enter the turret and get out 'Curly' Howden the tank commander, Ray Evans and Corporal Peake all badly burned but still alive. In the hull the 76mm loader, Wally Mowle, had been killed outright as had Gunner John Stainbank. The driver, Gordon Barnes, and wireless operator, Frank Myers, were both alive though very badly burned and shocked.

The shell (believed to be from a mortar) had landed on the hatch above the 75mm loader's position in the hull. None of the Jap guns in the area were capable of penetrating the armour on the side of the tank but the plate was very thin on top of the hull. The Jap gunner had had the luck to hit the tank at its weakest point. The shell had broken open the charges of cordite attached to the 75mm shells which Mowle had laid out on the shelf for firing. This cordite had blazed up and sent a sheet of searing flame through the tank, lasting perhaps seconds but seemingly interminable to the crew.

In attempting to tow the tank back to base, the tank of the troop leader, Lt Eric Miles, caught fire and was eventually completely burnt out, the crew having been able to escape. Exactly how this occurred I cannot remember but it may have been due to the exhaust catching the grass alight.

Back in harbour we faced the bleak task of getting the dead men out and also all the live ammunition, much of which was singed and highly explosive. I shall not forget the burned and wizened, half-crushed head of the loader. In shocked silence they were passed through the side hatch and lowered to the ground. We dug two graves near the side of the hill and buried our two comrades. Padre Wallace Cox conducted a short service in the presence of the troop and rough wooden crosses were put up. White ants would soon have eaten the crosses and the jungle grown over the graves, but at the end of the war the bodies were removed to the Taukkyan Cemetery at Rangoon where they found a permanent resting place, commemorated by individual gravestones.

The other five members of the crew went into the MDS where they received such treatment as the doctors were able to give and it was possible to slip in and visit them.

Johnny Monger received the Military Medal for his conduct in this episode. The next day he received a complete replacement tank. Where this came from is something of a mystery as we were cut off from Reserve Squadron.

During the day 'A' Squadron gave close support fire to a successful attack on the feature 'Hammers' by the 4/15th Punjab of 33 Brigade.

What made the 11th February a memorable day for other people in the Box was the arrival overhead of four Dakotas at 1700 hours. They were the first of many missions bringing in supplies to the beleaguered garrison. The supplies were dropped by parachute on some open ground to the north of our harbour to be known as the 'dropping zone'. The crates, after recovery by Field Supply personnel, RIASC, turned out to be mainly aviation fuel and 75mm HE shells for us, at any rate, probably the most urgent requirements. This drop had been forecast by the message received on the 8th February.

To look up at the underbellies of these aircraft and see through the hatch doors the men who shoved out the crates as they swung low over the Box was a great boost for our morale – a reminder that the 'real' world still existed and thought of us, as opposed to the surreal world in which we seemed to live.

After the war Mountbatten explained:

> I was in a hell of a jam. There just were not enough aircraft for me to keep my promise that I would supply anyone in such a predicament. I therefore determined to rob the 'Hump' route to China, which President Roosevelt had expressly instructed should not be done under any circumstances. So I robbed the 'Hump'! This got me into trouble with the President – but it got me the planes to supply the fighting troops!

One difficulty was that Gen Orde Wingate's second Chindit expedition was being planned and needed aircraft for rehearsal. Mountbatten's action not only saved us but avoided delay in the launching of this expedition.

The 'Hump' was the air-supply service run by the Americans over the south-eastern end of the Himalayas where they meet north Burma. It was the main supply route for China.

12th February:

The night had been fairly quiet, for us at any rate. However the Japs were still very much in evidence on Artillery Hill, so called because it was defended by the men of the artillery acting as infantry. The hill dominated much of the southern part of the Box including a lot of the stacked ammunition on Ammunition Hill, the entrance to the newly-sited MDS and the track from the Box's water-point. It was also very close to Box HQ.

It was therefore urgent to dislodge the enemy from this position and an attack using tanks, artillery and infantry was formulated. Two troops of 'C' Squadron fired HE at enemy positions whilst two platoons of the West Yorks under Lt C.H. Dean advanced up the hill. The sound of this bombardment was so great that it was heard by 5th Indian Division on the other side of the Mayu Range. At a certain point the infantry commander fired a Very light as a signal to the tanks to change from HE to AP and to fire their machine-guns over the crest. The infantry could continue its advance under this fire until it was very close indeed to the enemy, due to the accuracy of the tank guns (and gunners). At the same time the infantry mortars fired on the reverse slopes to disorientate the enemy. Then the tanks ceased to fire and the infantry rushed the enemy positions with grenades and bayonets. Even so it was not until 5.25pm the same afternoon that Artillery Hill was recaptured. Lt Dean having been killed in the final stage and some Jap snipers remaining in thick undergrowth half way up.

An account of this incident, from a different viewpoint, is given by RQMS Murgatroyd RA:

> Artillery Hill was attacked by a strong force of Japs who first mortared and machine-gunned, then made a bayonet charge. The defence was overrun by superior numbers and the positions had to be evacuated. Our LAD lost L/Cpl Moss and Craftsman Kew killed, and Craftsmen Riley and Itzinger missing believed killed. The top defences of the lower ridge of Artillery Hill were doubled by personnel of the 139 and 136 Field Regiments and 284 Anti-Tank Battery. At 1315 hours the tanks blasted

the Japs from the positions just evacuated. Unfortunately the tanks could only just clear the lower ridge but not the trees. RQMS Murgatroyd, Sgt Deldenfield, L/BDR Ruderham and Signalman Lawrenson had the unpleasant experience, along with the personnel of 136 Field Regt, of being at the receiving end of the tanks' guns. The first shots felled a tree within 4yds of our trenches and pinned a bombardier of the 136th to the ground. While he lay there he was hit in the leg by a piece of shrapnel. Our trenches were only about 15ins deep as we had not been there long enough to get properly dug-in.

Every member of the party received some shrapnel in his person or his equipment. The strafing of the hill continued for 30 minutes and, after an interval of the same period, was repeated. The second bombardment seemed to us worse than the first because the Japs had come down the north side of the hill and the tanks had to aim lower. The West Yorks attacked and re-occupied the hill at dusk. The Punjabis relieved them.

This infantry/tank technique, worked out originally by Major Ley, had been used in the attacks on Tortoise at the end of January. However, as all parties gained experience, the technique was refined and the changes in the gun-fire were more accurately judged. A good tank forward observation officer, right up with the infantry, was needed and Major Ley mentions Capt Malcolm Marwood (later of 8th Hussars) as such a man.

Whilst this technique was designed for and ideal for Arakan, it was not necessarily so for other theatres such as the Imphal plain where the 3rd Carabiniers were to operate. The small coastal hills of Arakan were much steeper and covered with thick bamboo and were unclimbable for tanks who had to fire from below. In the Imphal area the tanks were able to climb many of the hills with the infantry – and did so with great success.

At 2pm that day two tanks of 'A' Squadron in the Box took supplies to the 'A' Squadron tanks of 33 Brigade. They were fired on as soon as they came out of the Ngakyedauk village by what was thought to be a 37mm anti-tank gun. They located it approximately but were not sure whether they put it out of action. They returned in the evening with three prisoners from 33 Brigade who had given themselves up in recent fighting in the north Buthidaung area. The Diary reports they were thought to be the first Japanese to give themselves up without a fight. This could well be the case. At this stage the Japanese usually fought to the death or committed suicide rather than be taken. Curiously, when taken, they were quite prepared to give information and seemed almost in a daze. Col Frink said their existence was finished as far as Japan was concerned. A wire cage had to be constructed in the Box to take prisoners.

Brig Evans used to pass this cage from time to time and, whenever he passed, one of the prisoners would make elaborate Japanese gestures of submission and obeisance. This annoyed the Brigadier intensely but there was little he could do about it.

Meanwhile, at 5th Indian Division on the west side of the Mayu Range, General Briggs was anxious to press on with opening up the Okeydoke Pass. For this purpose he intended to use the 2/1st Punjab, 4/7th Rajput, 1/18th Garwhali Rifles, some other Indian units and the Reserve Squadron of 25th Dragoons, which had remained at the side of the Pass. The advance started on the 12th February, the Punjabis and Rajputs pushing up the Pass, whilst the Garwhali Rifles held Point 1070 that commanded the centre of the Pass from the northern side.

Quartermaster Bill Nicholson afterwards wrote:

During this operation my main contribution was to feed Reserve Squadron and to maintain daily contact with our tanks, which were blasting away at Japanese bunkers on the west side of the Mayu Range, and to keep them supplied with ammunition and fuel. This could be a tricky business, particularly when the tanks were in various hidden positions and enemy road blocks appeared overnight. Every day I sent a 3-tonner with two men with a requisiton to an Indian supply unit wherever there was one. On one of these excursions I went with the lorry and was returning with supplies along the brick-made road, which was full of vehicles travelling both ways and exposed to enemy positions on the hillside, when a freak tropical storm broke and the road was an absolute quagmire. There was a hold-up in the traffic and I alighted from the vehicle and walked forward to find the cause of the stoppage when the Japs opened fire from the hillside just as we were trying to straighten a vehicle which had slewed round and caused a blockage. We fellows on foot immediately took cover on the opposite side of the road and then the convoy got moving. Quite rightly my driver started up and moved on with the convoy and I spent a very uncomfortable 24 hours getting back to my squadron which had moved to another position since I left it the day before.

On another of these trips I had gone with supplies to two of our tanks which were harbouring in a tiny village of bashas (huts of straw and bamboo) when one of these bashas caught fire, which quickly spread towards our tanks. We spent a hectic few minutes jumping in the vehicles to move them away from the fire and extinguishing the fire inside the vehicles which had ignited the ammunition in the machine-guns. The whole village was burnt down but our wounded men were removed from a basha in time.

I often wished our lorries had 6 inches of plating round them, particularly on the occasion when I was in a truck with my driver, with a third man sitting between the cab and the body on the camouflage nets with his rifle at the alert. We heard some rifle fire on our left but thought no more about it until the fellow sitting behind us said his back felt as though it was burning. When we stopped and examined him, we found that he had a huge score from a bullet across his back – a lucky miss. On several occasions we had to use the machine-gun to dispose of Japs lying in wait for us en route. Whenever we came across a stream we made full use of it for bathing and doing our laundry, provided the Japs were not too close.

Miles away at Bawli Bazaar the following message was received:

> I am following your battle with intense interest. Remember what matters is the 'Will'. Concentrate everything on destroying the immediate enemy.
>
> (Winston Churchill to XV Corps, 12th Feb 1944)

Sunday 13th February:

During the night two companies of 7/2nd Punjab arrived from 89 Brigade (from Awlanbyin to the east). They had a difficult time getting through and were caught in the open in a strong enemy bombing attack and suffered many casualties. One company was put in charge of Artillery Hill but enemy snipers were still there. 'C' Squadron carried out another shoot on the hill in support of the Punjabis but the hill remained uncleared.

The remaining seven tanks of 'A' Squadron left the Box at 10am to join the rest of the Squadron at 33 Brigade for operations with them and 89 Brigade.

There were two chaplains in the Box, our own, Padre Wallace Cox (C of E), and a Free Church padre. The latter I do not remember meeting. Wallace Cox, however, managed to organize some services during the siege, on Sundays as far as I remember. These were of course entirely voluntary and in no sense 'Church Parades' and were well attended. Presumably a special dispensation was issued by Brig Evans to allow people to come together for this purpose.

A problem arose for the Free Church padre when Gen Messervy wished to dispose of the bodies of a considerable number of mules, who had been killed or 'put down' because of wounds, and sent for the bulldozer in the Box to dig a pit. It then occurred to him to deal with the bodies of a number of dead Japanese at the same time. When the Free Church padre heard of this, he protested against the burial of human beings and animals in the same pit. The general however would not change his mind. Whether Padre Cox was involved in the argument I do not know.

Our troop leader 'borrowed' a staff car for the duration from the 'Ascot Car Park' and, I see from a letter home, 'we went to church in it one Sunday morning'. Also the Padre himself acquired a similar vehicle.

At 2.30pm in the Box further air supplies were dropped consisting of 75mm ammunition, POL and rations. It might be thought that dropping supplies was a cushy job for the air crews. Not so!!

Paul Chadburn, a reporter from *SEAC* newspaper, volunteered as a 'kicker-out' on one of the flights and wrote as follows:

> They collected every available transport plane, every conceivable sort of supply – rations, fuel, ammunition, spare parts, medical supplies and vast quantities of parachutes. Besides the crews, volunteers were needed, air stevedores to heave the supplies overboard from mid-air. An SOS was circulated among all men of the 7th Indian Division who, for one reason or another – sickness or leave – had left their unit before it became encircled.
>
> We volunteered our services, the only way to see what was done as they were taking no passengers on the run. We sat on the bamboo crates with two men of the division, a Yorkshireman and a Londoner, as the heavily-freighted plane swayed towards the Arakan front.
>
> We were now well within range of Zeros and it seemed at least a point of view that this 'Carter Patterson Circus' would be easy meat. Some of the planes – not ours – had two small machine-guns firing from the removed emergency exits on either side, but it was not a formidable armament and bullets would be deflected by the airstream. The look-out

man was reassuring. First of all he pointed to the sky; there above us were confidence-restoring Hurricanes. 'They give us a cover for the last part of the run,' he told us, 'and their patrolling makes the Jap pilot think twice about getting into the air. The whole supplying force has only written off one plane so far.' He pointed out of the side window. 'That's Buthidaung – Jap pockets all around there.' It seemed to us we were flying very low, considering. It was hilly country, jungle-covered with a good many clearings in which you could see the cattle browsing peacefully.

Civilian life was going on here as usual but a couple of miles away spouts of smoke came off the ground, probably shell bursts.

'We'll be dropping the stuff in a few minutes now.'

The two wireless operators and air gunners left the cabin and we scrambled after them over the crates. From then on, during the next half-hour, everything went 'nuts'. The plane seemed to go crazy, rolling and pitching and at intervals frantically buzzing (the pilot's signal to heave away), the ground kept rising against the open doorway (we'd taken the door off). Bofors guns seemed to be pointing at our heads like pistols, foreshortened figures were standing about on the sides of green precipices: we had gone crazy ourselves, frantically scrambling among the crates, heaving them into piles by the door, tying them with cords to a fixture in the door-frame, and then as the buzzer wildly and insistently rang out, hurling them overboard into the rush of the airstream, where the carefully tied cords broke and the parachutes opened.

The volunteer from Yorkshire lashed himself to the fuselage to stop his body following bales. We were stripped to the waist, running with sweat; the bamboo crates tore your fingers; the lurch of the plane as it rose suddenly to clear a hill-top (we dropped the supplies from 250 feet) sent us blundering about like drunks, only a sudden horrible drop enabled us to avoid collision.

With an escorting Hurricane, we began circling erratically; the turns jerked our hearts into our mouths. Round and round, following the plane in front that seemed to be behaving so soberly, sailing round slowly on an even keel . . . and what was happening to the ground or whatever it was that kept on blotting out the view of some blue sky across the hatch? It looked as though it had been strewn with great multi-coloured bits of confetti, green, red and black. The parachutes, of course, the parachutes . . . but to men who have been on the job every day – with a night trip thrown in very often – it was just routine: for they weren't through when the last bale of ration biscuits and bully, the last load of shells, had snapped their parachute cords.

(Chadburn: *SEAC* Souvenir Issue)

The colours of the parachutes denoted the type of supplies attached. The whole operation was visible to the Japanese from the surrounding hills and was within range of their mortars and small arms. It was always possible that the Japs might try to rush the collecting party from the edge of the jungle. In consequence some tanks stood by to cover them.

Some mail was brought in on these flights but I did not receive any myself. Johnny Leyin celebrated his 21st birthday in the Box and received a card from his mother in the shape of a key. It was duly hung on the side of the tank which he eventually joined.

About this time Tanahashi issued the following statement to his troops:

> Tanahashi Butai have completely surrounded the enemy. However, the enemy are still continuing their hysterical resistance. I am going to make great demands on you in the struggle against this doomed enemy.

The note of melodrama in this statement suggested that it was the Japanese, rather than the defenders of the Box, who were getting hysterical.

Wireless communication was established with Col Persse who was with 5 Division force trying to make its way over the Ngakyedauk Pass from the west. Lt Johnson's troop of 'B' Squadron went with two platoons of West Yorks under Major Dunlop along the Pass road from the east. They were able to proceed some two miles, after which the infantry was held up by a blown-up bridge and it was decided to return. On the way back they came up against several huge tree trunks blocking the track – an ambush. There was no way of getting round them so Lt Johnson ordered his troop to blast them out of the way with 75mm high-explosive and armour-piercing shells. The Japs fired on the tanks with mortars and machine-guns but Lt Johnson managed to get all three tanks back to the Box safely and undamaged. However, the infantry suffered serious casualties who were brought back on the tanks. The remainder had to work their way round through the jungle as best they could.

About 4.15pm the harbour was dive-bombed by enemy aircraft. Three or four bombs fell amongst the vehicles in the harbour but very little damage was done. One tank caught fire but was soon extinguished. Major Horne received bomb splinter wounds in the face and arms and was evacuated to, MDS. Lt MacFarlane was very slightly wounded and four non-commissioned ranks also. Further dive-bombing later hit the ammo dump and 25-pounder ammunition was exploding until put out by the dew. Splinters landed in the harbour all night and kept everyone awake.

It is interesting to compare Tanahashi's statement with Mountbatten's entry in his Diary for the 13th February. After outlining the situation he wrote:

> This battle, which is now at its height, is of the utmost importance to us in South East Asia, as it is a battle of morale. In importance it will rank with El-Alamein. The same troops that were so badly defeated by Rommel rallied themselves together under Alexander and Montgomery and inflicted a crushing defeat on him. The same troops that ran before Tanahashi last year have stood firm to the last man this year and I feel confident of ultimate victory.

14th February:
During the early hours of this day, some two hundred Japanese continuously attacked the Garwhali positions on Point 1070 from east to west. The attack was made regardless of cost to themselves and, just before first light, they managed to drive the 1/18th Garwhali Rifles from the hill. This was a serious setback in the process of opening up the Okeydoke Pass, since the hill commanded the Pass from the north.

Inside the Box further efforts were made to clear Artillery Hill. Troops of 'A' and 'C' Squadrons supported the Punjabis in attacks from the north-west and the north-east. The remaining Japs were now in the saddle just below the top and this attack finally finished them off.

Division Signals intercepted a message that an attack was to be made on the Box at 1700 hours but it did not materialize until the following morning.

'A' Squadron with 33 Brigade carried out a destructive shoot on Ngakyedauk village and feature 457519. The whole squadron fired for twenty minutes and destroyed the village. For some time it had been clear that it was a main Japanese supply centre and also a collecting place for Jifs. Its proximity to the Box made it a danger which could not be allowed to remain and it is safe to say that its Burmese inhabitants had long since left. The brigade occuped the area the following night.

One troop of 'C' Squadron in its operation with Gurkhas met an anti-tank ditch just beyond the Y junction of the tracks Awlanbyin and Buthidaung to the east of the Box. At first sight the ditch looked perfectly crossable for a tank but when the first tank nosed down into it the sides gave in. The tank went right down and the 75mm barrel stuck in the ground. Clearly the sides of the ditch had been lightly propped up and camouflaged. The Japs started mortaring and grenading but the rest of the troop was able to cover the tank and tow it out without loss, with cover from the Gurkha escort. The troop was able to carry out the first part of its shoot to the south but could not get round to the east as was at first intended. 9 Brigade reported a further road block to the north on the Awlanbyin road. These two road blocks meant the tanks could not operate to the east until they had been removed.

In the early afternoon two small air supply drops were made, followed by a double one in the evening. During the latter a Jap infantry gun opened up again and dropped about six shells in the middle of the harbour. HQ squadron leader's 15cwt truck went up after a direct hit and the Quartermaster Sergeant, Harold King, was wounded – the only casualty.

That afternoon the two companies of the 4/8th Gurkhas, who had on the 6th February lost contact with the rest of their battalion turned up on the southern edge of the Box. They had crossed to the west of the Mayu Range on the 7th February and had now crossed back again through the 2/1st Punjab on the crest of the Range. With them came a line party from the 5th Indian Division Signals and for the first time in a week telephone communication was established with the 5th Division. The line was immediately used by the two divisional commanders, Messervy and Briggs, and other senior officers but within three hours the cable over the hills had been found by the enemy and cut. Thereafter, until the end of the siege, only wireless communication was possible.

During the last two days I had been able to slip into the MDS and visit Gordon Barnes (driver) and Frank Myers (wireless operator) who had been burned in Howden's tank three days before. Each day they grew weaker, their voices fainter, their movements slower or none at all. The dead skin formed itself into rolls across the body. They had no 'wounds' but they were dying just the same and they must have known it. What did they think about, lying there in the heat under the trees? It seemed hopeless because nothing could be done for them. On the 13th February Gordon aged 22 died and on the 14th, Frank died aged 20. They, together with many other wounded of every description, were laid in the open-air 'ward' under the trees. The other members of the crew, in the turret, were not apparently so badly burned and two did in fact survive to re-join the Regiment many months later. Howden was, however, very badly shell-shocked from the blast and I do not think ever returned.

There was a continuous stream of wounded to the MDS and the doctors and medical staff had to work day and night, with restricted medical supplies, to give these people the best possible chance of surviving. A bamboo basha had to do as an operating theatre. The MDS was soon overflowing and wounded were laid on stretchers in nullahs and trenches, wherever it was possible to put them. By now the total was over 450. Cases of malaria and dysentry increased the number.

There was no landing strip in the Box but there was a track to the Box of 114 Brigade to the east whose strip took supplies for the bulk of the division. A small number of small strips were constructed during the battle and from these some of the most seriously wounded were flown out by light aircraft eg Austers, Fox Moths. They were often flown by American pilots operating on their own.

Every day and night the Japanese attacked or broke into one sector or another of the perimeter of the Box and had to be kicked out by a joint infantry and tank operation. With the shelling and sniping, the heat and the dust, the blazing ammunition and the falling shrapnel, not to say the basic necessities of living, it was, without exaggeration, 'One Damn Thing After Another'. Spirits were kept up, not only by the regular air drops of food, ammunition and medical supplies, but also by the great sense of comradeship and the ultimate belief in victory.

7

Signs of Relief

During the night of the 14th/15th February the Technical Adjutant, Captain 'Pigeon' Winters, had died in the MDS. Col Frink says that he had a bullet in the spine whilst another source refers to gun-shot wounds in the shoulder. Perhaps he suffered both. He failed to give the correct password at night to a guard and was shot out of hand. He was a Regular officer who had started in the Royal Tank Regiment, 'An excellent chap who can ill be spared,' said Col Frink; 'The salt of the earth,' said Major Ley. This tragic incident emphasizes the strict security in force in the Box after dark.

15th February:
A 'recce' party consisting of the squadron leader and troop leaders of 'C' Squadron with Major Burrell of 401 Field Squadron Indian Engineers, went out in two Bren-carriers to investigate the possibilities of repairing the two roads to the east of the Box. Major Burrell was able to deal with the first road block and by 4.30pm Capt Alexander (who had taken over command of 'C' Squadron from the wounded Major Horne) reported that Tattenham Corner was clear for movement. The Gunners repaired the north road block with the Gurkhas covering the party.

Tattenham Corner was presumably so named by our cavalry officers after the bend at the race-course on Epsom Downs. After leaving the Box it did indeed swing round to the left as do the horses at Epsom. Any other resemblance between them and our 26-ton tanks would be quite coincidental.

Shelling came in from the south-east, a new position, and set off the ammo on the north side of Ammunition Hill. The fact that the shells came from the south, went over the top of the hill, and dropped on the north slope, suggested that the gun had a high trajectory and was of 105 or 150mm. The ammo continued to explode for the rest of the day and scraps of metal landed all over the harbour. Capt Burton of 'B' Squadron was wounded and three other ranks. Several 'soft vehicles' and one tank were put on fire.

The attack that had been expected for 5pm the previous day took place that morning. It was against 'C Company Hill', on the west side of the Box just north of the Pass road. The enemy approached through thick jungle so close to the Yorkshires' trenches that the latter were taken by surprise and driven from their positions. From this hill the Japanese could command vital areas of the Box and they had to be moved out.

'B' Squadron was called upon to co-operate with 'A' Company of the West Yorks to re-take the hill before the enemy could dig itself in. The same method was used as for Artillery Hill and by the evening the hill was back in our hands.

'C' Squadron, by giving concentrated fire prior to the attack, was able to put the 4/8th Gurkhas onto the small hill features north and south of the gap to the east, thus opening the road leading to the 'eastern gate' of the Box.

Soon after 3.30pm a large air drop, mainly of rations, took place. These usually consisted of dehydrated potatoes, bully beef, biscuits and jam. Sometimes on these drops the parachutes drifted outside the Box, in which case they had to be speedily recovered before the Japs could get them. (The Japanese were by this time shorter of rations and supplies than we were, their supply lines having been drastically interfered with by the various units of 7 Division in the jungle.)

Whilst the night was quiet in 'B' and 'C' Squadron areas, firing continued through most of the night to the north-east of our harbour area and to the south of the old MDS.

A scruffy, bearded man on a motorbike used to pass through our lines from time to time. We understood him to be a member of V Force, the intelligence-gathering service which was of great help to all units in this confused maze of jungle. Bill Harding of 139 Field Regt described one of these officers:

> Capt Irwin of the V Force passed through 33 Brigade area about this time . . . Ginger-bearded and armed with a Tommy-gun, he was wearing a floppy bush-hat, khaki shirt, native lungi – a piece of coloured cloth, ankle length and wrapped around the waist – and chaplis (Indian sandals). Accompanied by three local Arakanese with slung rifles, he was to make his way back to Bawli by walking through the dense jungle of the foothills and over the Mayu Range by little known footpaths.

Captions to photographs on following pages

1. Aerial view from the direction of Maungdaw towards the Mayu Range. The 'Razabil Fortress' of the Japanese is in the trees upper centre with Tortoise hill to the left. The road to Buthidaung runs from the bottom, through the 'Fortress' and into the Mayu Hills. (IWM)

2. General Lee/Grant tanks of 25th Dragoons on the second day of battle, moving forward, watched by local workers employed to maintain the tracks and roads for heavy traffic. (IWM)

3. Tanks moving forward in the Razabil area – January 1944. (Lt Col C. Auchinleck)

4. The Road over the Ngakyedauk Pass. (IWM)

5. Bengal and Madras Sappers and Miners repairing the Pass Road after enemy bombing. (IWM)

6. 'C' Squadron 'O' Group in the Admin Box. Left to right: Lt B.O'C. Roberts, Lt R.J. Charles, Lt W. Childs, Major O. Horne, Capt C.W. Alexander. (Lt Col C. Auchinleck)

7. The Admin Box from Ammunition Hill towards the eastern entrance. In the middleground is the area occupied by 'C' Squadron tanks. Beyond the clump of trees and to the left is the hill held by 3/4th Gurkhas. (IWM)

8. Crew belting .30 Browning machine-gun ammunition in the Admin Box. (Lt Col C. Auchinleck)

9. The Admin Box, North West side, with parachute descending. (IWM)

10. Ammunition Hill with tanks along the base and a Dakota, some parachutes and two vultures overhead. (Lt Col C. Auchinleck)

11. Tank attacking Point 1070 near the top of the Ngakyedauk Pass. (IWM)

12. Men of Reserve Squadron during a lull in operations to re-open the Ngakyedauk Pass. (IWM)

13. 7th Division medical staff are relieved when the first ambulance convoy arrives to evacuate the wounded after the re-opening of the Pass. (IWM)

14. Ambulance Convoy with tank escort gets through to the western foot of the Pass. (IWM)

15. 'Unbeatable'. Many of the tanks were named. (Lt Col C. Auchinleck)

16. A crew takes time off for a much needed wash. (Lt Col C. Auchinleck)

17. 'Tokyo via Ngakyedauk'. The Indian Army points the way at the western end of the Pass. (Lt Col C. Auchinleck)

18. The Maungdaw–Buthidaung Road and the Letwedet Chaung near Buthidaung. (Major K. Spooner)

19. 'Camel': part of the ridge of hills of which Point 551 was the peak. Attacked on 15 April 1944. (Major K. Spooner)

20. 'Hump': Point 551. Attacked on 15 April 1944. (Major K. Spooner)

21. Valentine Bridge-Laying Tank. The Corps Armoured Group had a Troop of six of these. (Lt Col C. Auchinleck)

22. Ward la-France. The Corps Armoured Group had two of these. (Tank Museum, Bovington)

23. Brigadier H.R.C. Frink DSO. Commanding Officer of the 25th Dragoons from 1941 to June 1944. (Mrs J. Frink)

24. A group of 'C' Squadron in harbour with camouflaged tank, the Mayu hills in the background. (Lt Col C. Auchinleck)

25. A crew of 'C' Squadron at work on tank maintenance. (Mr Norman Hamer)

TORTOISE
EYE
1

2

3

4

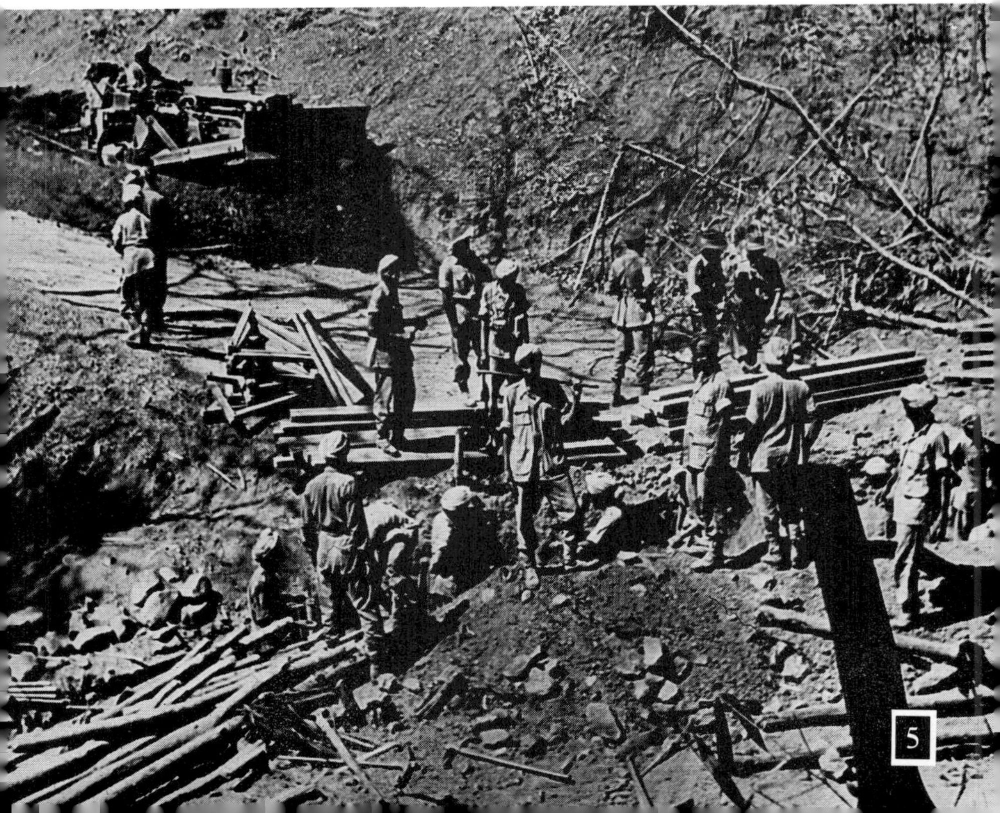

5

6

7

8

9

12

13

14

15

16

17

18

19

20

21

22

25

23

24

The V Force was an 'Intelligence' formation composed of groups of local natives led by British officers who penetrated the enemy's lines to gather information. It was extremely hazardous work and the members of the force could expect no quarter if captured.

16th February:

During the night 89 Brigade HQ and three companies of the 2nd King's Own Scottish Borderers came into the Box through the 'eastern gate'. They had however suffered a severe attack on the way. The mule convoy of Brigade HQ was stampeded by mortar fire and many animals were lost or killed in the darkness. It was thought at first there could be few, if any, survivors. In fact the muleteers had rallied after the attack, then dispersed, remained in hiding and two days later arrived in the Box with most of their mules.

The West Yorks had borne the brunt of the fighting to take and re-take the hills surrounding the Box and had now suffered some 200 casualties and desperately needed some help and relief, which the KOSBs could give them. Brigadier Crowther of 89 Brigade took over responsibility for the eastern perimeter of the Box from that day.

At 7.30am news came in that some of our own troops were approaching Point 315, to the north-east of the Box. Firing in the night had been heard in this direction. One troop of 'C' Squadron with Capt Alexander, a patrol of Scout Troop and a detachment of sappers moved out to try and make contact. At 10.05am they had contacted the 1st Battalion of the Lincolnshire Regiment. This was the leading column of infantry of the 26th Indian Division, which had made its way over the Goppe Pass, and moved south towards the Box.

Our party had been fired on by an anti-tank gun but they considered they had put the gun out of action. One tank had been hit in the bogeys but not put out of action. All these tanks were later hit by a 37mm AP shell but were undamaged.

The adjutant of the Lincolns was brought back to the Box by a 'C' Squadron tank and reported to 7 Division HQ at noon. It appeared that they had received orders to attack and take Point 315. Battalion HQ and two companies had gone to the area of the old 7 Division HQ, whilst the rest of the Regiment was in the Badana area. They had attacked 315 in the early hours. The Japanese were extremely well dug-in on this hill and were virtually impregnable. The Lincolns were halted on the open approaches and ultimately failed to take the hill. It was in the course of this operation that a company commander of the Lincolns gained the only Victoria Cross of this battle. The citation reads as follows:

> Capt (temporary Major) Chas Ferguson Hoey MC, The Lincolnshire Regiment (Vancouver).
>
> In Burma on the 16th February 1944, Maj Hoey's company formed part of a force which was ordered to capture a position at all costs.
>
> After a night march through enemy-held territory, the force was met at the foot of the position by heavy machine-gun fire.
>
> Maj Hoey personally led his company under heavy machine-gun and rifle fire right up to the objective. Although wounded at least twice in the leg and head he seized a Bren-gun from one of his men and firing from the hip led his company on to the objective. In spite of his wounds the company had difficulty keeping up with him and Maj Hoey reached the enemy strong point where he killed all the occupants before being mortally wounded. Maj Hoey's outstanding gallantry and leadership, his total disregard of personal safety and grim determination to reach the objective resulted in the capture of this vital position.

The tragedy of Maj Hoey's bravery is that the operation was in the end a failure, despite the impression to the contrary given by the citation. Pinned down, the Lincolns were obliged to wait for the cover of night before pulling back.

In addition to Maj Hoey there had been a number of casualties and when the adjutant returned to his regiment on the 'C' Squadron tank he took with him some medical stores. When the tank returned it brought back four wounded to the MDS.

Meanwhile, in the Box there were air drops in the morning, at lunchtime and in the evening. 'C' Squadron remained in the Tattenham Corner area all day and had several opportunities of opening up on Jap anti-tank guns. Two troops supported 4/8th Gurkhas in their move to increase their holds on the features north and south of the road.

By 5.30pm the Lincolns had been ordered to pull back about 2000 yards for the night. Lt Roberts with two tanks covered their withdrawal from the area of the old Division car park. Near Tattenham Corner, when they were nearly home, one tank got bogged down and another, commanded by Cpl Bob Smiles, was hit by a mortar bomb which went into the air-vent and caught the tank on fire. The tank came to a standstill and the crew all scrambled out before the tank blew up. The only casualty was Bob Smiles who had a load of shrapnel in his back. The crew had to remain there for the night, and were able to get the Browning-machine-gun out and mount it on a tripod. They lay down in a ditch for the night including Bob Smiles who was later taken to the MDS in the Box. The other members of the crew were N. Hamer, Len Talbot, E. Craber, F. Holmes, W.O. Hollingsworth and Fred Payne.

At some point the Gurkhas mounted an ambush by the tanks. The following day the crew moved in with the Gurkhas, who were very pleased with the machine-gun, and stayed with them until the 20th February when (as will be seen) a party came out from the Box to clear the track.

The Regiment's casualties from the time we left Chamba on the 4th February were as follows: 1 officer died of wounds, 1 officer wounded, 2 officers slightly wounded, 2 sergeant-majors wounded, 7 non-commissioned ranks killed and 26 wounded. Of the wounded the majority were treated in Doc Gaunt's underground regimental aid post and did not have to go into the over-crowded MDS.

During the siege the 25th Dragoons had their own cemetery in the Box and Archie Mitchell of 'A' Squadron, who was an artist, painted the regimental badge on a sign, little knowing that he himself would be buried there later. Bill Nicholson wrote:

> I think the most thankless job I ever had in Burma was when I had to write personal letters regarding colleagues who were killed and inform the relatives, usually parents, how their son had died, without giving the details.

Later Bill Nicholson had the bad luck to be wounded by a Japanese mortar bomb exploding beside him. He was sent back to base hospital and eventually ended up with a punctured ear-drum, which prevented him from ever re-joining the Regiment.

Following behind the Lincolns was the 1st Battalion of the Wiltshires, also part of the 26th Division. Lt Col Houghton Brown had now become Commanding Officer and he described how, on the night of the 10th February, he led his battalion over the Goppe Pass:

At mid-day I got my orders. The Battalion was to move that night under cover of darkness over the Goppe Pass to Goppe Bazaar on the eastern foothills of the Mayu Range. I sent Major Magawilly, OC 'D' Company, with a small advance party to move over the Pass that afternoon. I then settled down to prepare the details of my orders for the move. We had never done a battalion move before with only mule transport, and it took a lot of working out.

As soon as it got dark the mule companies arrived; 500 little animals moved into our perimeter. I soon realized we had a lot to learn about mule loading. It is a tricky business to load a mule correctly so that his back is not rubbed and the load equally dispersed both sides of him. At 1930 hours the long chain of men and animals moved out towards Garretts garden. This is a resting place on the western slope before one starts the steep ascent over the Pass. We waited here an hour to re-adjust loads and make the animals comfortable. Then the move started.

The Pass is a narrow track only fit for animals to pass over in single file. The long snake crept up the narrow dark path overhung with dense jungle. A moon occasionally glimmered through the gaps in the foliage. In front of me was a little round mule's rump, behind me flapped another's long silky ears. The animals dug their little toes into the dirt and gradually bumped their big loads up the winding path. It was a perilous night's adventure because if a mule stepped wrongly he was hurtled down over the precipices into the chaung below. We carried all our supplies with us including 1st line ammunition and four days' reserve rations.

We marched all night, only stopping for a ten minute 'breather' every hour. When daylight came we had crossed the main ridge and were descending towards the Kalapanzin valley. As we marched into Goppe Bazaar, aircraft were already busy dropping supplies by parachute, and sacks of rice were falling out of the sky like hail. In fact, that night two of our men became quite serious casualties because heavy bags of supplies dropped on their sleeping bodies. We rested that day and the following night in the old bashas that surrounded the Bazaar . . .

That day I got our orders from brigade. The Battalion was to be the advance guard for a move south of the Brigade to relieve the 7th Indian Division who had been cut-off in the Sinzweya Box.

On the 13th February our advance started. 'C' Company, under Major Tom Dutton (who afterwards got the MC), acted as vanguard and 'B' Company as rearguard. One company always had to be detailed to load, unload, and protect the mules. We moved along the banks of the sluggish Kalapanzin river and then hugged the eastern foothills of the Mayu Range. The country was strangely beautiful. On our left stretched flat strips of yellow padi stubble and on our right the great towering jungle.

The first day was uneventful. 'C' Company dug-in for the night at Badana West. 'A', 'D', HQ, 'S' and BHQ took over positions from the Lincolns at Prinkhaung and the rearguard followed to Manyindaung.

The Lincolns under Lt Col Sinclair, DSO, had been given the task of moving south to 'demonstrate' against the Japs on a feature known as 315 and thus relieve the tension on the '7 Div Box'. This they did to some tune, passing through the enemy's lines and eventually attacking the objective itself.

That night, 13/14th February, we got our first serious battle casualties. We had been drilled into always sleeping under mosquito nets. 'C' Company had a large perimeter to hold and at dead of night was attacked in force by the enemy. At one place they overran the sentries, penetrated the position and bayoneted some of our men before they could get out of their nets. Tom Dutton gathered up the men of his HQ around him and counter-attacked. He drove into the enemy with tommy-guns and bayonets. He killed many of them, he personally shooting the officer who had led the attack. The remainder fled in panic. However, it was a nasty blow to us, six of our lads being killed and eight wounded. Of course after that it was impossible to order men to sleep under nets and I got permission from the Brigadier to give up nets when in contact with the enemy.

For the next few days we had a busy time. The Jap harassed us every night, firing automatics and tracers into our positions. He tried to draw our fire and thus make us give away our localities. We soon learnt his game and the rule then was never to fire at night unless one could actually identify the enemy. Sometimes he even tried to molest us by day, and on one occasion a small party of Japs walked right into our positions. We shot them up well and for the first time I saw the dead of our enemy. They were brought in and laid in a row on the ground. They might have been part of the 'bag' after a mixed shoot at Pertwood but the soldiers, reverent always, insisted on covering their faces with blankets.

Corps continued to supply us by air and at night we had to light bonfires out in the padi to direct the aircraft to our positions. This was an unenviable task and at this stage was organized by my support company commander, Major Joe Panks, MC. The first night he and his CSM Bull spent most of the night up a tree near the fire, occasionally jumping down to pile more bamboo on to the furnace. Of course this was good fun for the Japs who used to fire constantly at the figures that fluttered round the flames.

In the morning the padi field would be littered with parachutes and stores and then a company would have to go out and collect our supplies.

The enemy planes seemed to make little attempt to interfere with our aircraft at night, although their Zeros would occasionally come over by day and bomb the long lines of mules that moved backwards and forwards along the routes to the forward units.

17th February:
Lts Evans and Roberts with a patrol of the Scout Troop went out to the two 'C' Squadron tanks abandoned the previous night. One had completely burnt out and the other could not be recovered without one or perhaps two D8s. All equipment was removed from the tank and it was decided that recovery was impossible until the infantry position became more firm.

There was some shelling during the morning on the south-west portion of the Box and the usual air drop arrived. Captain Copeland, second-in-command of 'B' Squadron, and Squadron Sergeant-Major George Devenport went to the support of 9 Brigade 'B' Echelon to knock out three machine-guns and evacuate some wounded. About 2.30pm Capt Copeland was fatally wounded in the head by a machine-gun bullet. In attempting to get his tank out, the SSM himself became bogged down and found that recovery by one D8 alone was impossible. The tank was rendered ineffective and left for the time being. The death of Capt Copeland was something of a shock and a loss to the Squadron and to the Regiment. He had been with the Regiment since its days at Risalpur and before.

A troop of tanks was sent westward up the Pass but was unable to get far owing to enemy road blocks. Between 5 and 6pm, 'B' Squadron's harbour area was mortared from the hills to the west and attempts were made to set the grass and vehicles alight with incendary mortar bombs. These bombs burst on hitting the ground and sprayed phosphorous pellets over the area for 30 or 40 seconds. The danger of fire was dealt with by shovels of earth. Major Burrell of 401 Field Squadron, IE was wounded in the foot. The night was quiet so far as our part of the perimeter was concerned but there was a fair amount of firing to the north and south-east.

18th February:
One troop of 'C' Squadron supported the 7/2nd Punjab onto a small hill feature behind Artillery Hill. The operation was entirely successful and a number of enemy dead were found on the position when the infantry went in.

HQ Squadron tanks gave twenty minutes' destructive fire on

Point 315 in the afternoon but the position remained in enemy hands. There was no air drop on this day but one troop of 'C' Squadron covered the collection of supplies dropped outside the area the previous night. They also supported the Gurkhas in a small attack near Ngakyedauk. One troop of 'B' Squadron supported the 7/2nd Punjab in a further attack in the Artillery Hill area. Meanwhile Lt Evans had spent the whole day with cover from a troop of tanks, trying to unditch 'B' Squadron sergeant major's tank with two D8s. He was unsuccessful and the work had to be continued the next day. Lt Grey carried out a 'recce' on a chaung and reported it a possible crossing for a squadron of tanks.

By this time many tanks began to take on a pock-marked appearance, the result of well-aimed but unsuccessful shooting by Japanese anti-tank guns of insufficient calibre. The solid shot did not penetrate the thick armour plate on the front of the tanks but drilled neat conical indentations perhaps two inches deep. The implications were a bit frightening but at the same time reassuring.

These operations give an idea of the incessant and infinitely variable jobs which the tanks were called on to carry out every day, apart from the major attacks on vital positions. They were on call to any part of the Box at any time of the day, where and when their mobility and firepower were required. What ultimately caused the strain was the necessity of keeping watch throughout the night. As a troop sergeant of 'B' Squadron says:

> After a fortnight of this, combined with sleepless nights, we all became rather punch-drunk and one morning after we were 'stood down' my corporal and his complete crew were found to be fast asleep. The troop leader went berserk and threatened to have them all court-martialled and shot. He and I had a flaming row and I was also threatened with court-martial. As usual we left the Box without even a cup of tea and did not return until just before 'Stand To'. I had another word with the troop leader but he was adamant that the next morning he would report the incident to Major Johnstone and ask that they be court-martialled. Next morning I found the troop leader and his crew fast asleep. There was no more talk of anyone being court-martialled!

At night those who were not claustrophobic could sleep in the trench alongside each tank or, perhaps, under the tank. One man in the trench and one in the turret remained on watch throughout the night. All members of the crew took turns so that you had one hour on and two off. In the event of an emergency all wireless sets were to be switched on. In the trench were a couple of machine-guns, a Tommy-gun and grenades. In the turret was a canister of shot in the 37mm gun.

In front of our tank was 50 yards of open ground, bordered by the jungle perimeter. You watched the edge of this jungle for movement and, of course, saw it – but it was just the night breeze stirring the tall plumed grass and the bushes – or was it a figure? Were you to raise the alarm and awake the whole camp over nothing? I could have fallen asleep over and over again whilst on duty. As the night wore on, eyelids grew heavier, falling down over the eyes, the head sank forward and each time had to be jerked up again. It would have been fatal to sit down, yet I found it curiously difficult to get any sleep during the periods of 'rest'. How long could this go on?

For those on the perimeter, surrounded as they were by jungle, it was even more tense. They had to maintain absolute silence themselves in order to catch the sound of any approaching enemy. The Japanese well understood this situation, imitating animal calls or softly calling in English, 'Tommy, Tommy, here I am. Come and get me.' No one ever shouted back or did anything to give away their position. They had cleared the jungle around them so that they would see anyone who came out into the moonlight. The eeriness and tension of those nights could never be forgotten.

19th February:

By this time the Box was becoming a shambles. High-explosives had flayed the leaves from the trees and pulverized the undergrowth; the one-time padi of the villagers had become a baked mud arena churned up by the tracks and wheels and surrounded by gaunt tree stumps. Charred skeletons of lorries and carriers and an occasional smoke-blackened tank were scattered over it willy-nilly. It was becoming a mass of flies. There was the possibility of disease setting-in. Two Japanese bodies had been found in the water point. Each morning, or whenever the opportunity occurred, you borrowed the tank spade and went in search of a surviving shrub or two to perform your duty in modest cover, hoping not to meet a Jap doing the same thing.

In the MDS, Corporal Pearse of the West Yorks, who had been badly wounded by a mortar, found the patients were being looked after by personnel from a Graves Registration Unit who had come to map out a cemetery (the army thinks of everything!). They were all that could be spared. The two surgeons who worked ceaselessly throughout the siege were Major Crawford and Major Lilwall. Although working in primitive conditions, they had the advantage of being on the spot. They might operate on men within five minutes of their being wounded.

Major (later Lt Col) Bernard Lilwall DSO, MS, FRCS, died on the 9th July 1987 aged 72 and his obituary in 'Dekho' reads:

> Lilwall and his anaesthetist were extremely lucky to be taken prisoner (during the Jap attack on the MDS on the night of 7th February), and not long afterwards to escape and crawl back to the British lines, where they were nearly shot by a sentry who was much impressed by the richness and fluency of the oaths with which they greeted the challenge.
>
> They immediately resumed surgery and continued working untiringly for the wounded in appalling conditions. For his superb conduct, Lilwall received the DSO. Later when the hospital was again attacked, he helped to beat off the Japs, firing a 2-inch mortar from the hip. For this exploit he gained a Bar to his DSO. In the most difficult and testing circumstances he performed more than 250 operations on sick and wounded men.

Turning to dental surgery, Major Ley developed raging toothache during the Box and went to the dental unit in the MDS. The dentist said, 'Out with it.' and assured him that there was more than enough pentothal coming in on the air drops to allow him to have it out painlessly without depriving the wounded.

The only problem was that the dentist had been wounded in his tooth-drawing arm which was strapped to his waist. However, with a stretcher balanced on four paraffin tins and the use of his knees to produce the necessary leverage, the dentist was able to perform the best extraction that Major Ley had ever had before or since. He also had the bonus of a couple of hours sound sleep on the stretcher, of which he had had little during the past week or so.

Six Dakotas had appeared overhead at 7.30am. They came again at 10.30am but this time – great catastrophy – 'large quantities' of rum were lost due to the failure of some parachutes to open. Commando planes were also used on these drops. Sometimes, it is said, there were nasty accidents as when an aerial stevedore would fall out with the crates, due to the lurching or even somersaulting of the planes as a result of air-turbulence and the uneven contours of the hills.

Lt Evans and two D8 tractors were able to recover the 'B' Squadron tank from the area of 9 Brigade 'B' Echelon by 2pm sufficiently to enable the crew to work on the tracks and finally bring it in.

One troop of 'C' Squadron and two Bren-carriers went out at 2.15pm to the area south-east of Tattenham Corner to search for wireless equipment belonging to 89 Brigade. This had been lost on the night of 15th/16th February when 89 Brigade HQ had been attacked on its way to the Box and the mules carrying the equipment had stampeded. Very little equipment was in fact found but there were no casualties.

Another air-drop came at 4.20pm but the majority of the load landed outside the harbour area. The company of the 4th Bombay Grenadiers with the Scout Troop with all jeeps and Bren-carriers available went out immediately to recover these before the Japanese did. In fact they were able to bring back about 80% of the drop.

In the evening unconfirmed reports reached regimental HQ that Buthidaung and Sinobyin were in flames and that the Japanese were moving from west to east across the Kalapanzin river. On top of this the Air Force was said to have had a successful fighter sweep in the Buthidaung area. The implication of these reports was that the Japanese were retreating east in a hurry. Whilst they were undoubtedly putting into effect a plan of retreat by this time, it was by no means a hurried or disordered affair and it would be another week before they were clear of our area. It is now known that Col Kubo's force on the west side of the Mayu Range were weak and even dying from starvation, being without any line of supply.

So far as 'B' and 'C' Squadrons were concerned there followed a fairly quiet night but 33 Brigade HQ was attacked by about twelve Japs and there was much firing but no casualties.

* * *

Meanwhile the relieving forces from the north were gradually mopping-up the enemy and moving towards us. Col Houghton Brown continues the experiences of the Wiltshires:

We were impatient to push on and on 17th February the 2/13th FF Rifles took over our positions at Prinkhaung. I then moved up our Battalion HQ and two companies to Badana West and stepped up 'B' and 'D' Companies to Yinboungyaung. 20 Mountain Battery was now supporting us and they dug-in their guns in our main battalion perimeter.

All this time our patrols from all companies were probing the enemy to our front and flanks. However, he hid himself well in the thick jungle and it was difficult to pick him up in any strength. At night he would come out of his hidden lair and try to molest us. He would fire into our positions, attack any isolated parties and generally make a nuisance of himself. He caused few casualties amongst us but did succeed in keeping us awake.

Again we moved on – I pushed up 'B' Company to act as a 'firm base' on the high ground overlooking the Prein chaung and passed 'C' Company across the river towards the 'wings'. I knew we were coming into the old battle area as flocks of long-winged vultures hovered over the padi. As I moved my Battalion HQ across the chaung I saw those birds, their heads covered in gore, rising in flocks from stinking carcasses. The place stank of rotting human flesh. I watched 'C' Company creeping round the edge of the jungle towards the 'wings'. As their leading platoon crossed the narrow strip of padi that divided the 'wings' from the jungle, they were suddenly met by a fusillade of fire. Japs were again dug-in on the high ground. Snipers lay hidden in the tall grass. The leading platoon wavered and then, covered by their own LMG fire, crept on again. In a flash the dry padi was afire and the breeze blowing towards us fanned the flames into the faces of our attacking troops. In a few moments it had extended and spread right across our front. It had either been ignited by the Japs or by the bursting of the grenades. Anyway it happened very suddenly and drove the company off. Fighting men, stretcher-bearers and 'walking wounded' all fell back to the line of the chaung. One platoon of 'A' Company held on in a corner of the jungle to the west and this was then reinforced with the remainder of the company. Another Jap force crossed the chaung and tried to outflank us to the east. To counteract this I pushed out 'D' Company to cover this flank. When darkness fell suddenly, we had reorganized and were digging-in again on the high ground, but it was a near go as the Battalion had nearly walked into a cleverly laid trap.

The next day we skirted the 'wings', which was now under fire from our artillery, and advanced south to some high ground south of the Prein chaung. The whole Battalion was now up so we 'dug-in' around a compact perimeter. Our position overlooked the padi to our east but was still dominated by the lower foothills of the Mayu Range.

Not being at all satisfied with this position, I immediately sent patrols forward to feel their way towards the Laung Chaung. They met Japs everywhere, entrenched in cleverly dug foxholes on the paths leading up to the higher features. We then discovered that there were three Jap bunkers (known as the three pimples) that were well established overlooking the Laung Chaung and commanding all the approaches to that river.

The enemy was now apparently angry that we had half penetrated their positions. At night they attacked us in turn from all corners of the compass. By day they occupied their defensive positions in strength, only sending out snipers to molest us. Our own trained snipers tried to pick them off but they were very cunning.

Sunday 20th February:

First thing this morning two D8 tractors, with two troops of 'C' Squadron and a patrol of Scout Troop as protection, went up the north-east track to Tattenham Corner where the two tanks had been abandoned on the night of the 16th/17th February. They were able to drag the burnt-out tank of 'C' Squadron off the road and push it down the hillside and recover the other tank which had been blocking the road northwards.

One troop of 'C' Squadron supported the KOSBs in a small attack on features to the south of Artillery Hill during the afternoon. Another two troops of 'C' Squadron went north-east in the afternoon to try and contact the 1st Battalion of the Wiltshire Regiment, part of 4 Brigade of the 26th Division. They were thought to be near the site of the old 7 Division HQ. Unfortunately the first tank became bogged-down in exactly the same place as the other two tanks had done and completely blocked the track again.

Lt Evans was called upon again and was able to recover this tank by 5pm. The expedition had to be abandoned and the tanks returned to the Box.

During the day 'B' Squadron carried out tests on their derelict tank with a Japanese magnetic mine. It was found that, when exploded, the mine made a bulge on the side of the tank but did not penetrate. When placed on top of the tank above the wireless operator's seat, the mine blew a hole through the top of the tank, out of the bottom and some 10 inches into the ground. A report was at once made suggesting that wire frames be made to keep mines away from the top plates of the tank.

Capt Briggs of 401 Field Squadron, with Divisional Sappers, went out to work on the track round Tattenham Corner as it was by now badly cut-up and not easily passable for tanks.

About this time Brig Evans received a call from Capt Smith on his walkie-talkie at 89 Brigade Mobile Workshop 'box'. They had been attacked by some Japanese, many of whom had been mown-down by the astute work of some Gurkhas. Capt Smith continues in his own words:

> The force of the automatic fire, the surprise and the number of casualties were so great, the Japanese retreated at once, taking their wounded with them. In the morning twelve dead Japanese were left lying in that open space. There had been no other attack on any part of our position during that night.
>
> Out in the open, between the Sikh position and the jungle, lay one Japanese wounded. He had dragged himself that far but could go no further. I reported what had happened on the walkie-talkie and the Brigadier's opinion was the attack had been by starving men as their food would have run out long ago. They had been subsisting on what they could find for many days. They were very much weakened and their attack was thus not determined. He said he would send a tank so we could capture the prisoner safely without risking an ambush from the jungle nearby. Few prisoners had been taken at the Box because the Japanese literally preferred to die rather than suffer the martial shame of captivity. Another live prisoner, he said, might therefore prove useful in some way to our intelligence people.
>
> A tank arrived and took up position between our island and the jungle, on the far side of the wounded man. It turned its turret with its machine-guns towards the jungle side, for there was no knowing how many of the enemy might be hidden there. A group of us came into the open and walked towards the man. He moved on the ground and threw a grenade towards us which he had been holding ready in his hand. We flattened ourselves down to the earth but escaped death and injury because the pin had not been removed. The man lay back knowing there was no more he could do against us. We brought out a stretcher and stood looking down at him. He was dirty, unshaven, and with a wild look on his face. He was badly wounded in the legs, his uniform filthy. A British

private knelt down, lit a cigarette and put it to his lips. At first he didn't seem to know what to do. He had, a few moments ago, been in a state of exaltation, ready to die for his Emperor. Now he was treated with kindness but acceptance of it would lead him towards a future of disgrace and imprisonment. He was given first aid but his wounds were severe and there was little we could do for him. He was taken away on the tank to the Admin Box.

Once again a peaceful sunny morning lay all around us. There were no sounds after the tank had gone but the scene of savage death we saw on our return brought us back to the war and the strain of what might still happen at any moment. I bent down by one of the dead men and took out his pocket book. There was a photograph of his family, stiff and unsmiling. There was another of a back porch of a wooden house where a young girl was sitting on a bench with her hair piled up wearing, what might have been, a ceremonial dress. There was money and an army book in another pocket. I put all the things back. None of us took anything. We buried it all, including rifles and bayonets.

* * *

Several Vengeance dive-bombing attacks were carried out on hills and nullahs round the Box during the day and by 6pm that evening Capt Briggs reported the road round Tattenham Corner fit for any number of tanks. Orders were issued for part of 'B' Squadron to go out next morning and contact 4 Brigade of 26 Division in the area of the old 7 Division HQ.

During the night a detachment of 89 Brigade Sappers went out with a patrol of the Gurkhas to 'recce' the track over Laung Chaung for mines, a necessary precaution before 'B' Squadron's expedition the next morning. Also that night defensive fire was brought down on the hills and nullahs to the north of the Box.

21st February:

Just before sunrise, a Japanese force of about seventy marched through the 'eastern gate' of the Box. However Gurkhas were posted in that area and duly attacked them. The Japs then tried to overrun the forward Gurkha post. As dawn broke they fell back into the jungle. It is thought they may have been lost, thinking themselves at Laungyaung. At 7.30am 25th Dragoons RHQ received a message that 'a platoon of Japanese had got onto a feature between the 2 companies of Gurkhas.' One troop of 'C' Squadron went out to Tattenham Corner to support the Gurkhas in removing the enemy who were not dug-in. They carried out a bombardment and it seems the action was successful. The Gurkhas found at least twenty-one enemy dead when they combed the area afterwards. The bodies were completely lacerated by high-explosive. As one infantryman said of the tanks, 'They fired so hard, you could see the country change before your eyes.' The troop returned to harbour about 3pm.

At 7am the same day two HQ tanks of 'C' Squadron went out with two Bren-gun-carriers to inspect the Valentine bridge in the Laung Chaung area to see if it was still fit for tanks. Returning at 8.30am they confirmed the bridge was still in good condition.

At 9am eight tanks of 'B' Squadron, under Major Johnstone, moved out as ordered to make contact with 4 Brigade in the old 7 Division HQ area. By 10am they reported that contact had been made. During the afternoon they supported the 1st Wiltshires and the Frontier Force in a small advance south from Prein Chaung towards old 7 Division HQ. The infantry did not come up against much opposition and the tanks were not able to give much fire support as no reasonable targets were located. They returned to the Box about 5.30pm.

So far as 'A' Squadron were concerned, they posed yet another problem for the Japanese. Whether they attacked the Admin Box or 33 Brigade defensive positions, they were likely to be met with tanks, something they were never able to overcome, but 'A' Squadron's role was as much attacking as it was defensive.

On the 17th February they gave close support to 'A' Company of the 1st Queen's Royal Regiment in an attack on a map-referenced hill feature. The attack could not be pressed home that day but on the 18th when this was done the enemy were found to have vacated it (perhaps during the night).

On the 19th February it was reported that 500 Japanese were thought to be in the area of Point 129 and north from there, and some 200 in the area of a spur nearby. A force commanded by Capt Munro, consisting of two troops, moved to the area at 3.15pm and by 4pm were shelling the re-entrant and the spur. An infantry patrol later reported that many Japanese had been caught by this shelling.

On the 20th February the Squadron went out with Capt Munro and a patrol of the 1st Queen's Regiment to 'recce' a possible route for operation against the hill called Abel, on the north side of the Buthidaung road. After much hard work the route was reported possible. On the following day Capt Munro and Lt Mair checked their 'recce' for tank crossings and reported one good and one possible. At 11.30am on that day the Squadron was ordered into action against the feature Sikh Knob. They were in action from 2pm and the feature was taken and occupied by 1/11th Sikh Regiment, who had used their bayonets in the final attack.

Fighting patrols of 33 Brigade had sometime ago discovered the Japanese supply routes and were able to destroy the convoys, which kept on using the same routes. It was now clear the Japanese had decided on retreat and patrols were sent out to catch them as they crept south. 'A' Squadron formed night patrols to assist the infantry and one patrol under Capt Munro was successful in causing enemy casualties. This was not the most popular type of operation with tank crews! On the 18th February, for the first time, a carrier convoy from the Box reached 33 Brigade without being attacked on the way.

As the situation began to ease and spirits rose, one tank of 'B' Squadron optimistically broke into song each time they left the Box on a 'duffy'. Led by Freddie Holdaway, they sang lustily above the noise of the engine:

The bells are ring–ing –,
For me and my gal.
The birds are singing –
For me and my gal.
Everybody's–been–know–ing
To–a–wedding–they're–go–ing
And–for–weeks–they've–been–sewing,
Every–Susie–and–Sal.

They're con–gre–gat–ing –
For me and my gal.

and etc.

8

Last Days of Siege

At 11.15am on the 21st February the KOSBs asked for the same troop of 'C' Squadron to support another small attack in their movement south of Artillery Hill. Lt Charles and Major Alexander carried out a 'recce' with the CO of the KOSBs and at 2pm Lt Charles' troop supported the attack of the KOSBs. It was entirely successful and the KOSBs established themselves on the ridge. At least six enemy were found dead and the troop returned at about 5pm.

No casualties were sustained by 25th Dragoons during these operations, but RHQ calculated that we inflicted up to 40 casualties on the enemy, with a good many more suspected, during the day.

Col Persse, on the morning wireless transmission from across the Pass, said that things were going well in clearing the Pass and that he hoped to see us much sooner than he had expected. In fact on this day Point 1070 to the north of the Pass, which had previously been taken by the Japanese from the Garwhalis, was attacked by the 2nd Battalion of the 1st Sikh Regiment with a company each from the Garwhalis and 4/7th Rajputs under Major Sarbjit Singh Kalha. The attack was successful and the hill was again occupied by the 1/18th Garwhali, after ten days of battery by aircraft, artillery and tanks. A landslide caused by the bombardment unearthed another score of enemy, who continued fighting until no longer capable. This was the penultimate event in the opening of the Pass.

At 6.30pm the familiar Japanese 105 and 150mm guns opened fire on the Box from the direction of Buthidaung. 6th Medium Regt RA, whose position in the Box was close to 'C' Squadron, opened up very quickly in reply. The Jap 75mm also fired at the same time. There were no casualties.

The ever-present possibility for everyone in the Box of being shot by an enemy sniper in the hills is illustrated by a corporal of the 2nd West Yorkshires.

The corporal detected a slight movement in a tree on the opposite ridge. He knew what it was. He went straight to the nearest Dragoon tank and said to the commander, 'Sir, can you see what that is up in the tree there?'

'What is it then, Corporal?'

'I'm sure it's a sniper, Sir.'

The commander took a quick look through the binoculars and gave orders to his gunner. The machine-gun laced the tree. Something flopped out and hung like a rag doll. 'Like to have a look at him, Corporal?' handing him the glasses.

It now seems amazing that, after the number of shells of all sizes, bombs, mortar bombs and small arms fire discharged into the Box over a period of three weeks, not to mention the explosion of our own ammo on Ammunition Hill, so many of us survived with barely a scratch.

22nd February:

During the night 9 Brigade 'B' Echelon on the southern-most point of the Box was harassed and there was confused fighting. This incident is described in some detail by RQMS Murgatroyd RA in his account of the siege:

> On the night of the 21st/22nd, a strong force of Japs attacked our position. At about 0115 hours his grenades were heard exploding and shots fired about 20 yards away. Capt (QM) Wallace was killed. The trench next to him suffered two casualties from bayonets. Capt Wallace had apparently exhausted his stock of grenades and left his trench to get more. On the way down he was wounded by a Jap grenade and four shots were fired into him as he rolled down the hill. Gunner Williams, his batman, shot the Jap responsible and L/Cpl Messenger got another seconds later. We were fired on all night but gave answering fire from the front of the hill.
>
> At about 0510 hours we heard voices and footsteps coming along the front of our position. A party of Japs came along with no attempt at concealment at a distance of 25 yards in front of us. Eighteen were counted before the leading man reached a distance of 4 yards from the Bren-gun on the right flank which opened fire. Every man on the hill opened fire with small arms and grenades. Five enemy bodies were recovered and tracks of blood led us to the remainder.

At 0610 hours a patrol was organized and seven Japs were discovered asleep in three trenches. They were prodded with bayonets but refused to come out so we shot them. All the bodies were centralized and searched. All equipment including LMGs, rifles, ammunition and important documents were collected and sent to Div HQ. The Japs were apparently half-starved and some of their wounds were days old and had received no attention. During the night they had rifled vehicles and kits, emptied their ammunition pouches and filled them with our cigarettes, matches and clothing. They were all wearing WD clothing under their own. The total bag killed was 34 and two prisoners, one of them a lieutenant.

Breakfasters were somewhat disturbed by shelling from the 105mm at 7am over the 'day' positions of 'C' Squadron. No casualties were suffered as the Squadron had not yet moved out from its night positions.

Troops of 5th Division were now reported to be well over the top of the Pass and it was decided to send two troops of 'C' Squadron up the Pass in the hope that they might make contact. They left at 10am with two companies of the KOSBs. Soon they were held up by the same obstacle as 'B' Squadron had reported previously. This was repaired by the Sappers but could not be crossed until 4pm.

The Regimental Diary continues:

They were again held up a very short distance further on by another road block. The tanks were in very close country and they were not able to operate with any success against Jap machine-gun positions in steep hills on either side of the road.

Considerable casualties were suffered by the infantry and the commanding officer of the KOSBs, Lt Col McLaren, was killed. They remained in position in the area of the first road block for the night and the tanks returned to the Box about 5.30pm.

Meanwhile further up the Pass 5th Div were having more success. In an elaborate flanking movement the 2/1st Punjabis stormed Sugar Loaf hill from the north, a position held by the Japanese on the col. The manoeuvre had a demoralizing effect and the enemy fled.

Reserve Squadron, moving up the west side of the Pass with 5th Division troops, was under the command at this point of Major James Allason. He was an officer of 3rd Carabiniers, an old and famous cavalry regiment, equipped with tanks, who went to the Central Burma Front. 25th Dragoons had been formed in part by officers and men of 'the Carbs'. GHQ had sent Major Allason to this area on a fact-finding tour. Instead he found himself taking part in the action.

'A' Squadron reported from 33 Brigade that Brigade HQ had been shelled from 3.30pm to 6pm by a 150mm gun but 'A' Squadron had not suffered any casualties.

In the Box the 105mm opened up again at 6pm and dropped shells all round the tank harbour but there were no casualties nor were the tanks damaged. There is no doubt that the Japanese hated the tanks as they did the artillery. They were major obstacles which they could not cope with and seemed to thwart all their attacks and intentions.

Brig Evans says:

> They (the tanks) had twice put the West Yorkshire Regiment in a position to re-capture vital points which had fallen to the enemy and it was largely their presence which prevented the Japs from rushing the dropping zone during the parachuting of air supplies. At almost exactly the same time each day, from the direction of Buthidaung tunnel, the enemy opened up with a 150mm gun in the hope of destroying the tanks. At no time did they succeed.

They therefore decided to try and get their infantry close enough to throw grenades and place explosives to get the tanks on fire.

At dusk one evening a large party, bayonets fixed, descended from the hills near Point 315 with a view to rushing 'C' Squadron tanks. They first of all met the 3/4th Bombay Grenadiers who were in slit trenches in front of the tanks, precisely to meet such a move. Standing in his slit trench, it is said, an Indian officer saw one of the enemy coming straight towards him and shot him dead at short range, but the Jap was carried by his own impetus right into the trench, knocking the officer down and pinning him on the ground at the bottom. His shouts for assistance attracted the attention of another of the enemy who, jumping into the trench, landed on top of the dead Japanese. He put his arms round the dead body and reaching down to the Indian officer began to strangle him with his bare hands. Hearing the shouting a sepoy in a nearby trench threw a grenade which landed on top of the second Jap, exploded and killed him. The officer was unhurt.

The remainder of the Bombay Grenadiers acted with similar bravery and, with some firing from the tanks over their heads, the attack was defeated. Not a single Japanese soldier reached the tanks.

This was little less than a suicide attack, a Kamikaze before its time. Col Frink puts the number of Japanese killed by 25th Dragoons up to this point at 'a conservative estimate of three hundred'.

Meanwhile the Wiltshires were fighting their way further south towards the Box. Col Houghton Brown wrote:

On 22nd February, in order to find the extent of the enemy's 'bunkers', we probed their positions with two companies – 'A' Company from the north and 'B' Company from the east. It was strongly held and every time we got near the top of the ridge we sustained casualties. However we could now pinpoint the actual main bunker positions, so I 'stood back' the Companies and let the medium artillery have a crack at them. The next day we tried again. This time, as a diversion, I took the carrier platoon (less their carriers which, of course, had been left behind) to 'demonstrate' on one flank and attacked with a company from the other. In order to show the platoon commander exactly where I wanted him to place his LMGs I went out personally with him and my escort. We crept along the edge of the padi and then ascended a small animal track that led up towards the bunkers. We had hardly gone thirty yards when some Japs, well camouflaged in some deep foxholes, suddenly popped up their yellow heads a few yards in front and opened fire on us at point blank range. The two leaders of my escort fell back, severely wounded. I had a slight wound through the corner of my wrist. We fired our weapons into the Japs and then side-stepped into the jungle. The enemy was indeed holding out in strength. My wound was only slight and after the MO had bound it up and put my arm in a sling it gave me no trouble. In a week it was all right again.

The next day 'C' and 'D' Companies had another 'go'. By dark they had driven in the outside rim and had, in fact, penetrated the crust. They laid up that night under the Japs' noses but could not pierce the main bunker defences. Once more we had to stand away to let the gunners 'soften it up'. The medium artillery then gave the bunkers a final rending. We followed this by concentration from our Mountain Battery, 25 Pdrs and 3″ mortars. This kept the heads of the enemy down whilst we attacked again – this time with success. By 11am on 25th February 'B' Company had occupied all three bunker positions. I reported back on the 'air' to Brigade and that afternoon moved our advance BHQ up into the bunkers. I was flabbergasted at what I saw. The ridge was precipitous to the west and unclimbable. The other three sides could only be approached through the jungle by small animal tracks. On each of these paths were cleverly sited foxholes, dug deep and strong. These were connected back to the main bunkers which were like small caves, dug in from the reverse slopes of the hill, being at least eight feet underground. Telephone lines connected up this intricate system of defence. No wonder our men had failed to capture these commanding hills until they had been 'cracked' by the hundred pound shells. When I got to the scene all the 'bunkers' had been torn open by our medium artillery. Trees had crashed through them and the bamboo and foliage were smouldering. It looked as if some giant had been up there destroying all he saw. Sticking out of the half-covered foxholes and bunkers were parts of dead Jap bodies, partially buried by the effects of the artillery. Flies buzzed over the devastated scene. Odd mess tins with half-cooked rice lay in the trenches. Jap equipment and weapons littered the hilltop. He had indeed suffered punishment and had paid heavily for trying to hold up the 'Moonrakers'.

Advance BHQ stayed that night in the central bunker surrounded by 'D' Company. Having captured our objective and, having had no sleep for about a week, we lay down exhausted. Even the stinking Jap dead, smelling like the old ferrets house at home, could not keep us awake. However, we were up as usual just before first light for 'stand to'. We had a beautiful view on both sides of us. The misty jungle to our west on the Mayu Range looked magnificent. To the east the sun rose over the yellow padi stubble, dotted periodically with little jungle-clad hillocks like islands in a sea. The distant view looked peaceful enough but I knew that even then two of our companies were struggling towards their objectives.

23rd February:

After a quiet night one troop of 'C' Squadron was sent up the Pass to join the KOSBs again. Two bridges were repaired and a road block cleared. Movement up the Pass road continued and no opposition was met. The KOSBs eventually made contact with 2/1st Punjab and 4/7th Rajput of the 5th Indian Division. The Pass was, at last, open. Yet it remained for the infantry to secure the surrounding features and comb through and clear the jungle on both sides if the road before the Pass could be used. The main anxiety was to get the 500 wounded in the MDS away and over the Pass.

One troop of 'B' Squadron and a patrol of Scout Troop gave protection to a column of carriers and one bridging-tank to the old Div HQ. The carriers went to collect 300 rounds of ammunition for the 6th Medium Regt RA. The bridging-tank went to collect its bridge. They encountered some mortar fire but were able to complete their tasks and return by noon.

Two tanks of 'C' Squadron took Brigadier Crowther of 89 Brigade over to 1/11th Sikh Regt at Awlanbyin during the afternoon. Also there was a very large air drop of ammunition and supplies.

The troop of 'C' Squadron returned from the Pass at 5pm without casualties.

One troop of 'A' Squadron commanded by Capt Munro escorted Lt Evans with one Valentine bridging-tank back to the Box from 33 Brigade. This was done to enable it to be used on the Pass but as things turned out it was not necessary.

No enemy shelling all day, followed by another quiet night, suggested that the enemy had left the area and the battle was over – but not quite.

24th February:

One troop of 'C' Squadron left the Box at 7am to continue operations on the Pass. By 8.40am they had reported that the road was clear so far as the second bridge. By 11am the whole Pass was open. Major General Briggs, commander of the 25th Indian Division, had spent the night with 123 Brigade HQ, who had been mainly responsible for clearing the Pass from the west. He now appeared in one of our tanks, entering the Box from the Pass road, to be met by Messervy and Evans and other senior officers. I was not present at this memorable moment but it is reported that he leant down into the turret and produced a bottle of whisky which he handed ceremoniously to Messervy. All seemed to be over but that turned out not to be true so far as we were concerned. Nevertheless, convoys were now able to proceed both ways over the Pass throughout the rest of the day and the majority of the wounded (416 in all) were evacuated by nightfall. I wrote home afterwards:

That was the happiest day of all for everybody: it was what we had all been waiting for. I went down to see some of our fellows off. It was extraordinary to watch how talking and laughter took the place of what had been just silence or groans before, so bucked were they at the prospect of getting out of that place.

Whilst watching the convoys move out, I suddenly realized that I was standing next to General Frank Messervy who was doing the same thing. Being very junior and very young, I did not open the conversation but he did not hesitate to say to me how very thankful he was to see them all going off.

In the meantime 7 Division had ordered 25th Dragoons to make contact with 4 Brigade in the area of Prein Chaung (north-east of the Box). Col Frink describes this expedition as follows:

In the morning the division commander (Gen Messervy) sent for me and said he wanted me personally to go out and contact 4 Brigade Commander (Brigadier Lowther), in the area of his (Messervy's) old HQ, which was still in Jap hands. This meant running the gauntlet in front of an anti-tank gun hidden away in the foothills.

I moved off in my tank with the adjutant in his at 1300 hours with a troop of 'B' Squadron as escort. On the way out we were hit twice by the gun, the second shot putting me on fire. The adjutant, in the tank following, rang me up and told me. This meant a rapid evacuation in an unpleasantly exposed spot. We managed to tow the tank to a safer place and extinguish the fire. I then changed tanks and proceeded to the rendezvous with 4 Brigade. We fetched up safely and we made our plans. Just as I was going to return to my tank, a Jap opened up on us with an automatic at short-range. He nicked my wrist with one shot and put another through my sock. Rotten shooting but I was certainly moving. I then went back to try and get my old tank going. Whilst repairing it, the gun opened up on us at about 600 yards with 75mm. He put down three quick shots, luckily all near misses. Fortunately we picked up his flak and dust. My tank and the adjutant's tank were quickly manned and on about the fourth or fifth shot there was an orange flash, a mass of smoke and sticks and he bothered us no more. The Japanese are beginning to dislike tanks.

We had to leave 'Defiant' – my tank – in the care of the Frontier Force as we couldn't get her going and pile into the other tanks. On the return journey our old friend, the 37mm, opened up again. This time he hit me three times – good shooting – the third shot just hit the top of the cupola and exploded. Roberts, who was with me in the turret, took a nasty crack on his tin hat which saved his life, though he got a nasty scalp wound. I got the balance in my right arm and back – purely superficial and can go on with my work. We were extremely lucky. Today I'm gunning for that gun and am hatching a plot to conceal two tanks to shoot him up when they see his flash. They ought to get him unless he is cunning enough not to open up.

Felt a bit weary and shattered after rather an eventful and full two hours and was relieved to know that the rum ration was up. Four of us were hit but none seriously.

This party took with it a Valentine bridging tank and a platoon of Gurkhas with carriers to collect stores from the old 7 Division HQ area.

The 37mm gun which caused the trouble was hidden in a bunker on the hillside of Point 315 overlooking Tattenham Corner. It was well known for firing on tanks proceeding along that track to the old Div HQ area. The Adjutant's tank was hit on the side, just penetrating the side plate, small flakes of metal hitting two of the crew. The fire on the Colonel's tank was extinguished in the Valentine bridge area, where it was eventually left.

From there the Colonel went forward in Lt Grant's tank of 'B' Squadron with the Adjutant and met the Brigadier at 2.30pm.

Thus the forces inside the Box had formally met and joined up with the relieving brigades of the 5th and 26th Indian Divisions on the same day. Whether Brig Lowther, commander of 4 Brigade, had a bottle of whisky ready for 'Frinkie' is not recorded.

On the return journey 2/13th Frontier Force asked for support to be given to two of their companies who were trapped in a nullah. Lt Grant gave them covering fire for twenty minutes and returned to the Box by 5.30pm, the platoon of Gurkhas with their carriers having returned at 3.30pm.

Col Frink, who had remained with his tank, ordered one troop of 'C' Squadron to go out and cover the return of the Valentine bridging-tank (less bridge) and also his own tank. While in this area another gun opened-up and was probably destroyed by the fire of the three tanks. The Colonel's tank would not start, so it had to be dismantled and left under the protection of 1 Company of the Frontier Force Regt. The Colonel and his crew returned in the 'C' Squadron tanks by 5pm. 'Roberts' was Lt Roberts of 'C' Squadron.

The Colonel's tank 'Defiant' was not the only tank to carry a name. Others were 'Unbeatable' showing a hand of cards with three aces and a joker, 'Nil Desperandum' ('B' Squadron), 'Surrey', 'Manchester' and 'Oxford' ('A' Squadron) and 'Bamber Bridge Hellcat' (Lt Auchinleck). So far as 'A' Squadron was concerned, all the tanks were named after the driver's home town and the naming had been done before leaving Ranchi by a professional sign-writer in that squadron, Alf Banbury.

During the afternoon Lt Charles' troop of 'C' Squadron had a shoot in the old 'Delhi' area in support of an operation by part of the KOSBs. In the Box, Major Youens and Col Persse came over the Pass with one troop of Reserve Squadron and the latter was attached to 'C' Squadron. Six Ammo and six POL trucks, under Corporal Fairweather of 'A' Squadron, arrived about 5.30pm. Maj Youens and Col Persse returned before dark to 5 Div.

There had been continuous shelling from the 105mm and yet more of the ammo on Ammunition Hill caught fire. Apart from this 'a reasonably quiet night followed', as the diary reads.

25th February:

One troop of 'C' Squadron was again sent up the Pass to assist in dealing with any enemy who might still be in the area. Twelve echelon vehicles went back over the Pass taking further wounded.

In view of the trouble caused by the anti-tank gun in the Tattenham Corner area, Lt Briggs made a 'recce' to find an alternative route to the north. This was urgent because tanks were required by 4 Brigade to help them in their drive south towards Point 125 and the old 7 Div HQ. If a new route could not be found, the tanks would have to pass in front of the gun again, with the risk of yet more being knocked out and further casualties. Lt Briggs found a fresh route but it involved an impassable bridge which would take eight hours to repair.

'B' Squadron was therefore ordered to go by the old route. Lt Charles made a 'recce' south of the Ngakyedauk chaung to find a position to cover this gun should it open again. The gun was well dug-in and defiladed in the hills, ie positioned so that it could not be hit by sweeping fire across the hill and this was why it had not been possible to silence it.

Twelve tanks of 'B' Squadron under Major Johnstone left at

1pm. One troop of 'C' Squadron with a forward observation officer and a patrol of Scout Troop took up a position from which it was thought they would be able to cover the anti-tank gun should it open fire.

As this was a journey and not a battle, the tank commanders did not close down the hatches on the turrets but kept their heads out. The gun apparently allowed a number of tanks to pass and then opened fire. It failed to hit a tank but blew off the head of one of the commanders, Sergeant Clive Branson, and his lifeless body fell down into the tank.

The troop of 'C' Squadron, directed by the FOO, were able to shoot at the gun as soon as it opened up. No definite hits were recorded but the gun did not shoot again when the squadron made its return journey the following day.

The Squadron continued on its way to 4 Brigade, where it harboured for the night in the area north of Prein Chaung.

Clive Branson was well known in the Squadron for his left-wing views. He had trained as an artist at the Slade School and his idealism had led him to become a Marxist. He had fought with the British Battalion of the International Brigade in the Spanish Civil War and had been taken prisoner and spent many months in Franco's prison camps. His letters to his wife from India with some of his drawings were subsequently published. He left a wife and a baby daughter whom he had never seen, born a few months after he left England.

The composer, Bernard Stevens (1916–1983), admired Branson as an artist and a man of action. He, though in the Army, had been able to compose a symphony during the war which he called a 'Symphony of Liberation' and which he dedicated to Branson. It was first performed at the Royal Albert Hall, London by the London Philharmonic Orchestra under Malcolm Sargent and has now been recorded.

Meanwhile in the Box the Regimental HQ troop leader went out with a piquet and the Colonel's crew to the Valentine Bridge area. They were able to recover the Colonel's tank. Also an attempt was made to set alight the jungle on Point 315, which was still in the hands of the Japanese, using mortar smoke bombs but this met with little success. However that night it was reported to RHQ that at least two companies of Japs had left 315.

The Wiltshires and 2/13th Frontier Force Rifles were two of the three regiments that comprised 4 Brigade. Col Houghton Brown continues his story and tells how they came across the old 7 Division HQ area:

I had sent 'B' Company round about a mile to the west of the bunkers to try to cut off any of the enemy who might try to escape that way. I got through on the air to 'Needle' (OC 'B' Company) and heard he had a hard time. They had had to cut their way through the jungle, there being no tracks. They had met an enemy strong-point the evening before and had sustained some casualties before they could clear them out.

After twenty-four hours hard plodding they had arrived on the Laung Chaung and were now digging in on the high ground. I told 'Needle' I would come down and meet him on the chaung itself and give him further orders. With my escort I then moved forward down the south path from the bunkers towards the Laung Chaung. When we rounded the path and saw the little river below us, we all halted in amazement. There was a clearing in the jungle both sides of the chaung and this had apparently been used as the administrative area by our 7th Division. When the Japs had overrun them three weeks before, our troops had evacuated the place in a great hurry. The scene that met our eyes was a deserted bedlam. Smouldered bamboo huts and tents lay scattered over the area. Files and papers littered the ground. Camp beds, stools, tables, typewriters, wireless sets, plates, mugs, bottles, gramophones, were all strewn about everywhere.

We moved down cautiously towards the chaung. As we penetrated towards the river we were again met by the stale smell of rotting flesh. Semi-decomposed bodies lay in all directions. In some cases one could just discern the different nationalities. The high cheek-bones and yellow legs of the Japs; the turbans lying near the corpses of the Indian sepoys; ribbons of green battledress hanging round the remnants of the British soldiers.

Never before in my life had I met 'departed spirits' face to face. They were here in earnest – they seemed to whisper to us as we passed through the bamboo. The place was haunted by sinister beings who appeared to watch us as we stalked through the tangled mess of bodies and equipment.

I was relieved to meet 'Needle' with his escort. He looked even thinner and more drawn than usual. He had obviously been through a tough time and he and his men all looked as if they had nearly had enough. I explained to him that the chase was almost over. We now only had to move a few miles further before we would be in touch with the 7th Div Box. 'B' Company was to cover our flank for this final advance.

We returned to HQ for a hurried breakfast of fried 'bully', biscuits, jam and a hot cup of 'char'. During my absence the IO had been searching some of the enemy dead for identifications. He found a lot of interesting information which we passed back to Brigade. Apart from military belongings, each man carried a little miniature 'Buddha' tucked inside his belt. In his wallet he had a photo of his family at home, in the middle of which was usually a fat baby (presumably the son and heir) around whose tummy was draped a small flag of the Rising Sun. Apparently the chief amusement of the Jap when resting in his bunker is to draw obscene pictures of sexual intercourse. His mind seemingly is spent at home with his wife or girl and his pencil follows his imagination in portraying the latest fantastic method of procreation. Each pocket book had half-drawn or completed pictures, obviously done by himself. Apart from being an expert seducer, the Jap is also no mean acrobat. It would require a superb gymnast to perform some of the antics which I saw portrayed in many of the sketches!

Well fortified with food we picked up our gear and moved south again. When we got down to the chaung, Joe Panks was already there busily building a bridge over the river with his pioneers. They had (quite rightly) boasted that they had always managed to build a bridge over each obstacle before the sappers came up. As we crossed over we suddenly saw a small party of Japs leading a single mule. They were obviously the remnants of the retreating enemy, trying to escape. Our troops who were 'covering' the bridge builders, opened up on them. Two dropped quivering into the tall grass. A third pulled out a grenade from his pocket and blew himself up under our very noses. He lay twitching near the river, his yellow mouth twisted in agony.

As we moved on there were more signs of the Jap retreat. We passed bamboo stretchers on which were strapped dead Jap corpses. Most of them looked as if they had only been there a few hours. This showed that the enemy had fled from the Mayu Range in a great hurry. His plan for the cutting off of the XV Corps had failed. He had obviously run out of supplies and what remained of his force was now in full retreat. Up to date, we had found the Jap very careful to always get away and bury his dead. He was now apparently too exhausted even to do this. His morale must have dropped severely.

'C' Company had gone forward as vanguard to contact 7 Div itself. Tom Dutton got through to me on the 'air'. He had taken his objective with little fighting and was at Pt 315 overlooking the 7 Div Box. He had contacted one of the Gurkha battalions and thus the relief of 7 Div was almost complete.

That night we dug in again on a pleasant green patch of grass just outside the Box. 'A' Company remained behind on an island covering the Laung Chaung. 'D' Company were employed mopping up enemy stragglers in a little village nearby. 'B' Company continued to cover our flank.

26th February:

Today for the first time it was considered unnecessary to send a troop of tanks up the Pass. Nevertheless during the morning there was further shelling from the Jap 105mm and Trooper William Graham of 'C' Squadron was seriously wounded. Indeed he died the following day. Most military historians have ended the Battle on the 24th February with 'Briggo' and his bottle of whisky, but for us and many others the shooting and killing continued on to the 27th. Only at the end of that day can it be said that the Japanese had finally drained out of the area.

(Airgraph) 26th February 1944

My dear Mother and Dad,

It is well over a fortnight since I have had a chance to write you a note. I have not any of your recent mail to hand but hope to have some in a day or two. The last weeks have been pretty hectic but we've inflicted a good deal of damage on the Japs and completely upset their plans. If you listen to the Arakan news every day, you will get some hints as to what is going on. When I have the time I hope to write about all this in more detail. Meanwhile what you really want to know is that I'm quite safe and well and feeling as fit as ever.

As every tank has a wireless set, we get the world news most days and don't lose our perspective. I hope you are keeping cheerful and well at home. Remember me to everyone as I haven't time to write to them all.

Thank goodness we're getting on with the job at last. I hope it won't take too long but there is a long way to go before we get leave in Tokyo!

Love

In fact, that same evening the Cook's lorries arrived from the Pass with 17 sacks of mail – a sure sign of the return of normality, in so far as such a thing exists in war.

27th February:

The pressure was now off and we could afford to relax a bit, get washed and cleaned up, and catch up on the news of our 'B'

Echelon troops who by all accounts seemed to have had a bad time, especially for people not expecting to do any fighting.

Some journalists were brought over the Pass and let loose on us, so that this 'historic victory' could be written up 'in all its glory'. I remember noticing that their main object was to find a neat string of facts or incidents which would make a 'story', rather than take down 'boring' details of what life in the Box was actually like. One Australian took a picture of the whole of our crew sitting on the tank and said it would be published in a book he was writing about his travels in India.

One section of 72nd Workshops was by now established at the western foot of the Pass and tanks were sent back from day to day to be overhauled and have their engines checked. They hung out a notice: 'Wee Drag 'em Inn'. One troop of 'C' Squadron with the Colonel's tank went back today in exchange for one more troop from Reserve Squadron. From now on it was the intention to keep fifty-five tanks on the east of the Mayu Range fit for action and to send back any tanks for repair over the Pass. The LAD, now under the command of Capt R.H. Ferguson REME came over complete to do minor repairs and fit searchlights. One troop of 401 Field Squadron IE also came over the Pass.

Even now the fighting was not quite finished. The Japanese were as stubborn as ever in their retreat. During the afternoon a troop of 'C' Squadron had to go out and give fire support to the Gurkhas in clearing up a pocket of resistance in the old 'Delhi' harbour area.

Bill Nicholson was also still in the fighting area:

> Although the Pass had now been cleared, the Japs were still occupying several neighbouring features with code names like 'Hop', 'Skip', 'Step', etc (on the west side of the Mayu Range). Our infantry sent three or four platoons into one feature after it had been dive-bombed by our Vengeance planes and attacked by our 75mm guns plus the heavy artillery, without dislodging the enemy. When this feature was eventually cleared, we found that the Japs had dug narrow trenches and bunkers round the side of the hill, in which they had lived for days without contact with their main unit. Somehow they all disappeared one night without being detected and it seemed incredible that men had existed in such cramped conditions without supplies of fresh food and water. The booby traps they had made were very simple, such as tin cans on string or wire . . .

We took some prisoners during these mopping-up operations and they looked pathetic little figures but when they were in their hordes they were a different proposition. One prisoner had in his possession a photograph showing a British Army officer being beheaded with a Japanese sword by a Japanese officer and watched by a ring of Japs. This was a form of propaganda we did not appreciate!

During the operation when the Pass was being re-opened, one of our fellows, Trooper David Vagg, volunteered for a particularly dangerous job when he climbed in and drove some Bren-gun carriers and trucks which were blocking the Pass and were exposed to enemy fire. He was awarded a Certificate of Gallantry by General Giffard.

Back in 1943, when the Regiment left for Calcutta for 'the Front', Vagg was left behind. I think he was sick but this did not prevent him rejoining the Regiment in Burma within a few days. When he reported to me for duty, he said that he went to Dum Dum airfield in Calcutta with a forged permit and was on the next plane to Chittagong!

28th February:
The Colonel and the Adjutant returned over the Pass to visit the Repair Section and to clear up outstanding correspondence etc at Rear HQ at Bawli Bazaar. A 'recce' party was sent to the 'Delhi' area to prepare for the movement of the Regiment back there, thus leaving the Admin Box to revert to its original function of 'Corps Administrative Area'. In short, things were returning to 'normal'. It had been a defensive victory. We were now free to proceed with Messervy's original plan to attack Buthidaung, the Road and the Tunnels. The Japanese had reverted to their original lines.

However, things were not quite the same. Gen Slim later said, 'The Battle of Arakan was the first occasion in this war in which a British force had withstood the full weight of a major Japanese offensive, held it, broken it, smashed it into little pieces and pursued it. Anybody who was in the 5th and 7th Divisions and was there has something of which he can be very proud indeed . . . Judged by the size of the forces engaged, it was not of great magnitude but it was, nevertheless, one of the historic successes of British arms. It was the turning point in the Burma Campaign.'

Such was the loss of face for the Japanese generals in charge of the campaign, Hanaya, Tanahashi, Sakurai, Tohutaro and others, that they all made immediate application to the Emperor for permission to commit hari-kiri (maybe the Japanese army kept a stack of application forms on hand from then onwards). The Emperor refused on the grounds that grave command problems would result in the Burma theatre of war. He did however grant his divine permission for these acts when Japan had victoriously concluded the war. The fact that Japan lost the war placed them in a somewhat embarrassing position!

In the meantime those seventeen sacks of mail had been sorted and I had received my share. I was able to write a letter acknowledging it all:

(Airmail) 28th February 1944

After a period of three weeks without any mail I have just received 12 letters and about half-a-dozen papers and magazines . . . I have also had AMLs from Aunts L. and G. and 'Laugh with the Forces' from Aunt G. The latter is refreshingly above the normal standard of humour usually dished out to 'the Forces' and the crew are enjoying it . . .

I am writing this in the Ngakyedauk area on the east side of the Pass. I understand the whole story was broadcast on the news last night, so you might as well know that *we* are the 25th 'Indian' Dragoons.

Well, cheerio. I hope you are keeping as fit and well as I do.

In the meantime the Wiltshires were able to march into the Box and Col Houghton Brown described it as follows:

On the morning of the 29th February, the Battalion moved forward into the Box itself and took over from the West Yorks. We marched down the dusty track, hot, tired but happy. We really felt we had done a good job of work.

The Box was a vast natural arena surrounded by hills about 300 feet high. These had previously been covered in bamboo but now were scarred and burnt. The Japs apparently had held these heights for many days and had fired directly into the flat of the arena at the 7th Division. However, they had retaliated to some tune. They had fired back with artillery and tank guns, firing over open sights, and had literally blasted the enemy off the hills. When we arrived the Japs had gone, leaving the Division in complete command of the situation.

The level part of the natural basin was covered in six inches of grey dust. In this were dug the trenches, dug-outs, and command posts, in which our troops had put up such a magnificent stand. One could see in a moment what a murderous time they must have had. It was in fact remarkable that they could have held out for three weeks under such conditions.

As we marched down the track we passed the mouth of the famous Ngakyedauk Pass. This was now open again. Dust-covered lorries and ambulances were passing through it freely.

We saw the Main Dressing Station which the Japs had broken into. The enemy had proved to us what good soldiers they could be and it seemed strange that they could also be such inhuman, cruel devils.

I now pushed 'B' Company right forward to dig-in on the heights overlooking the next river, the Tatmin Chaung. 'C' and 'A' Companies took over the hills surrounding and guarding the mouth of the Ngakyedauk Pass. The remainder of the Battalion dug-in at Waters Meet about a mile south of the Box. Here we made ourselves quite comfortable, using old Jap foxholes for my battalion HQ.

29th February:

The entry in the Regimental War Diary for today is marked 'Delhi' and speaks for itself:

> Group HQ moved to old 'Delhi' area at 1000 hours. The CO and the Adjutant in their tanks visited 33 Brigade during the afternoon to discuss future operations. A quiet night followed.

Sergeant Fred Oxtoby of the orderly room, a Manchester journalist in civil life, prepared a news-sheet dated 'Leap Year Day 1944'. With journalistic enthusiasm he headed it:

FOURTEENTH ARMY SCORES
FIRST MAJOR SUCCESS AGAINST THE JAPS

Victory with important effect on entire
Burma War

In the course of the sheet he addressed the infantry regiments with whom we had been fighting and said, 'How very greatly everyone in the 25th admires your grit and your gradely spirits, your coolness under fire and your daring and pluck. A million thanks to you lads of the infantry, Indian as well as British. Every mile you win means a hundred miles nearer home for us all.'

The cook-house, feeling we needed some fresh food after the monotonous round of tins during the last three weeks, produced some live chickens. A group of odd-bods were detailed to catch and kill them. Regrettably they were not all experts at wringing chickens' necks and so a considerable number of headless chickens were running frantically about the harbour.

At top level, congratulatory messages were beginning to flow:

I congratulate the 14th Army heartily upon the successful outcome of the series of fierce encounters with the Japanese in the Arakan. It must be a great satisfaction to all ranks and races engaged in the common effort that the Japanese have been challenged and beaten in jungle warfare in Burma and that their boastfulness should have received a salutary exposure.

Winston Churchill, Prime Minister

You have gained a splendid victory. Your splendid spirit was clear to me when I visited you recently.

Now that spirit, that temerity, that courage, have been demonstrated to the enemy and to the world.

I salute you!

Mountbatten, Supreme Commander SEAC

Col Frink described the battle as 'the strangest and also one of the bitterest battles of modern times'. He himself had commanded a squadron of tanks in France in a rearguard action before Dunkirk in 1940 and was therefore one of the last to leave Dunkirk. He wrote:

In my opinion it was immeasurably worse than Dunkirk, owing to the ability of the enemy to get close under cover of jungle and chaungs. We have had to sit around for days and nights, an easy target from every angle. The worst aspect has been the wounded who have had to lie in an MDS in a chaung. The flies and smell are appalling. I've managed to get most of mine out into an underground hospital we have built in the perimeter.

The Padre, Cox, has been magnificent and has consistently brought in the dead and wounded quite irrespective of shelling and bombing. It has been a situation in which seasoned troops would have found it difficult to compete. The youngsters of the Regiment, for whom it has been the first major action, have behaved magnificently and are cheerier than I have ever known. They are a very fine example to all others. I regret that many other troops have not been so staunch. I have a long list of awards and mentions to go in and I only hope they will be recognized. There have been so many cases of unselfish gallantry that it is impossible to record them. It has made past operations of my experience like peacetime manoeuvres, France '39–'40 included.

Col Frink received a special message from Gen Slim congratulating all ranks of the besieged force on the way in which they had held out and placed the Army in a position to put in an offensive on a thoroughly disorganized and weakening enemy.

Figures vary as to the number of Japanese taking part in this offensive. The overall figure was probably about 12,000, of which some 7,000 formed the main striking force under Tanahashi. Reinforcements are thought to have been brought up during the battle. The original force had been given rations and ammunition for seven days.

A pertinent question to be asked with hindsight is how this large force managed to infiltrate north through the dispositions of 114 Brigade without challenge in the course of one night. The story is told of how a runner, moving from one unit of 114 Brigade to another during that night, came across a mule train. He stopped for a moment and a soldier, whom he took to be a Gurkha, said, 'You go, Johnny.' So he crossed and continued his journey. Later it was established that no Gurkhas were in that area that night. He had in fact passed through the Japanese forces moving north.

The victory was possible because of our superiority in air power and the failure of the Japanese airforce to seriously impede the dropping of supplies. It was also possible because of the presence of 25th Dragoons tanks on the eastern side of the Mayu Range at the crucial moment. The historian of the 5th Indian Division very generously says:

> The debt owed to these tanks and their crews cannot be overemphasized. It was their accurate high-velocity, close range blasting which put our infantry back whenever the Japanese penetrated our defences or captured any vital position.

This compliment can be repaid by simply saying that ultimate victory must belong to the infantry. It was the infantry who finally went in, exposed and single-handed, took the positions and held them. In particular the 2nd Battalion of the West Yorkshire Regiment of the 5th Indian Division were responsible for most of the vital attacks in the defence of the Box. They lost 144 men killed or seriously wounded in eighteen days. Gen Christison said:

It is rare in history that one regiment can be said to have turned the scales of a whole campaign. The West Yorkshires were in the Box for 25 days. Every single hill overlooking it was captured by the Japanese and every single time the West Yorks, supported by tanks, drove them off.

When the Wiltshires arrived and took over, the survivors of the 2nd West Yorks marched back over the famous Pass to rejoin 5th Division. Their regimental history says:

> The night was dark and moonless and over the sombre defile hung the sickly-sweet smell of death, for British, Indian and Japanese lay dead, undiscovered and unburied, in the dense jungle on either side of the road.

Some 5,000 Japanese dead were counted in the jungle round the Box and many others may have been retrieved by their comrades. XV Corps are said to have suffered 3,000 losses.

* * *

Lt Gen Hanaya, commanding the Japanese 55th Division, afterwards explained his defeat:

> At Sinzweya however we were confronted with the obstinate resistance of infantry and artillery formations of the enemy as well as its tank brigade. As there was no collaboration in our airforces, our operations could not progress as pre-arranged.

For the first time since Pearl Harbour, a Japanese land offensive had failed. From this moment until their surrender in August 1945, the Japanese were never to win another major victory.

* * *

Three years later Compton MacKenzie, the writer, visited the site of the battle:

> Nothing now remains to recall that desperate struggle in the Admin Box, except for a few tanks and the slit trenches gradually filling up. Cattle are grazing tranquilly. We sat beneath a tree and surveyed a scene of Arcadian peace . . .

9

The Fall of Buthidaung

This they told me was war;
This waiting, crouching, silent fumbling on
Through crazy undergrowth;
These dead and wounded men and mules;
This melody of the mysterious bullet
Sung straight through the discord of green;
The sepoy crying for loss of limb and sight:
This wounded Jap prisoner, gabbling fanatic:
This long, long darkness, smoking not allowed.

From *The Arakan*
by Graham Cherry
(Staff Officer, 7 Indian Div)

(Airmail)

'B' Squadron 25th Dragoons
RAC Indian Command
1st March

My dear Mother and Dad,

I hope you have got my telegraph by now. I thought I had better send one as I was unable to write during the last 3 weeks. We have been too busy dealing with the Japs. However, now we have a week or so's rest and maintenance and I shall try and answer some of the many letters I have received all at once . . .

. . . I'm looking forward to my next leave in Calcutta – or Akyab!

Akyab was the next port south down the Arakan coast. Apart from being a port it also had airfields and was of considerable military value. It was not captured for another ten months.

The Battle of the Admin Box had been a defensive victory, but it meant that when the Japs launched their great attack at Imphal on the 9th March, the XIVth Army was ready to meet it without having to worry about its Arakan front. Ultimate victory in Arakan depended on the vigour with which the battle was followed up, crushing the Jap military strength and morale in this area before the monsoon. This was not an easy task, for the Japanese persisted tenaciously in all their positions, sometimes re-occupying them after they had been taken. They were, of course, aided greatly in this by the thickness of the jungle. It is easier to hide in the jungle than to search out the hidden.

A number of awards for distinguished service and gallantry were made but were not published in the *London Gazette* until 18th May. Col Frink received the DSO as did Col Cree of the 2nd Battalion West Yorkshire Regiment, Col Patrick Hobson of the Signals and Col R.B. Cole of the Artillery. Brig Evans received another bar to his DSO. Now that his job as Box Commander was over he was appointed to 123 Brigade of 5 Division and Brig Salomans resumed command of 9 Brigade. Later Evans was promoted to command 5 Division and later still, 7 Division, as these two divisions proceeded through to Rangoon.

The West Yorkshires and the 3/14th Punjab, together with 9 Brigade HQ, crossed over the Pass to join the rest of 5 Division on the west side of the Mayu Range. We were now left with 7 Division and the newly-arrived 26 Indian Division on the east side.

At this time Messervy asked Major Ley if he would like to become his senior staff officer (GSO1). Ley had already observed that the general was giving his present GSO1 a bad time and had said to Frinkie, 'Much as I like old Frank from pre-war days and playing polo together at Sialkot, I wouldn't be his GI for all the tea in China.' So Ley had to think quickly. Sensing that Col Frink would almost certainly be promoted when the campaign ended, he said, 'Thank you very much, but if there is any chance of getting command of 25th Dragoons, I would prefer that.' Messervy replied, typically, 'Of course, I agree with you. I'll send a signal to Delhi to find out.' So the matter rested for the time being.

Some adjustments were made to the XV Corps Armoured Group as from 27th February. Lt Col Frink, as commanding officer of the 25th Dragoons, now had under his command:

25th Dragoons (52 tanks plus 3 FOO tanks)
25th Dragoons LAD (Light Aid Detachment) Workshop
1 Troop 401 Field Squadron, IE
'A' Company, 3/4th Bombay Grenadiers (motorized)
6 tanks, Bridging Troop.

Thus the LAD was now included whilst the West African Recce Regiment and the mechanized wing of the Gwalior Lancers went elsewhere. Also another armoured squadron arrived in the forward area, 'C' Squadron of the 149th Regiment of the RAC. About fifty men of the 25th Dragoons were sent home on repatriation as 'time-expired' men.

'A' Squadron of the 25th Dragoons returned from their attachment to 33 Brigade, so virtually the whole regiment was now together at 'Delhi', grandly re-named 'Tank Valley'.

It was while we were there that I was rudely awoken in the night of 2nd/3rd March just before dawn. I was sleeping under my mosquito net as per orders, the top end of which was attached to the top portion of the track of the tank. I was lying at right angles to the tank so the net sloped down to my feet. Vaguely I heard the familiar sound of distant firing but was too tired and sleepy for it to register. Suddenly a voice bellowed, 'GROUNDS, GROUNDS, get UP.' It was Squadron Leader 'Bumper' Johnstone who had all but tripped over my legs. Everyone was rushing about in a great flap. It emerged that some 100 to 200 Japanese were digging themselves in north-east of the Valentine Bridge beyond Tattenham Corner. Two troops of 'C' Squadron were sent to support the 1/18th Gurkha Rifles in an attack. The Japs retreated through the hills. It was thought they were remnants of Kubo's battalion which early on had climbed over the Mayu Ridge and descended so unexpectedly on Chamba and Briasco Bridge. They had been cut off from supplies and were now desperately trying to re-join their comrades to the south in the Buthidaung area.

Nevertheless, this was basically a time for rest, recuperation and maintenance and renewal of the vehicles. In his Order of the 29th February, the corps commander, Gen Christison, began by saying: 'No victory is complete without pursuit . . .' and, indeed, as soon as the Box was relieved, Messervy had returned to his plans for attack on the Buthidaung area which had been so rudely forestalled by the Japanese attack of 4th February.

The main objectives of the corps were now:

a) to drive away the enemy from Razabil fortress on the west of the Mayu Range, which we had signally failed to do before the Battle of the Box. This would be the job of 5 Division.

b) to capture the two tunnels through the Range and the whole of that area, which would be carried out by 26 Division from the east and part of 5 Division from the west.
c) to capture Ledwedet and Buthidaung in the east, to be implemented by 7 Division.

As we were already in the east side of the Range, it was not surprising that we were to continue operating with 7 Division. Some officers of the 1/11th Sikh came to us to discuss joint operations and the following day were given a demonstration of tank-fire support for infantry. Planning conferences took place and preliminary 'recces' were carrried out. The workshops worked overtime to get the tanks in top condition. On 5th March operational orders were received from 7 Division. Advance Base Workshops came over the Pass during the afternoon and established themselves in the Admin Box. Nine tanks and crews of Reserve Squadron were to remain there also, in readiness for use as required.

Sapper 'recces' were made during the nights of 4th, 5th and 6th March for tank crossings being constructed over the Letwedet Chaung and its tributaries. On 6th March a conference was held at 25th Dragoons' HQ involving the CO of the 1/11th Sikh, 'A' squadron leader with the CO of 4/15th Punjab, and 'C' squadron leader with the CO of 1st Queen's Royal Regiment. An operational order for 25th Dragoons was issued that afternoon. The operation, 'Staghound', was to be carried out by 33 Brigade which was before Buthidaung on the west bank of the Kalapanzin. The two tactical HQs were set up, one for 33 Brigade itself and the other consisting of Col Frink, the Adjutant and Major Dunlop (OC 'A' Company 3/4th Bombay Grenadiers).

'A' and 'C' Squadrons moved out with 25th Dragoons tactical HQ to join 33 Brigade that evening. 'B' Squadron was not involved. At 0300 hours on the morning of 7th March the Tactical HQs went on foot to the hill feature 'Abel', on the north side of the Maungdaw–Buthidaung road and some way to the west of Buthidaung itself. This hill had been held by the 4/1st Gurkhas for some weeks, despite repeated attacks by the enemy. Its importance was that it commanded the main road into Buthidaung, as well as being overlooked by five features on the south side of the road:

Cain (opposite Abel), Rabbit, Poland, Point 142 and West Fingers – all occupied by the enemy.

SKETCH MAP OF THE ROAD FROM THE TUNNELS TO BUTHIDAUNG

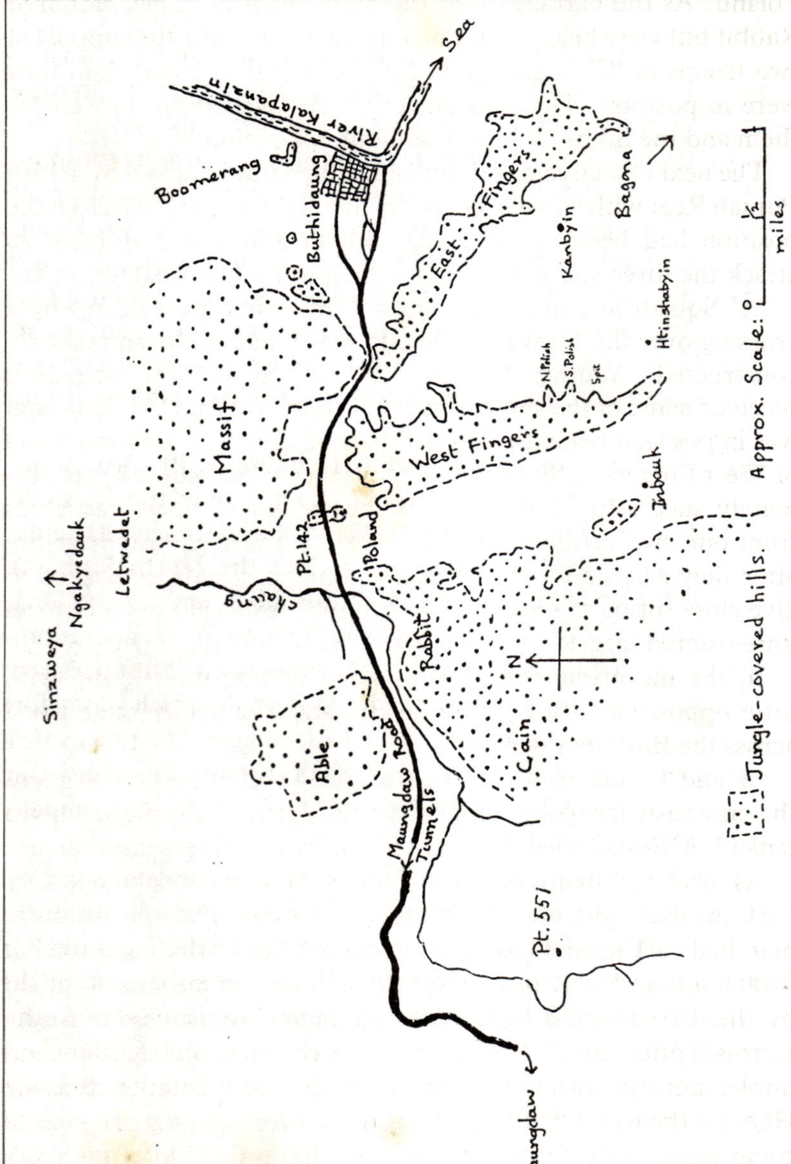

The previous evening the 1/11th Sikh Regt had moved out in bright moonlight east of Abel. At 10.15pm the Kalapanzin Valley was shaken by the roar of 100 guns as our artillery put down a tremendous barrage on the first two objectives, Rabbit and Poland. As the barrage lifted the Sikhs went in. They captured Rabbit but were held up on Poland. They asked for the support of two troops of 'C' Squadron at first light (6am). By 6.45am they were in position. The Japs however had decided not to wait for them and the Sikhs took over without opposition.

The next objective was Point 142, which was attacked by 4/15th Punjab Regt with equal success. By first light on the 7th March the position had been consolidated and the Punjabis re-formed to attack the three spurs to the east which were their final objective.

'A' Squadron had moved out at 4am but were held up by a crossing over the Letwedet Chaung which had not been properly constructed. Another barrage was put up and the Squadron received some of the shells which fell short. By 7am 'A' Squadron was in position ready to support the Punjabis attacking the spurs of West Fingers. This continued for most of the day and was ultimately successful. However, the Punjabis had thirty casualties from our own artillery gun-fire and nine more from mortar-fire after they arrived on the positions. The guns had been asked to give close support, some of them from 12 to 14,000 yards onto an unregistered target.

In the meantime the Queen's attacked and took 'Cain' with little opposition. By evening 33 Brigade was firmly established across the Buthidaung road.

'A' and 'C' Squadrons returned to 'Tank Valley' in the afternoon, the only casualty being the death of Bill Foote in the night when a tank of 'A' Squadron overturned on the way to the assembly area.

As has been mentioned, the Tactical HQs set out on foot after dark on the night of 6/7th March. Col Frink and the Adjutant marched to Tatmin Chaung and reached the Buthidaung road at 0100 hours and 33 Brigade HQ at 0330 hours, in the area occupied by the 4/1st Gurkha Rifles. The Brigade Commander was Brig Loftus-Tottenham. Col Frink spent all day in this HQ: 'a hot and unpleasant day with enemy attacking all round. Infantry Brigade HQs are the worst-run formations it has ever been my privilege to come across. Intercom as we understand it is non-existent.'

At 1900 hours that evening Col Frink and the Adjutant set out to find their way 'home', not a pleasant walk as they missed the convoy and escort and had to make it on their own. With a march of three miles across open country with Japs moving off the hills and our infantry being ignorant of their identity and route, anything might happen. In the event, nothing worse occurred than the loss of Col Frink's pet hand grenade out of his pocket.

In the meantime Major Ley had prepared and issued operational order No 4, code-named 'Badger'. The objective of 'Operation Badger' was the destruction of enemy dumps and installations to the south-west of West Fingers. It was to be carried out by 'C' Squadron with 'A' and 'D' Companies of the 1/11th Sikhs. The order stated it was to be 'pressed with the utmost determination, with no regard for civilian life or property. No prisoners to be taken – no room for them on the tanks, except for the odd one for interrogation'.

At a conference with Gen Messervy before, Major Ley said he was happy to take command provided the country was 'tankable'. Should they have a 'recce'? Messervy said this was not necessary and produced a photograph of the area showing tank tracks. This was accepted as evidence that tanks had been there before without difficulty.

At 4am on the morning of the 8th March 'C' Squadron under Major Ley moved out as ordered but, as 1/11th Sikhs had been continuously counter-attacked during the night and were still involved at first light, the operation had to be postponed until noon. When the tanks eventually moved forward, a tank on the flank got bogged down and the leading tank reported a Bren-gun carrier stuck in the bog in front. It seemed clear that the tracks in the photo had been made by this carrier. The ground was very 'untankable' and Major Ley reported on the wireless for orders. It was agreed he should get the infantry onto a hill feature half-way down West Fingers so far as he could. This he was able to do but the rest of the operation had to be abandoned.

The Squadron was back in harbour by 5pm, one tank having become bogged down well to the south. It was not recoverable that day and an ambush was set on it for the night. A Jap patrol came along during the night and set alight to it and it became a write-off. Nevertheless the ambush killed three of that patrol.

While all this was going on, 5 Division surrounded and finally captured the Razabil fortress, thus opening the way for an attack on the tunnels.

To the east, above Buthidaung, the road passed over a col between two jungle-covered hills, that on the north called 'Massif', that on the south 'East Fingers'. As this ridge was crossed by the road, it was called 'Astride'. It was this which now barred the way to Buthidaung and along which the Japanese now dug-in.

The next objective for 7 Division was the taking of 'Astride'. During 9th and 10th March several minor actions were fought to secure jumping-off places for this attack, and to secure the right flank by establishing posts on the south end of West Fingers still held by the enemy. The feature taken by the infantry supported by 'C' Squadron on the 8th came in very useful in this action.

On 10th March, Lt Grant of 'B' Squadron and Lt Briggs of 401 Field Squadron IE with two men from Scout Troop went out on patrol in the area between East and West Fingers. A glance at the sketch map shows the area and, of course, the enemy were in occupation of East Fingers as well as the south-end of West Fingers. They reached the small village of Bagona. Near Kanbyin they encountered some Japanese and killed three of them with a Tommy-gun. Considerable firing followed and in the confusion Lt Briggs became separated. The patrol had to return without him and he was never seen again. Nevertheless they brought back a very extensive ground and enemy position report.

This patrol was part of the preparation for the attack the next day by 1/11th Sikh Regt, supported by 'B' Squadron, on East Fingers. Early in the morning 'B' Squadron moved out to the Letwedet area with one patrol of Scout Troop, one D8 tractor, a Regimental Aid Post and a detachment of 401 Field Squadron (also 5 days reserve rations) all under the command of Major Johnstone. He met the officer commanding the Sikhs at 0630 hours in the area of 'Poland', the Sikhs themselves forming up for the attack behind the north-end of West Fingers before daylight. The attack was scheduled for 1030 hours but the enemy observed the Sikhs getting into position and shelled and mortared them, causing some casualties.

The attack was preceded by an air strike and at 10.10am our

artillery laid a heavy smoke screen on the left flank and in the centre. Our mortars and medium machine-guns opened fire and the tanks and infantry moved forward to the start-line under cover of the smoke. A tremendous concentration of fire was then put down by our artillery, so intense that the infantry had to lie flat on their faces to avoid splinters from the shells dropping 500 yards ahead. The undergrowth on the objective caught fire and the smoke and dust obliterated it. Over 700 shells were fired on a front of 500 yards in fifteen minutes.

The artillery fire lifted and we moved forward with the infantry. Despite the smoke, direction was fairly easy to maintain. We gave overhead covering fire to the infantry with the tank machine-guns and from West Fingers further supporting fire came down. The artillery resumed on targets at the enemy rear and the Sikhs charged shouting their war-cry 'Fateh' (Victory). Altogether the effect must have been awe-inspiring.

The attack was entirely successful but, when we reached the defile through Astride itself, it was found that an anti-tank ditch had been dug and mines laid. Work was immediately started on clearing the road through the defile. However the infantry were able to continue the advance, the Japanese offering little resistance and retiring in some disorder. Large bodies were seen streaming south in front of Buthidaung. An artillery observation officer with the leading company managed to bring down effective fire on them. Buthidaung itself was shelled and set ablaze.

By 11.30am Astride was taken and the reserve companies of infantry passed through and secured the position without meeting the enemy. Patrols pushed ahead and entered Buthidaung without opposition. To secure the right flank it was decided to send three troops of tanks carrying two platoons of Sikhs south along the west side of East Fingers and advanced on Buthidaung from this direction. The party was delayed until 1400 hours due to anti-tank mines. Then the Sikhs clambered on the tanks and Major Johnstone led them down as far as Kanbyin. Being unable to go any further due to the ground, he turned back and went through a defile in the middle of East Fingers and thence into Buthidaung. It was deserted. The Squadron drove right through the town without opposition. Unfortunately Lt Johnson's tank struck a mine to the north in the area of Boomerang (a small hill so shaped). Damage was caused to the track and a bogey but there were no casualties. It could not be repaired that day, so the troop remained in that area for the night with one platoon of Sikhs to prevent it falling into enemy hands. The remainder of the Squadron returned through Astride, leaving the newly-captured positions in the hands of the Sikhs and the 4/8th Gurkha Rifles who had come through after midday. The Squadron was back at Tank Valley by 2100 hours.

The operation had been a bigger success than expected and to consolidate further the 4/8th Gurkhas were moved that evening to positions that covered the southern approaches to Buthidaung. Col Frink commented, 'This squadron certainly has plenty of drive and Tony Johnstone and his chaps have done a lot of damage to the enemy.'

During the night the enemy tried to infiltrate back onto their old positions. They managed to re-occupy a small hill called 'India'. This was not defended by our troops, apparently because of the platoon assigned to guard the damaged tank at Boomerang. 'India' was a knife-edged ridge with jungle-covered slopes, too close to our own positions to allow artillery and mortar support. It was extremely difficult to attack.

After daybreak the platoon of 1/11th Sikhs was able to leave Lt Johnson's troop at Boomerang and proceed to 'India' to retake it. In the meantime, 'A' and 'C' Squadrons had left Tank Valley and passed through Astride on their way to a new harbour. As they did so the officer commanding the Sikhs asked for a troop of tanks to clear a pocket of resistance which was holding him up just south of Astride. A troop of 'C' Squadron was dropped off for this purpose. This 'pocket of resistance' seems to have included 'India' and a section of Sikhs under Naik (Corporal) Nand Singh was ordered to drive the Japs out, after some harrassing fire from the tanks. In an amazing and fearless attack Nand Singh led his section in and took the positions and his conduct earned him the Victoria Cross. He was the first man in 7 Division to receive this decoration. The citation reads as follows:

No 13068, Sepoy (acting) Naik Nand Singh, 11th Sikh Regiment, Indian Army.

In Burma on the night of the 11th/12th March 1944, a Japanese platoon about 40 strong with medium and light machine-guns and a grenade-discharger infiltrated into the battalion position covering the Maungdaw–Buthidaung road and occupied a dominating position, where they dug fox-holes and underground trenches on the precipitous sides of the hill.

Naik Nand Singh commanded the leading section of the platoon which was ordered to re-capture the position at all costs. He led his section up a very steep knife-edged ridge under heavy machine-gun and rifle fire. Although wounded in the thigh he rushed ahead of his section and took the first enemy trench with the bayonet by himself. He then crawled forward alone under heavy fire and, although wounded again in the face and shoulder by a grenade, which burst one yard in front of him, took the second trench at the point of his bayonet.

A short time later when all his section had been killed or wounded, Naik Nand Singh dragged himself out of the trench and captured a third trench, killing all the occupants with his bayonet.

Due to the capture of these three trenches the remainder of the platoon were able to seize the top of the hill and deal with the enemy. Naik Nand Singh personally killed seven of the enemy and, owing to his determination, outstanding dash and magnificent courage, the important position was won back from the enemy.

The London Gazette
2nd June 1944

It is said that of the forty Japanese who originally occupied the feature, thirty-seven had been killed.

Many months later Mountbatten attended a parade in front of the Red Fort in Old Delhi, when the Viceroy presented the VC to, amongst others, Naik Nand Singh. He spoke to him and notes: 'He was a magnificent-looking man, who had completely recovered from his wounds.' He also said, 'I could not help feeling from the citations that the standard of the 14th Army VCs was higher than the 8th Army,' with which Slim agreed. Nand Singh was eventually killed in action in 1947 in Kashmir when serving with 1st Battalion The Sikh Regt of the new Indian Army.

By 7.30am 'A' and 'C' Squadrons were in harbour with the Battalion HQ of the 4/8th Gurkhas, west of a hill feature called 'Shoe'. A reconnaissance was made for a secure base in the area of another feature 'Big Tree' and settled on. Mines were discovered everywhere on the tracks and the first fifteen were picked up just south of Shoe where a carrier had been blown up, though with little damage.

Spare parts were sent to Lt Johnson's troops at Boomerang by a platoon of the 3/4th Bombay Grenadiers. Yet further mines were discovered in that area.

All defiles to the south through East Fingers were also found to be mined. 'A' Squadron sent out a patrol of two troops and a platoon of 3/4th Bombay Grenadiers with orders to move south to the Bagona area. The leading tank struck a mine in a defile through East Fingers which killed the driver and the 75mm gunner, Norman Wagstaffe and Albert Woolmer, and wounded the 75mm loader and tank commander. The tank completely blocked the defile and further movement south through any possible defiles was out of the question until extensive sapper 'recces' and mine lifting had been done.

Sergeant Herbert Greatorex and Troopers William Eastham and Edward Hammond of 'A' Squadron went on foot about 500 yards forward of the harbour area towards the Kalapanzin river to investigate reported Japanese movement there. They were never seen again, although no firing was heard from their direction.

Col Frink feared they had gone too far and walked into a Jap ambush. 'The hills are still full of small parties of them and it is not safe to take any liberties. A fighting patrol sent out to find them failed, losing two men in doing so, but they killed six Japs. It's beastly unsatisfactory country to work in, thick and hilly and difficult to clean up.'

This had been a bad day for 'A' Squadron, five men killed or missing (eventually presumed killed), all aged between 21 and 27, and two wounded.

A company of the Gurkhas moved north through Buthidaung and took up positions in the area of Boomerang. They at once came under fire from hills to the north-west. A sapper detachment lifting mines in this area had three casualties.

Replenishment for 'A' and 'C' Squadrons in their new harbour south-west of Buthidaung arrived at 10.30pm that evening by carrier. It consisted of POL, ammunition and medical stores.

There had been slight mortaring in the harbour area but no casualties. One troop of 'C' Squadron had had a shoot at a feature called 'Dragon' during the afternoon where movement had been seen but results were not known. The Squadrons, together with Regimental HQ which was with them, had a 'reasonably quiet night' with little Japanese patrol activity. The forces in this harbour or box, including 4/8th Gurkhas, were all under the command of Col Frink and called 'Frinkforce'. The object of this force was to consolidate the ground and to hem in and destroy what was left of the enemy in the area.

Col Frink wrote:

We felt a bit isolated and lonely the first night, virtually surrounded by Japs in unknown quantities, but by being active next day we found there weren't so very many about and those that were there weren't for showing themselves and getting to grips. We consolidated a bit more ground, cut his L of C and blew up a large number of his dumps.

The Jap has a large force contained in the South and must be very worried. I believe he is trying to pull out to a line a long way south. He will find it difficult as there is a pretty strong ring round him. He will need a lot of reinforcements to re-establish himself. Estimates are that there are only about 3,000 effective left of his original assault force of 9,000. He has plenty more no doubt, if he can get them up and maintain them. It will be no easy matter.

The Japanese Buthidaung emplacements were well worth looking at – miles of tunnelling into the hills and under the houses, well supplied with stores, ammunition etc. It had obviously been one of his main HQs and supply centres for operations in this area after we had withdrawn last year. All yesterday was spent locating them and blowing them up by my sappers and Bombay Grenadiers. They thoroughly enjoyed it and made a good job of it. The town was in flames and ammunition dumps were still going off when we left. The troops got a large number of trophies and we sent in boxes of maps and papers to Div HQ. The Div commander came out in the evening to see us and told me to inform all how pleased he was.

Our operations were badly restricted by intensive mine-laying which must have taken place quite recently. Every track was mined indiscriminately as were all defiles and approaches. They must have realized that their ordinary mine did not do us much harm, as they had tied two together and fastened about 5lbs of gelignite to the base, enough to blow up a house. Four tanks struck them but only one with fatal results. The explosion hit the bottom of the tank and blew up the driver and 75mm gunner and wounded the 75mm loader and tank commander. The tank is a complete write-off. It was very bad luck. Our sappers had been all over the ground ahead and must have missed it.

* * *

Meanwhile 'B' Squadron, apart from Lt Johnson's troop, had remained in Tank Valley. At 7.05am on 12th March two troops and Squadron HQ moved to the area of 89 Brigade HQ where they made contact with a company of the KOSBs who were to clear Sinobyin village and a neighbouring feature. Sinobyin was a village almost due north of Buthidaung close to the west bank of the Kalapanzin river and a sharp bend in that river. The Squadron carried the KOSBs up to 'Mont Blanc' which was the start line for their attack. They then transferred their attentions to a company of the 7/2nd Punjab.

On the west bank of the Kalapanzin, opposite Kyaukit, was a feature called 'the Bulge', consisting of a group of small hills covered with thick undergrowth. It had been occupied by the 7/2nd Punjab on the 8th March, having been formerly held by the Japanese, of which the many tunnels and bunkers were ample evidence. On the night of the 10/11th March the Japanese infiltrated through the Punjabi outposts and by morning were on a ridge overlooking Battalion HQ. The CO personally led a counter-attack but was killed while doing so and the counter-attack was repulsed.

A carefully-planned attack with artillery and tank covering-fire was now to be made and started at 2pm that afternoon. The undergrowth was blasted away by an artillery bombardment and the enemy bunkers could be clearly seen. 'B' Squadron gave the usual supporting fire and the Punjabis moved in. The tank gunners were able to give very close support. Although held up several times by the Jap bunkers, the attack eventually proved entirely successful.

At the end the whole position was strewn with bodies and arms and equipment. The whole garrison of 127 Japanese had been killed – except one who was taken prisoner. He stated that they had been ordered to occupy the feature and stay there until annihilated. The two officers in command had committed suicide during the battle. As against this, the Punjabis had suffered heavily, losing nearly 150 men killed or wounded. As the 7th Indian Division historian says, 'It was probably one of the toughest battalion actions fought during the Arakan campaign.'

'B' Squadron returned to their harbour in Tank Valley.

* * *

The main task of 'A' and 'C' Squadrons with RHQ, in their harbour south-west of Buthidaung, was to clear the area north of Buthidaung between the Massif and the Kalapanzin. Owing to the number of mines about the place (over 60 had been picked up by now), movement was restricted to those areas which had been 'recced' by sappers and only a few sappers were available.

On the 13th March 'C' Squadron moved to the area north of Boomerang to support a company of 4/8th Gurkhas onto a feature. The feature was taken, but no enemy were found and the company was able to withdraw – just part of the mopping-up operation. The whole area of Buthidaung was searched for dumps. Apparently during the operation some of the tank shells went 'over the top' of the feature and fell into the area of 503 Battery of 139 Jungle Field Reg. A gun-sight was hit but no damage was done.

One platoon of the 3/4th Bombay Grenadiers, engaged in clearing a small feature to the east of the harbour, killed some six enemy but lost two killed and four wounded themselves. By now it seemed there were few Japanese left north of Bagona, apart from those installed on the Massif – Point 162. The latter, as will be seen, were to cause a good deal of trouble in the next few days.

Meanwhile in Tank Valley Major 'Bumper' Johnstone was inspecting an old Japanese position on a hill overlooking his squadron area. Suddenly he tripped and fell flat on his face. There was an explosion and part of his buttocks was blown away.

He was reportedly furious, not so much about the buttock, but because he had been telling everyone else to beware of booby traps and now he had fallen into one himself. He was no doubt lucky not to be more seriously wounded but, as it was, he remained away from the Squadron for some three months. It was a great loss to the Squadron at that time.

As a footnote to this day, it is said 'A' Squadron fired on a party of Japs bathing in a chaung (not playing the game, quite?) but results were not known.

On 14th March the only fighting seems to have been done by two troops of 'C' Squadron who supported 4/8th Gurkhas in their task of completing the encirclement of Massif. There was difficulty in pin-pointing the enemy and they were not able to do a great deal.

At 2pm the divisional commander (Gen Messervy) and the

Brigadier came to RHQ for a conference. It was decided that 1/8th Gurkhas should take over the positions of 4/8th Gurkhas the next day. The 1/8th Gurkhas were part of 36 Brigade of the 26th Indian Division. 'A' Squadron was to remain under the command of 89 Brigade for operations against Massif from the south-east. Consequently, at 5pm, 'C' Squadron, RHQ, 3/4th Bombay Grenadiers, the bridging troop and sappers returned to Tank Valley, leaving however one platoon of the 3/4th with 'A' Squadron who were to remain on their existing harbour.

During the afternoon of that day, a detachment of the 401 Field Squadron IE and the 3/4th Bombays burnt or blew up all dumps on old enemy positions in the Buthidaung area. These included ammunition, mines, food, clothing and other military stores. One dump, consisting of smoke bombs, set alight a large part of the town. All houses and surrounding features had very considerable earthworks, confirming Japanese confidence in retaining their HQ in this forward area and their determination to stay there.

In view of a slight lull in activities, at any rate as far as 'B' Squadron was concerned, I found time to write an airmail home:

(Airmail) 14th March 1944

. . . I was very interested to hear that Christopher was in a Punjab regiment in Burma. We have been working in co-operation with Punjabis recently.

I was glad you felt like that about 'China' week. Besides the Chinese Red Army and Kuomintang Army under Chiang-Kai-Shek, American-trained Chinese under Gen Stilwell are fighting in Northern Burma. The latter seem to be doing pretty well but there is no news of the fighting inside China.

I am sorry if my letter in January was a bit of a shock but I thought it best to tell you what was happening, instead of leaving you to guess.

As a matter of fact, we were in two more engagements recently, both of them entirely successful; we had no casualties. The capture of Buthidaung was announced the other night on the news, so you might as well know I was there.

I hope we shall be out of Burma by the time the monsoon breaks. We shall then be due for a good stretch of leave.

The next operation was code-named 'Neptune' and its object was 'to reduce Massif 162 by killing the garrison piecemeal, stopping supplies by raids, artillery and air strikes, and by burning the undergrowth'. It was to be carried out by 33 and 89 Brigades of 7 Div. 'Recces' were made eastwards of Letwedet Chaung for firm positions leading to the west and north faces of Massif. On the night of 15th March the KOSBs put in an attack to see if they could take the position without support. It was found that the features were strongly held and the attack was not pursued further.

About this time 'A' Squadron leader Major Sloan left the Regiment on repatriation. His command was taken over by Captain W.A.H. Munro.

'A' Squadron was south of Massif and had two troops out supporting 4/8th Gurkhas during the afternoon onto isolated features to the east of the main feature. There were no 25th Dragoon casualties but two enemy bunkers were destroyed and five mines were picked up. However it should be added that in the mopping-up operations in this area the Gurkhas had a bad time at the hands of the enemy artillery and mines. Three officers were among the many wounded by shell fire and the Colonel and his Adjutant were both killed when their carrier ran over an artillery tank mine.

The Ledwedet Massif, as it was called, was the only area west of the river, and within the territory recently captured by ourselves, that still contained Japanese units in force. It was a mass of jungle-covered hills, a labyrinth of spurs, re-entrants, ridges and steep slopes, honeycombed with camouflaged enemy bunkers connected by tunnels and crawl trenches.

No change occurred in the situation on 16th March, as the attacks were not to take place until the next day, so I had time to write again:

(Sea mail) 16th March 1944

Whilst I have the opportunity I thought I would write another letter.

An organization has been set up through which we are able to send parcels home from the Burma front. It is run by the 'Lady Voluntary Workers of Calcutta'. There is a list of specified parcels from which to choose. I am going to send you one containing:

1 Tablecloth
2 Turkish Towels
2 Pillow Cases
4 yds curtain net

This was the best assortment on the list, although personally I would rather have sent you some food, which you would probably have found more useful. You will have to regard this as last year's Christmas present! I expect it will take some time to arrive.

On 17th March 'B' and 'C' Squadrons left harbour in the early morning and made contact with the KOSBs. A very heavy artillery barrage was brought down on the north and north-west faces of Massif, which lasted 45 minutes. 25 Pdrs, mountain guns, mortars and medium guns poured down 9,000 shells. Then the tanks blasted the objective from close range with shells and machine-gun fire. From their start-line in Letwedet Chaung, the Queen's and KOSBs moved up onto the shell-torn ridges. There was little opposition, though a certain amount of hostile shelling in RHQ area. The only casualty for 'B' Squadron was caused when an HE shell exploded on the turret of a tank, wounding the tank commander, though not too badly. By noon the KOSBs had taken all their objectives with six casualties.

Col Frink had moved off that morning at 5am in a jeep to meet David McConnell commanding the KOSBs at the Tatmin crossing of the Ledwedet Chaung. There was still a good moon and a heavy ground mist. Col Frink continues:

I was doing the action on foot to enable me to maintain close co-operation with infantry by wireless to my tanks. At 0915 hours we started to move slowly up the chaung, which was very wet, just under cover from the enemy positions 200 yds away. Zero was 0930 hours for the artillery and tanks and 1000 hours for the infantry. We arrived at the Assembly area 200 yds from the position without incident.

At Z hour the artillery concentration came down onto the enemy position – 120 guns onto a target area of about 400 yds by 200 yds – it was simply terrific and quite terrifying. Being so close we got a lot of splash, and bits of trees and rocks were hurtling past us. To improve matters the tanks were firing close over our heads on a flat trajectory. It was by no means my first experience but it was quite the most frightening thing I have ever had to do. The Japs opened up at the same time and 150 and 75mms were falling all round us and the tanks. Nothing to do but lie very still behind a tree. I had to move out into the open to contact my tanks and got blown off my feet by a 75 which landed about 2 yds in front of me.

Col Frink makes the point that the above took place on St Patrick's Day and a party was organized that evening. His experience did not apparently interfere with his enjoyment of whatever the party had to offer!

In fact only the northern rim of Massif had been captured. The Japs were still well-entrenched on Point 162 and its approaches. However, 'B' Squadron and two troops of 'C' Squadron were ordered back to harbour, leaving two troops of 'C' Squadron in the area north of Letwedet Chaung in case further support was needed by the KOSBs in exploiting their success and moving eastwards towards Punkori. They did in fact give some support and returned to harbour at 4pm. As to the tank whose turret had been hit with HE, the damage proved to be slight.

In the meantime 'A' Squadron was able to return from the Buthidaung area and camp again in Tank Valley.

The following day the Queen's, less one company which remained in position on north-west Massif, was ordered to clear Pt 162. 362 Battery of 139 Jungle Field Regt supported the Queen's in this operation and their historian describes it as follows:

> Passing many deserted enemy dug-outs, the leading company of the Queen's reached a spur not far from its objective after walking through dense bamboo jungle and slithering down steep slopes. On being sent forward a platoon was heavily fired on by enemy LMGs and suffered several casualties. The following is in the company commander's own words:
>
> 'I ordered 12 Platoon to keep back under cover of our feature whilst I had the enemy positions plastered for ten minutes (by 362 Battery's mortars). This I admit was a big risk. I was just a little dubious, although I was pretty certain I knew where I was. I could not really be sure that the map was all that accurate as regards distance and we were only 100 yards away from the enemy. We heard the initial salvo come whistling over mighty close. What shooting! It was grand, right on the target first time – made us wince a bit, but we had no casualties.'
>
> High praise indeed for 362 battery.
>
> (Bill Harding, 139 Jungle Field Regt)

However, the Japanese were too well ensconced in their bunkers. Any attempt to approach them was met with deadly machine-gun fire. The jungle on either side of the track was almost impenetrable and made out-flanking impossible. So the operation was called off, but Pt 162 continued to be harrassed by both artillery and from the air.

10

Across the River

Preparations were now well in hand for pulling out 5th and 7th Indian Divisions from Arakan and transferring them to the central front at Imphal. The Japanese had launched a big attack in that area on 9th March (as indeed our high command expected). On 21st March the Japanese army had for the first time crossed the Indian border in their move towards Kohima. This may have been well foreseen by Gen Slim and had no great military significance. From a political point of view it did not pass unnoticed by the Indian leaders nor by the British civilian population who had for so long been able to assume the Indian borders to be inviolate.

West of the Mayu Range, the Razabil Fortress had been taken and attention had been moved to the tunnels and their fortifications. On 13th and 14th March important hill points had been taken by the Dogras, the Royal West Kents and the Punjabis.

The 26th Indian Division and 36th British Division were gradually replacing the 5 and 7 Divisions all along the front. Our last co-operation with 7 Division was to be with 114 Brigade who occupied an area *east* of the Kalapanzin, where they had been since before the Battle of the Admin Box. The three main objec-tives here were the Kyaukit 'fortress', the Pyinshe Kala 'redoubt' and Zadidaung hill.

In preparation for this the whole 25th Dragoons Group, less 'A' Squadron and a platoon of the 3/4th Bombay Grenadiers, moved on 18th March to a new harbour on the west bank of the Kalapanzin. This was a very much pleasanter place than the old 'Delhi'. We were to stay there at least a week and it was named 'Gulmarg'. It was in fact in the area of 26th Division with whose 71 Brigade we were also to work. Col Frink attended a conference at 71 Brigade HQ that day. He remarked 'a few days rest by the Kalapanzin river did us all a bit of good and I managed to get back to Reju Khal to see the wounded and fit in a bathe. It was glorious to be away from the dust and flies for a few minutes.'

During the next few days demonstrations of tank fire power

were given to units of 71 Brigade. Companies of the 1st Battalion Lincolnshire Regiment spent the day with 'C' Squadron practising loading onto the tanks and generally finding out how they worked. The following day they carried out an exercise with 'C' Squadron.

In the meantime 'A' Squadron seems to have joined us and started fraternizing with 114 Brigade. On 19th March the Squadron Leader went on a 'recce' with Col Persse and Brigadier M.R. Roberts of 114 Brigade in his area east of the Kalapanzin. On 22nd March a demonstration of fire power was given to units of the brigade. On the same day orders came through that two squadrons would be crossing the river by raft in order to operate with 114 Brigade, whilst the remaining squadron would work with 71 Brigade on the west side.

Operational orders were issued for the combined attacks with 114 Brigade. Reconnaissance was carried out by 'A' and 'C' Squadrons, Sappers and Scout Troop east of the river for the routes, harbour areas, and features that were to be attacked. 'A' and 'C' Squadrons were to support the 4/14th Punjab onto Point 124 and 'C' Squadron was to do the same for 4/5th Gurkhas on to the feature 'Whale' and the south of Zadidaung.

The 24th March was given over to getting 'A' and 'C' Squadrons, RHQ, two platoons of 3/4th Bombay and other supporting units across the river. The divisional sappers had constructed two crossings, each consisting of three ramps at varying heights on either side of the river to cope with the very quick rise and fall of the tide. The tanks were loaded on to rafts each consisting of four pontoons powered by outboard motors. The crossing of a tank took 18-20 minutes when things were going well, but the tide rose and fell even quicker than expected and there were periods when landings could not take place. However by the end of the day all vehicles were across and were harboured in 114 Brigade Admin area by 6pm. This brigade had never worked with tanks before and had had rather a tough and lonely time, placed as it was to the east of the river.

Meanwhile the Pyinshe Kala redoubt had been subjected to continuous harrassment by artillery, mortars and close-range sniping as a preliminary to the assault. The enemy suddenly abandoned the position, leaving behind light machine-guns, rifles and ammunition, which the garrison was presumably unable to carry. As the capture of this redoubt was a prerequisite to the attack on Zadidaung Hill, this evacuation simplified the position, and the assault on Zadidaung could be pressed forward.

This was put into effect on 25th March. At 8am the squadrons moved out, 'A' Squadron to the area north of a chaung, itself north of Pt 124, one troop of 'C' Squadron to a position facing 'Whale' from the north-east, and 2 troops of 'C' across the chaung facing 124 from the east. RHQ was at the south end of Pyinshe Ridge and the signals officer's carrier was at the foot of the hill.

Zero hour for the first attack was 9am. Supported by the tank the 4/14th Punjab put in their attack and this first phase was successful. By 10am the two northern knolls of Zadidaung had been taken, although some of the bunkers were inaccessible to tank action.

In the middle of this phase, however, a message came through that a battalion of Japanese had, during the night, infiltrated back into Wet Valley and onto the hills near the eastern entrance to the Admin Box, and one squadron was to return over the river as soon as possible. A feeling of 'Haven't we been there before' must have come into many minds.

However, the second phase of the attack on Pt 124 proceeded on the arrival of one troop of 'C' Squadron in the area south-west. The troop was in position by 1100 hours and the 4/14th Punjab was given support onto the top of the feature from three sides but was unable to consolidate owing to one large overlooking bunker which had not been put out of action. At this point 'A' Squadron and RHQ withdrew as per orders.

The regimental signals officer, Capt D.A. Robertson, was killed by a Jap shell while standing by his carrier at RHQ talking to the CO on the wireless. Col Frink said of him, 'A first class chap and I shall miss him a lot, both for his excellent work and as a friend. A main reason for the far too many casualties on my HQ is that the infantry commands will not site their battle HQs where they can see and conduct the battle. The result is that we have to push too far forward for safety to operate with any success. As we always have to operate outside our tanks, this inevitably leads to casualties.'

'C' Squadron remained to support the 4/5th Gurkhas onto 'Whale' at about 3pm and this was completely successful. The

Gurkhas went in very close under the tank fire and took the hill with only one casualty.

One troop of 'C' Squadron also supported the Punjabis onto the final feature of 124, but they were unable to clear it of enemy entirely and consolidated on the near features. The position was taken over by the 1st Somerset Light Infantry (very much understrength) and the Punjabis were sent to deal with another situation. 'C' Squadron returned to night harbour in 114 Brig Admin area. A Valentine bridge over a chaung, necessary for the tanks to reach the fighting area and return to harbour, had to be abandoned as it became hopelessly stuck in the chaung and badly distorted. 'A' Squadron and RHQ had crossed the river and were back in Gulmarg by 10pm.

Meanwhile, at 10.30am on the same day, 'B' Squadron, following the news of the Jap infiltration, had moved out of Gulmarg and was ordered to report to Brigadier Loftus-Tottenham commanding 33 Brigade. They covered the withdrawal of 33 Brigade to its Admin Base and engaged a number of enemy targets in the eastern area of the Box. The Japs, thought to be an understrength battalion with suicide orders, had occupied their old positions on Pt 315. The 1/11th Sikhs were already in that area and were ordered to attack the enemy in conjunction with 'B' Squadron and they succeeded in clearing two out of the three enemy positions before nightfall. No 3 Troop of 'B' Squadron covered the withdrawal of the medium artillery unit. The Squadron harboured that night in the familiar Admin area.

The following morning 'B' Squadron and the 4/15th Punjab, who were then en route from Letwedet to the Admin Box where 33 Brigade were concentrating to move out of Arakan, completed the task of clearing the enemy. They left sixty dead behind and much equipment (the War Diary reports they suffered ninety-three casualties). The survivors moved east to the Awlanbyin area where they were liquidated by units of 26th Division. Neither 'B' Squadron nor the infantry suffered any casualties in these actions.

As General Slim wryly remarked at one stage:

> It would be a pleasant change to fight someone who held up his hands when he realized that further resistance was quite useless.

Col Frink wrote at the time:

> The Jap is getting us rather puzzled. We have pushed some way to the south and he has started his infiltration tactics round the east flank. Last night he shelled us from the north. Personally I think he is trying to stop us consolidating our forward line and from reinforcing IV Corps by threatening tactics. He is succeeding to a certain extent but it will only be temporary.

* * *

The change-over of the divisions was gradually being effected. Command of the front east of the Mayu Range passed to Major General C.E.N. Lomax and the 26th Division on the 21st March. 33 and 89 Brigades were being eased out and replaced by 4 and 71 Brigades of 26th Division. 114 Brigade would be the last to go. The 5th Indian Division had already left, its place being taken by 36th Division. It arrived in Imphal on 27th March including its mules, guns, jeeps and supporting personnel and equipment. It was the first time that a division had been flown out of action on one battle front to fresh action on another front some several hundred miles away. It was Mountbatten's answer to the Japanese attempt to prevent reinforcements being taken from Arakan to the Imphal front in time to hold the new Jap attack there.

The air lift was carried out by American pilots in many cases and the whole journey took ten days and would have taken ten weeks by road and rail. It was a great achievement by the RAF and USAAF.

In the meantime, on 26th March, 'A' Squadron at Gulmarg was standing by ready for operations with 71 Brigade. They were to support the 1st Lincolns and the 1/18th Royal Garwhali Rifles in various attacks in the area south of Buthidaung. 'Recces' were carried out by 401 Field Squadron and a rendezvous was fixed for early afternoon at the east end of 'Wet Valley'. The Lincolns' advance was slow and by 3.30pm the defile it was planned to clear was not open. After half an hour the squadron leader with No 3 Troop and two tanks of Squadron HQ moved up through the valley into the defile. The second tank struck a mine and had its track blown off. The third tank, in reversing to by-pass the disabled tank, also struck a mine and had its track damaged. The leading tank had passed over these mines without touching them off. There were in fact no casualties in either crew. An alternative route had been cleared by the engineers but no guides or marks could be found to indicate its position.

The Lincolns failed to make contact with 1/18th Garwhali and the plan of action had to be changed. The Lincolns with tank support were now to attack another feature and went in at 4.30pm. The objective was gained with little opposition and two troops of tanks supported exploitation of this advance. The remainder of the squadron covered the retrieval of the two damaged tanks. One of these tanks was towed under the hill just taken by the Lincolns and left in their protection for the night. The other tank was repaired and returned to the squadron harbour by 7pm. One tank was called back to Wet Valley to eliminate an enemy machine-gun which was covering the road. This was successfully silenced and all tanks, apart from that with the Lincolns, returned to harbour for the night.

On the morning of 27th March 'A' Squadron was ordered to support a company of 1/18th Garwhali in an attack on a feature in the same area as on the previous day. Capt Munro led nine tanks into action and Lt Mair acted as liaison officer with the Garwhalis. Whilst co-ordinating the plan, Lt Mair and the Garwhali commander were both wounded by shell splinters from enemy fire. Lt Mair was taken to the MDS with facial wounds. The attack in fact failed and at 4pm another attack was put in on the same objective. This also failed mainly due, it is said, to failure of signals to lift supporting fire at the right time. The Garwhalis suffered thirty-six casualties, mainly wounded.

At Gulmarg 'C' Squadron spent the day on maintenance. At 5pm an odd incident occurred. The regimental provost sergeant reported that a large number of sampans had come up the Ngakyedauk Chaung, which formed the north-west boundary of the Gulmarg harbour. The boats contained about 230 people, presumably locals. It was decided 'as a precautionary measure' to detain them under guard for the night. During the night there was some hostile shelling of 'C' Squadron area by a 75mm gun but no casualty or damage was caused.

The following morning (the 28th) 'A' Squadron was sent to make another attempt on the feature which they and the Garwhalis had failed to take the previous day – this time with the Lincolns. A careful fire-plan was laid down, also as signals for the infantry to use when they wished to lift the tank fire, but it was specifically agreed that this support fire would not be lifted over the objective until the leading infantry were on top. This worked very well and the infantry took the objective without casualties to themselves or the tanks. The Squadron was back in harbour by 1.30pm.

On 29th March a number of medal awards were announced arising from the fighting in the Admin Box. Lt Col Frink and Major Johnstone received the DSO, Lt Johnson the MC, Trooper Monger and Trooper Williams the MM, Lt Briggs (who had been reported missing since 10th March) of the 401 Field Squadron of the Indian Engineers, also received the MC. The awards were popular and thought to be well-deserved. Col Frink said of his 'I can only think it was won for me by a damn good regiment which I am proud to command.'

An extract from his citation reads:

> Throughout the whole period from the 4th to the 28th February he was a constant inspiration, not only to his own troops, but to those others close to him, not only of how to hold on but also to strike back. During one of his offensive operations he was slightly wounded in the right arm and back but refused treatment until other casualties had been dealt with.

An extract from Major Johnstone's citation reads:

> Throughout the action at the foot of the Ngakyedauk Pass, Major Johnstone displayed outstanding initiative and drive. His courage, determination and energy for this sustained period of three weeks were very largely responsible for the high performance put up by his squadron.

Col Frink gives the regiment's casualties at this point as follows:

Officers:	Killed	3	Wounded	8
Other Ranks:	Killed	16	Wounded	34
Totals:	Killed	19	Wounded	42

Of the 42 wounded, 22 had remained at duty.

On this day 'A' Squadron was in harbour in the area of Ngakyedauk village, 'B' Squadron in the old 7 Div Admin Box, and 'C' Squadron with RHQ at Gulmarg. Lt Spooner of 'A' Squadron carried out a 'recce' in the area of East Fingers with a view to further operations with 71 Brigade to clear out the Japanese from their remaining strong points in the hills south of 'the Road'. They were to support the Lincolns in attacks on two hills called 'Seahorse' and 'Trinidad'.

'C' Squadron however, in the Gulmarg harbour on the west bank of the Kalapanzin, was ordered to cross the river at noon and continue the operations with 114 Brigade ('Boarhound') which had been so rudely interrupted by the enemy's sudden eruption on Pt 315 on the morning of 25th March. In fact the Squadron was unable to cross until 4pm owing to a very low tide. The crossing was without incident and each tank's crossing time was reduced to an average of ten minutes. By 6.30pm they were in harbour with 114 Brigade.

Extensive 'recce' was needed before the tanks could take part in the proposed attacks, which were to be against two features called 'Boot' and 'Horseshoe'. The squadron leader therefore arranged with the brigadier that the attacks should be postponed to 31st March.

The following day Capt Foxwell of 'C' Squadron carried out a 'recce' in the Bulge area with a view to supporting an attack on Kyaukit and other 'recces' were made in the Horseshoe area. Col Persse and Col Frink attended a conference at 114 Brigade HQ and final orders were issued that evening. The command of 114 Brigade had now devolved on Lt Col H.W. Dinwiddie, Brig Roberts having relinquished his command a little earlier to take part in a lecture tour on the lessons of the Arakan fighting for the benefit of those about to take part.

As a preliminary to the final attacks on Zadidaung and Kyaukit, the 4/5th Royal Gurkhas had attacked and captured (in part with the assistance of 'C' Squadron on 25th March) the two features 'Whale' and 'Khukri' which lay between them. On 27th March the Gurkhas had started the final operations to isolate Kyaukit, of which the operation now to take place on 31st March was part.

'C' Squadron moved out that morning at 8.30am and the attack started at 9.15am. The Gurkhas followed the support fire very closely, as they had done in the case of Whale, and took Boot without difficulty by 10.15am. The attack on Horseshoe was put in at 11.15am and again was completely successful. There were no casualties, either in the Gurkhas or in the Dragoons. 'C' Squadron were able to return to harbour by 12.30pm. A conference was held at 3pm at 114 Brigade HQ to decide on an attack on Point 106. This was to go ahead at 10am on 2nd April.

'C' Squadron carried out 'recces' with the 1st Somerset Light Infantry (71 Brigade). Very late in the afternoon of 1st April two of their tanks went out to assist 4/14th Punjab on Pyinshe Kala ridge. They were fired on by 37 and 75mm guns using armour-piercing shot at about 600 yards range at the Kwazon defile near the squadron harbour area. The harbour itself was also shelled but there were no casualties. These guns at the defile caused quite a bit of trouble. It was decided to postpone the attack on Pt 106 until they had been properly located and dealt with. Gen Messervy himself was at a conference at 114 Brigade HQ. An attack was planned for the following day with 'B' and 'C' Squadrons firing across the river from the west bank at the Kyaukit redoubt. 'C' Squadron harboured for the night on the east bank but crossed over to the west next morning. The CO with RHQ moved to the Bulge area (opposite Kyaukit) and met representatives of 'B' and 'C' Squadrons.

However in the early morning of 3rd April the Gurkhas occupied the main Kyaukit feature and it was now decided to support their further movement south along various features to Pt 109. The assembly area of the tanks was near Sinobyin and 'B' and 'C' Squadrons were there and ready for action at noon. Owing to the Gurkhas' success, however, zero hour was postponed until 4pm and only one squadron was to be used. 'C' Squadron therefore returned to harbour at Gulmarg. 'B' Squadron gave fire support from 3.45 to 4.15pm onto five features. A fair amount of destruction was caused but the Gurkhas were unable to get on owing to fire from the reverse slopes of the hills. Nevertheless they did infiltrate onto the first two objectives during the evening.

'B' Squadron returned to its harbour in the old Admin Box and moved out the next morning at 10.45am, refuelled and stocked up with ammunition. They were due to support the Gurkhas once more, now in their exploitation of the successes of the previous day, but zero hour was postponed from noon to 1pm.

A preliminary artillery barrage went down at 12 noon but due to the postponement it had to be repeated again at 1pm. At 1.17pm the tanks opened their support fire on Pt 109 and surrounding 'pimples' and at 1.37pm the fire was lifted onto Thankrwe, south of Kyaukit. Thereupon the Gurkhas advanced south down the features to 109 and established themselves on top with no difficulty but were soon subjected to fire from grenade dischargers.

HQ also came under the same fire and were heavily machine-gunned from concealed bunkers on the east of 109 and the small feature to the east of that. This latter bunker prevented any further advance beyond 109 and, as the Gurkhas were not intended to stay there, they decided to withdraw under cover of the tank guns. They sent a call for covering fire to quieten the bunkers on the south and south-east of 109 whilst they evacuated their wounded from Company HQ area. On completion of this evacuation a smoke signal indicated to the tanks that they should open up a destructive shoot on the two offending bunkers. This they did for five minutes but the damage could not be estimated because the feature was never re-occupied.

The 4/5th Gurkhas decided it was pointless to advance south of Pt 109 without complete fire support from tanks. This they could not give because the bunkers were partially concealed from the tanks and had about 6 feet of protective earth over them, so that only medium artillery would be likely to penetrate, but medium-guns could not bring down fire because observation was not possible. The Gurkhas could have continued their advance down the west side to Thankrwe covered by the tanks but the latter had insufficient ammunition left to give this cover. So the Gurkhas withdrew and the tanks remained until they were all clear.

The tanks were not called upon further in these offensive operations which were now coming to a close. It eventually became plain that, though putting up strong resistance on all features, the Japanese were for their own reasons evacuating these defensive positions, leaving behind every kind of booby trap. Their latest device was a lachrimatory or tear-gas grenade. Though its effect may have been mainly psychological, it was one more thing for our patrols to think about.

On 5th April a withdrawal of the whole of 114 Brigade east of the Kalapanzin River commenced. It might seem a waste of men and materials that, after so much hard fighting and sacrifice by the infantry regiments, these positions were to be abandoned. The decision had of course been taken some time beforehand at the highest level and was part of the arrangement to establish a firm line defensible throughout the monsoon, which was due to break in May. In order to ensure an unmolested withdrawal, it was necessary to keep the initiative until the last moment and to drive the enemy from any positions overlooking the withdrawal routes. An attack was planned on the Kyaukit position but before it took place several patrols found that the main keep was empty and the whole area was cleared of enemy before the evening. So ironically the whole area was in our hands at the very moment we were to abandon it.

The operation involved back-loading large quantities of stores and some 2,000 animals. 114 Brigade had been in this area since before the Battle of the Box. The enemy had observation points in the hills so all moves had to be made by night. A deception plan was mounted using both 25th Dragoons and Capt Lubeck's deception unit (55 Observation Squadron) made up of British and Sikh personnel. Capt Lubeck was a Czech whose motto was said to be: 'Eff you giff me one ball of string and some fuze I will arrange.' Whatever the allied troops might have been doing, he could persuade the Japanese they were doing exactly the opposite. Sadly he was killed before the campaign ended.

On the morning of 6th April a troop of 'C' Squadron tanks carried out a shoot in conjunction with the artillery onto Pt 109 from the Bulge area. Two troops also made noises near the tank ferry to simulate the crossing of tanks to the east. These noises were continued next morning by Capt Lubeck's unit on the other side of the river.

The withdrawal was completed by the night of 6th/7th April without the enemy being aware of what had happened. The Brigade went over the Okeydoke and back to Bawli. 33 and 89 Brigades were already withdrawn and this was the end of 7 Division operations in Arakan. So we said farewell to these famous regiments with whom we had co-operated since the beginning of the affair in the Admin Box. We also said farewell to Major Hugh Ley. Gen Messervy had received a reply to his signal to GHQ at Delhi. This was to the effect that Ley was sixth in seniority for command of an armoured regiment in the area. As there were only four or so in all and only two were in action, he felt his chances were rather remote. He therefore accepted (with some trepidation) the General's offer to become his senior staff officer. In fact, after one row, they got on very well and Ley stayed with 7 Division, first under Messervy and later under Geoffrey Evans until it reached Rangoon. He then left to command the 3rd Carabiniers and led them in the Victory Parade in Delhi.

7 Division followed 5 Division to the Imphal front and both were part of the great allied army that drove the Japanese across the Irrawaddy and out of Burma and then took up duties in the occupation of countries formerly under Japanese rule.

* * *

On 29th March 'A' Squadron were in harbour in Ngakyedauk village with Lt Spooner making a 'recce' on the area south of the Maungdaw-Buthidaung road in preparation for operations with 71 Brigade of the 26th Indian Division. The object was to clear out the remaining Japanese from their strong-points in the hills there.

The first operation was to be with the Lincolns in an attack on 'Seahorse' on 3rd April. If an attack by the 8/13th Frontier Force Regt (36 Brigade) was not successful by 2am of that day, then 'A' Squadron was to leave at 4am. In fact Seahorse was reported captured by 11.50pm that night so the Squadron was never called out. The next proposal was an operation with the Lincolns in the area of Htinshabyin and Capt Munro went to 36 Brigade with the intention of making a 'recce' of an anti-tank ditch in the area during the night of 4/5th April. He reported the next morning that the ditch was crossable at the east and that the 'Polish' features of West Fingers were all tankable. Two troops of 'B' Squadron were to join in the attack so they moved to 'A' Squadron harbour and came under 'A' Squadron command.

The attack took place on 7th April and the tanks, twenty-three in all, moved out of harbour at 4.15am under Capt Munro. They proceeded over the crossings of Tatmin Chaung and Letwedet Chaung, through the defile at Pt 142 and south between East and West Fingers. The two troops of 'B' Squadron were dropped off in this area to carry out their task of neutralizing features north of the objectives. They opened fire at 6.52am and 'A' Squadron was in its firing positions a few minutes later: one troop facing Polish North, another facing Polish South and one facing 'Spit' from the south across the anti-tank ditch. The Squadron opened fire at 7am on the objective and the Lincolns advanced across the padi from the chaung to the east at 7.05am. They attacked with two companies and got to the foot of the hills without casualties, covered by a very heavy concentration of fire from 'A' Squadron. Lt Ian Gray's tank was almost immediately hit by a shot from a 47mm anti-tank gun from Kanbyin village. It caught fire and Lt Gray was wounded. One member of the crew, Henry Newman, was killed instantly; another, Archie Mitchell, was badly burnt and died that night, and a fourth, Ken Griffin, was badly wounded in the legs and was eventually repatriated to 'Blighty'. James Tiley was in the tank immediately behind and remembers seeing the flash. His tank fired back immediately but the Japanese gun managed to fire six rounds before being silenced by the guns of Lt Gray's troop and HQ troop, which also set the village on fire. The gun had a very high muzzle velocity and was fired at 50 yards.

Col Frink observed that an important lesson was to be learnt from this action. The Japanese had dug an anti-tank ditch which looked as though it had not been completed. At this point there was an easy tank crossing and on this the two guns were trained on fixed lines. Luckily the Squadron was suspicious of this and only one tank was caught.

Two troops of 'A' Squadron, which had covered the infantry advance across the padi, went in very close between the two objectives and captured another 47mm gun, which was afterwards found to be completely intact. The Lincolns were thought to be on all their objectives by 7.30am, but there was considerable sniping in the Spit area and the position was obscure on South Polish where large numbers of grenades were exploding. By 8am North Polish and Spit were reported to be in our hands, but they were being heavily sniped from South Polish. No 2 Troop went in still closer and was able to stop this sniping with armour-piercing shell and co-axial machine gun onto South Polish. It was found that the main feature of South Polish was still strongly held by the enemy.

To break this situation Lt Grant of 'B' Squadron went up onto South Polish to get a clear picture and controlled from there what is described as 'a first class shoot' by one troop of 'B' Squadron and five tanks of 'A' Squadron. They fired onto South Polish very close over the heads of the Lincolns and very near to their flanking positions. This enabled them to take the hill and a period of consolidation followed.

The tanks remained in support until 11.30am, clearing up pockets of resistance, dropping ammunition and water to the infantry and carrying back the Lincolns' casualties to our regimental aid post. 'A' Squadron Sergeant-Major 'Taff' Haddon was ordered to move in close to the defile north of Spit and knock out a sniper who was causing casualties during the early stages of consolidation. He was unable to shoot from his tank so dismounted and shot the sniper with a Tommy-gun. For his conduct he was awarded the Military Medal.

The tanks rallied to the rear at noon and were back at Ngakyedauk village by 1pm. On the way they were heavily shelled at the crossing of the Letwedet Chaung by a 150mm gun but none of the tanks were hit.

This battle, lasting less than five hours, must have been one of the most hard-fought engagements of the campaign, since the beginning of March. It had been preceded by air-fighter strikes to the west of the features (enemy rear) and a very heavy artillery barrage which had been put down for forty minutes before zero hour. As well as the 1st Battalion of the Lincolnshires, one and a half squadrons of tanks had taken part in support, when normally not more than a squadron was used at a time. The final count of enemy dead was 164, excluding any killed by the fighter strikes or artillery barrage. The Lincolns lost four officers and fifteen other ranks killed, and twenty-five other ranks wounded. 'B' Squadron had one man wounded and 'A' Squadron suffered the casualties already mentioned when Lt Gray's tank was hit. That tank had burst into flames and the ammunition had exploded, thus leaving the tank a write-off.

As previously mentioned, Sgt Bill Nicholson was sent back to India after being wounded by a mortar shell. He eventually reached Secunderabad, a well-known and not altogether unpleasant military station in the hills in central India.

He wrote:

Here I visited the many hospitals, looking for any of our wounded and, luckily, found Ken Griffin some 24 hours before he was flown back to England. He was in a shocking condition but was surprisingly cheerful and he reminded me of a little matter of some 80 rupees, winnings from his card school, which I was holding for him and which he had given me the day before his tank was hit. Two members of the crew were killed and the other five wounded and burned.

The following day two troops of 'A' Squadron under Lt Spooner were called out at 8am to deal with a bunker on the south face of South Polish still in enemy hands. They gave the bunker ten minutes' concentrated fire after which the CO of the Lincolns considered that the bunker was destroyed. The troops were back in harbour by 9.30am.

* * *

'B' Squadron was now harboured in the Admin Box, to which 'C' Squadron also moved on 8th April. RHQ and 'A' Squadron were in the 71 Brigade Box not far from the river. Arrangements for gradually withdrawing the 25th Dragoon tanks from Arakan prior to the monsoon were now put in hand. 'C' Squadron left the Admin Box and moved over the Okeydoke Pass for the last time, had to wait until 4am for the tide before crossing the river and arrived at Bawli Bazaar by 5am.

139 Jungle Field Regiment was also pulled out via the Admin Box at this time and their historian describes it:

> In stark contrast to the tension, sleepless nights and bloody conflicts of February, the atmosphere in the Admin Box was one of light-heartedness and relaxation. Men strolled around and chatted in groups without fear of being sniped or shelled from the scarred and shattered hillsides. Life began to assume a slightly more civilized aspect after a good clean up and a beer and rum ration issue. The Army 'Rosa' rum was mighty potent stuff. Its fumes alone, when mug was put to lips, caused one to cough and splutter and drinking it was like swallowing liquid fire, but the searing gulp was followed by a relaxed feeling.
>
> (Bill Harding)

Shortly after, 139 were flown to Imphal.

In the pre-monsoon period the heat was becoming scorching and tiring. Already the sky had clouded over several times to give a few showers of rain which only temporarily damped-down the dust on the sun-baked padi. Nothing much happened the following day and consequently I was able to write a letter home:

(Air mail) 9th April 1944

. . . There was no mail waiting for me, so I expect I shall get a large pile all at once.

Our crew has adopted a very small pup. He has grown quite a bit and is now about a foot long or just over. I wish you could see him. He is black with white paws, a white nose and a white end to his tail. He has been into action with us several times and doesn't seem to mind the guns going off inside the tank. At the moment he is eyeing me suspiciously from a cool position underneath the engine doors.

Yesterday was Good Friday and the Padre held a service in the evening. As usual it was voluntary and there was a very big attendance. We all sat round on empty ammunition boxes.

Since we have been near the front (if it can be so called), congregations have increased tremendously, due I think to several reasons – firstly the Padre himself, who takes real trouble to get to know everybody and has an informal way of taking the services; secondly, being in action makes people feel the need for something stable when everything else seems to be going under, a natural reaction to danger perhaps; and thirdly, there is nothing much else to do when the services are on and no spit and polish. People can just wander across wherever the services are being held.

I hope you are all very well and cheerful. All my love.

The following day was Easter Sunday and an operation was considered involving support of an infantry attack on Inbauk. Lt Ryan of 'B' Squadron carried out a 24 hour 'recce' round the feature but as a result it was decided that, though tank support could be given, it was not a good proposition. Japanese troops were reported in the Punkori area but not in sufficient strength to justify the use of tanks.

Col Frink was able to attend the church services organized by the Padre on Good Friday and Easter Sunday. He says of Padre Cox, 'A very good chap and of great help to all ranks. All services are entirely voluntary and it is very gratifying to see the large attendance. I find him a great help too and shall always be grateful for his company.'

On Easter Monday Mountbatten arrived at the HQ of the 36th Division near Maunghnama on the western side of the Mayu Range. He was shown the tunnels area from this side and inspected the Razabil fortress now in our hands:

> It had been prepared for a siege, like the Rock of Gibraltar, with deep bunkers and fox-holes and tunnels, and might have withstood for a much longer time if our troops had not succeeded in completely encircling it. Before the artillery and heavy tanks could complete the encirclement, the last remnants of the Japanese garrison fled by night.
>
> (Mountbatten: Diary 10 April 1944)

The following day he took off from a small airstrip nearby on a Moth and flew over the Ngakeydauk Pass, landing at Laungyaung:

> Here I was met by Maj Gen Lomax who commands 26th Indian Division. The corps commander and our staffs had already arrived by jeep. We drove onto Wings Hill. Brig Lowther who commands 4th Brigade, and two of his battalion commanders described the battle for Point 315, when the Lincolns and the Wiltshires made their gallant advance to clear the Japanese off the east side of Sinzweya during the recent battle. We lunched in Lomax's HQ. The mess furniture was very simple. It consisted of a rectangular pit with some planks put across the middle. One sat on the edge of the pit and used the planks as a table. After lunch we met Frank Messervy at Sinzweya which was where his Administrative HQ were encircled for 17 days.

Messervy then led Mountbatten up the highest feature in the Box and spent an hour describing what has now become known as the Battle of the Box. Mountbatten was greatly impressed and concluded:

> The whole story is so thrilling that I am trying to get one of the MOI (Ministry of Information) writers from home to write it up in popular pamphlet form.
>
> (Mountbatten: Diary 11 April 1944)

I do not remember this visit but Col Houghton Brown did because he was called back to explain to the 'Supremo' how the Wiltshires had captured the bunkers on 'Three Pimples':

I went back in a jeep and met our general, brigadier, and the CO of the Lincolns. I was interested also to be introduced to our corps commander, Lt General Christison. This was the first and only time that I had the chance of seeing him.

Eventually, out of the sky dropped a small plane. It pulled up on the dry strips of padi stubble and out stepped Admiral Lord Louis Mountbatten, with his staff. I was immediately struck by his fine figure and forceful personality. The divisionial commander explained to him the general picture and then he turned to me for more detailed information. He seemed to have a remarkable grip of infantry technique and in a few moments he had the whole situation at his finger tips. Later in the day he came forward to see the troops. He spoke to them freely and clearly and explained the general situation throughout South East Asia Command. The men were all very impressed with their Supreme Commander and there was no doubt in all our minds that he was the right man for the job.

11

Battles for the Monsoon Line

On the 13th April the Japanese were still in the Punkori area and the 5/1st Punjab were not able to get them off two features to the south-west of Punkori. 'B' Squadron were called upon to produce two troops to give fire support to the Punjabis in a small attack. The troops left harbour at 4pm and were heavily shelled on the way to the area by a 75mm. Several shells landed within feet of the tanks but there were no casualties. The attack went in after ten minutes concentrated fire by the tanks and was completely successful, the infantry suffering no casualties. The following day a report was received that the bunkers had been completely blown-in and remains of the Japanese occupation found, with two enemy dead. If there were more they must have removed the bodies. 'B' Squadron returned to harbour in the Admin Box without incident.

About this time I received, and replied to, a letter from Joyce MacDonald, a Hoddesdon friend who had married after the war started and whose husband was now in a German prison camp. Somehow this letter has survived the years.

(Airgraph)

5 Walnut Tree Close
Hoddesdon
Hertfordshire
England

24-3-44

My Dear Tom,

Many apologies for not writing before but I haven't forgotten you. I won't tell you of the long series of illness but look to brighter things. First, how are you? Very glad to say I am quite well and so is Mac. News is very irregular but always cheerful from him and the Germans are allowing them many privileges which is a great comfort. However Mac said he had a few weeks in hospital with a poisoned foot and still wondering how he got it.

Remember red-headed Tony Forbes? He is not far from you but unluckily not continuing what he would very much like to do. After getting his wings was told he had no natural ability for flying so is now waiting to go on another course.

George Taylor was home last week. He looks as young as ever. Remember Dorothy Gray, now Mrs Douglas Lea? Well, she will be a mother when you read this. My 1st anniversary was on the 20th.

Cheerio, Tom, look after yourself.

Yours as always,
Joyce

About the same time I wrote home to my parents:

(Airmail) 12th April 1944

I have just received your parcel enclosing the socks, 'Herts Mercury' and letter dated 21st Jan. Many thanks for all these. It was the first correspondence I have received for nearly a month. We are still in Burma but hope to be coming out soon.

You may be interested to know that four people in the regiment were decorated, three in 'B' Squadron, as a result of the Ngakyedauk business. The CO received the DSO and so did our squadron leader. Everyone feels they both deserved it. Had it not been for their direction and organization during the first critical days after the Japs infiltrated, when things were pretty chaotic, I think what was announced in the press as the first major victory over the Japs on this front, might so easily have been a disaster for us.

A troop officer in our squadron received the MC. A driver in my troop received the MM for some very brave work on a burning tank.

I hope you had a pleasant Easter. The Padre held morning and evening services and communion which I was able to attend.

To the west of the hills the 5th Division had in mid-March taken features called Propeller and Wrenkat in the Rekhat Chaung area and Points 1079 and 1267 north and south of the tunnels, as well as Tortoise and the Razabil fortress itself. Their place had now been taken by 36th Division. By the 26th March 72 Brigade of that division had seized most of the ground round the west tunnel but not the tunnel itself. Several attacks had been made by the infantry supported by the Sherman tanks of 149 RAC Regiment ('C' Squadron) but had been repulsed. On the 4th April a shell from one of the tanks was fired into the tunnel and hit the ammunition dump. The whole thing blew-up and the explosion killed or wounded most of the defenders but a small group fought back desperately as the 9th Royal Sussex Regt moved in.

After taking the tunnel a heavy Howitzer was found near the east mouth which had clearly been used to shell the Admin Box. It had been withdrawn into the tunnel each time it had fired its scheduled number of rounds. It was in fact a tactic of the Japanese to fire a gun from one position and then move it to a new position before firing again, thus, making it very difficult to pin down. 72 Brigade then moved on to take the east tunnel, having handed over the west tunnel to 54 Brigade of the 25th Indian Division which had now come up to the front.

This however was not the end. There remained a hill to the south-east of the tunnels, Point 551, which dominated the road. At a conference on the 6th April between Gens Christison (Corps), Lomax (26th Div) and Messervy (7th Div) it was decided not to retain Buthidaung for the monsoon season but to take Point 551 at all costs. It proved to be a tough proposition. It had already been attacked by 4 Brigade of 26th Division from the east but without success. A large-scale attack was planned for 15th April.

The road from Buthidaung to Maungdaw ran for a few miles in a westerly direction and then turned due south and passed through the two tunnels. Parallel to the road at this point was a long ridge-like hill running north to south of which the peak was Point 551 near the centre of the ridge. At the north end of this hill were two pairs of smaller hills separating the road from the main hill. The eastern pair were named 'Hump and Camel' and the western pair 'Bullet and Barrel'. The Letwedet Chaung ran round the north edge of these hills and all five were in effect part of the same land mass. The four smaller hills all had defiladed slopes and all slopes were steep and thickly wooded.

Two distinct operations were planned for the 15th April. The main attack on Pt 551 was called 'Soccer' and 'A' Squadron was to support the 1st Wiltshires onto two of the peaks, 'Hump' and 'Camel', in the first phase. This however was to be preceded by a diversionary attack by 'B' Squadron and the 1/18th Royal Garwhali Rifles on Rabbit, onto which the Japanese had again infiltrated. This operation was 'Bunny'.

The attack on 'Hump' and 'Camel' was planned jointly by Col Houghton Brown and Col Frink. They appear to have got on well, perhaps because they were both keen horsemen and riders to hounds, though Houghton Brown was a Territorial and Frink a

SKETCH MAP OF PT 551 AND THE MAUNGDAW–BUTHIDAUNG ROAD

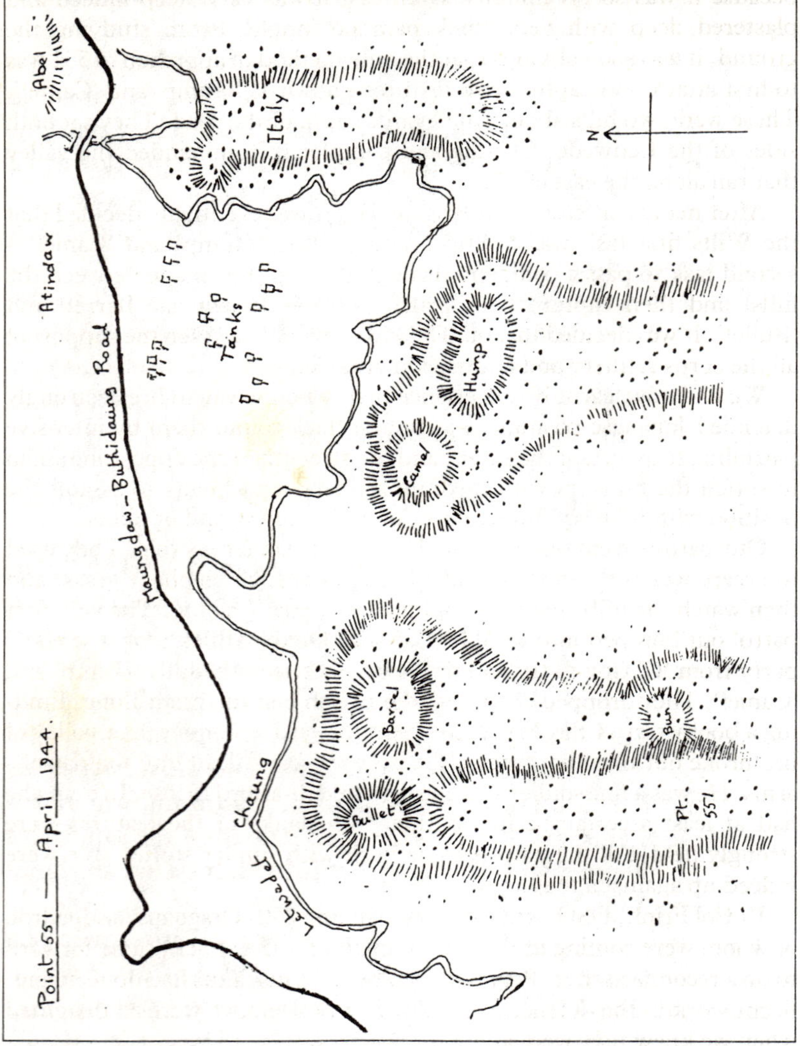

Regular. Col Houghton Brown, as CO of the Wiltshires, was in command of the operation. He wrote as follows:

The main objective of our division was the high feature known as *551*. This hill was known to be very strongly held by the enemy as it completely commanded most of the road from the tunnels to Buthidaung. It was almost impossible to approach this feature from the north or west because it was so precipitous. Even east it was very steep indeed and plastered deep with very thick bamboo jungle. From studying the ground, it was soon obvious that the only method of approach to 551 was to first attack and capture two features known as 'Hump' and 'Camel'. These were two hills about 1,000 yards south of the road. They sat both sides of the Ledwedet Chaung and completely commanded the valley that ran along the east of 551.

After many conferences at Brigade HQ it was eventually decided that the Wilts first task was to attack and capture 'Hump' and 'Camel' – second task to pass a company through the gap thus made between the hills, and then capture two further features known as 'Barrel' and 'Bullet'. It was decided that on 'D' Day we would be given the support of all the corps artillery and a squadron of tanks.

We had now learnt by experience that the only way to break strongly defended Japanese positions was to first 'feel' round them by intensive patrolling to ascertain the extent and the strength of the opposition; then to soften the bunkers with medium artillery, and finally to assault the position with infantry, under cover of field artillery and or tanks.

Our patrols went out every night on their dangerous role. They used to creep over the deserted road, through the high elephant grass, and then watch the hills that bordered the Ledwedet Chaung. The very first patrol out bumped into trouble. Captain 'Duke' Afflick took a selected party from 'C' Coy to try and find a way between the hills 'Hump' and 'Camel'. They dropped down into the stream bed and crept along. Finding a booby trap, CSM Priddeaux went forward to remove it. A volley of fire broke out from both sides. He dropped-back dead into the patrol's arms. He was a fine soldier and one we could ill-afford to lose. In dying he had at least ascertained for us that both flanks of the features were strongly held. All the patrols came back with similar stories. We were indeed up against a tough proposition.

Lt Col Frink, DSO, who was commanding 25th Dragoons, a squadron of whom were coming under my command for the attack, came forward to do a reconnaissance. Brilliantly led by him, his tanks had done magnificent work in the defence of the 7th Div Box and we were all delighted when we knew they were going to support us.

He and I worked together for one long day and planned every detail for the final attack. Eventually I took the company commanders forward for a final reconnaissance. We looked at the ground from every aspect.

On our return I had a sand model made, approximately to scale, of the area we were about to fight over. On this I gave out my orders. Then I explained in minute detail the situation to all the NCOs of both our attacking companies and the tank leaders of the Dragoons. We finished up with a joint 'tea party'. This meant that our Wiltshire Officers and

NCOs got to know the tank officers and NCOs. It was an amusing affair and everybody got very friendly. By nightfall there was no doubt that everyone knew exactly what to do.

On the last day, 14th April, I could not resist going forward with my escort to make quite certain nothing had changed. We slipped quietly over the sinister road and lay up in 'No Man's Land', deep in high elephant grass. I then moved along studying our objectives with my glasses. They looked strangely quiet. Both hills stood up grimly in the evening light. As usual, no sign of a Jap. I wondered if our patrols could have been wrong and if they were not strongly defended after all!

We got back safely and then moved my advance HQ on to the toe of 'Italy'. Briefly our plan was as follows: first, for 'B' and 'D' Companies to move up before light to the start line, which was the edge of the jungle 100 yards from the objectives, and soften all the main features along the front with artillery. Under this cover the tanks to move up. Then the artillery to lift on the reverse slopes to give the dust time to clear. Then at zero, for a company of the Frontier Force to our right, to attack some foothills of 551 and, at the same time, for 'B' Company to attack 'Camel' and then go through on to 'Bullet' and 'Barrel', leaving the Carrier Platoon to hold 'Camel' once captured.

'C' Company was to move up and be ready to exploit success of the Frontier Force and 'A' Company in reserve. The infantry attacks to go in under cover of the 75mm guns of the tanks. We were, in fact, going to use these monsters as mobile artillery, firing over open sights. I had arranged to have an advance RAP on the Road between 'Cain' and 'Abel' under the protection of the Rajputs. Here jeeps and ambulances could get up. Stretcher bearers were to be up with the leading companies, and the Regt police were to be dotted along the Road to direct the walking wounded to the RAP. Each company's reserve platoon was to carry up barbed-wire, extra water, ammunition and digging tools.

For many days the artillery had been registering their targets, and I felt certain that by now the enemy must have realised there was something suspicious in the wind.

(Houghton Brown: Farmer-Soldier)

On the morning of 15th April 'B' Squadron left harbour in the Admin Box at 5.45am and formed up in the area south-east of Poland. An artillery concentration was put down which was followed immediately (at 7.45am) by fifteen minutes firing from the tanks. The Garwhalis went in under the fire and were on to two of their objectives by 9am, and by 10am the whole objective was secured. Their diversionary task was now completed, the main attack being well underway, and they pulled off.

Col Frink wrote:

> They came in for a certain amount of shelling but no direct hits were scored. About 50 Jap dead were picked up. As it was to be 'B' Squadron's last action before going over the hill on the first stage of their pull-out to Cox's Bazaar, I told them they need not bring back any ammunition. They duly complied and gave Inbauk an almighty plastering with HE and smoke. This so upset the Jap that he opened up with all his guns on his own positions. They did not stop to count the damage.
>
> This Squadron has done exceptionally well and deserves the rest it will get before training-up again for next winter's campaign.

The Squadron returned first to the brigade area and then to harbour in the Admin Box. They had suffered no casualties but two tanks had developed mechanical faults which turned out to require second line repair.

Back to Jack Houghton Brown:

> Just as it was getting light I met the long files of 'D' Company creeping through the undergrowth towards their 'forming up place'. The men looked tired but fit and hard. I knew they would make a good account of themselves.
>
> My advance HQ was on the forward slope of the toe of 'Italy' and looked directly across 'the road' towards our objectives. The ground was fairly flat but was covered in high elephant grass and scrub. 'Hump' and 'Camel' loomed large and formidable. A slight hazy-blue mist hung over the jungle, showing that yet another day was going to be stiflingly hot.
>
> Avery had fixed up communications back to our rear HQ and to brigade. He was also running out lines with the advancing troops so that we would be able to contact the companies with both wireless and telephone. Adams, as always quietly efficient, had our HQ well laid out. There was nothing else to do but wait for the artillery concentrations to start. By 0800 hours both 'D' and 'B' Companies reported they had arrived safely at their FUPs. They had met no opposition and could see nothing of the enemy. Adams started chatting. We discussed ships, horses, theatres, girls – everything except the impending battle. We both pretended not to be anxious. I knew in my case I felt the same sinking feeling inside me as I used to get sitting on a young horse, waiting for hounds to find outside a cover in the Knoyle Vale. Mice appeared to be gnawing at my navel.

Suddenly there was a crash. The earth shook. Then roar upon roar – almost surely an earthquake. The hills to our front were being plastered with shells. A hundred guns of all calibres were loosing their projectiles on the enemy. Great clouds of greenish black smoke rose from the heights opposite. Soon they were covered altogether and could no longer be seen. Intermittent amongst the din came the resounding earth-splitting crashes as the shells of the medium artillery landed about the bunkers.

In the meantime 'A' Squadron had left harbour at 6.45am and arrived at their fire positions at 8.25am during the artillery barrage. They had crossed the 'road' (which had been cleared during the night of anti-tank mines) and moved to within 100 yards of the two hills.

Ten minutes before zero, the artillery concentrations lifted on to the reverse slopes of the hills. We had planned this to enable the dust to lift so that the tanks could see the infantry and then fire above them.

I looked at my watch. 0900 hours. Zero. Adams shouted 'They're off!' I could see 'D' Company moving across the narrow strip that divided the jungle from the hills. Then down into the clearing and up the other side. I was horrified to see the dust still shrouded round the hills. At that moment the infantry entered into the cloud of hazy dirt and disappeared. Not a sound from the tanks near 'Hump', although I could hear them firing smartly into 'Camel'. My worst fears were realized. The ten minute artillery pause on 'Hump' had not been enough. There was not a breath of wind and the dust still hung so thick that the tanks could not see our men and therefore dared not fire. The jungle was thicker and greener on 'Camel', which must have been the reason for less dust on that feature. I got through to 'Needle' (commanding B Co.) All appeared to be going well with his leading platoon, although the bamboo was so dense that the sections could only advance in single file.

A slight breeze ruffled the nearby foliage on 'Hump' and then I saw the leading platoon of 'D' Company had almost reached the top crest of their objective. The dust was now lifting but it was obviously too late. The tanks had not been able to give any support (on Hump). Suddenly the sound of the sharp crack, crack of Jap machine-guns. The artillery had not after all, squashed the enemy bunkers. They were firing and throwing grenades at our leading infantry. These poor lads were quite helpless. They required both hands to hold on to the scrub to enable them to scramble up the steep hillside. They could not successfully use their weapons. I saw the leading section pause and drop. Then I noticed long-legged Keith Falcon, the company commander, striding about amongst the troops. He carried his rifle over his shoulder and looked as if he was organizing the beaters for a partridge drive on his Norfolk farm at home. Another 'crack' and Keith dropped too, a bullet through his knee. Slowly the company were driven back. By 1100 hours I realized the attack on 'Hump' had failed. I got through to Captain Motion, the second-in-command of 'D' Company, and told him to reorganize what remained of his company at the bottom of the hill.

During this time Adams was in touch with 'B' Company. Here there had been little dust and the tanks had thus been able to give them good support. The leading platoon had climbed the hill, the tanks firing AP shells 10 yards above them rising as the men crept up. On reaching the summit they found the Japs, magnificent men of the Imperial Guard, cowering down in the bottom of their trenches. Young Newton, the platoon commander, led his men in. Hand-to-hand fighting then ensued. Newton got severely wounded by a bullet through his foot but encouraged his men on as he lay on the ground. Firing their weapons from their hips they charged in, eventually winkling out the Japs with their bayonets. They killed fifteen of them. The rest vanished.

'Camel' was ours. I got through to Joe Panks and told him to push up his carrier platoon to hold the feature with their many Bren-guns. I knew the enemy would almost certainly immediately counter-attack.

I now had to make up my mind what to do about 'Hump'. It was obviously impossible to carry out our second task until we had completed the first. However, now we had captured 'Camel' we had opened half the door and this would enable us to attack 'Hump' from two sides, both from the north and west.

I got through to the Brigadier and told him my new plan. He agreed. It was obviously impossible to collect up the company commanders again, so gave out my second orders on the air.

The new plan was similar to the old, except this time 'B' Company would help 'D' Company by simultaneously attacking from the flank. Also all the tanks would now concentrate on the one feature. There was a slight breeze blowing, so I knew we would have no bother with the dust. That would soon blow over. My chief worry was the tanks. It was a big risk leaving them up for such a long period. We had not seen anything of enemy anti-tank guns in this area but, if the Jap planes came up, they would give them hell. However, Col Frink agreed that this was a chance we had to take. We had seen little of the enemy airforce for many weeks.

Motion had reorganized his Company ('D'), but it was sadly reduced. He had suffered 40 percent casualties. However, he was determined to have another 'go', and this time I prayed it would be successful. I got through to rear BHQ and spoke to Peroy. He had been up to the advance RAP and found everything in order. The stretcher bearers had rather a long carry but once the wounded got back to the RAP the MO soon patched them up and sent them back to the Advance Dressing Station.

The second zero was for 1300 hours. At 1230 hours the corps artillery concentration started again. This time it seemed more effective than ever, all the shells landing on the one feature. At 1250 hours it again lifted. In the pause that followed, the dust blew off beautifully. The tanks then let fly with everything they had. Brownings and 75mm HE blasted into the hill. They seemed to make more noise than the artillery. Surely no Japs could live in this!

At zero, the infantry started climbing. I could see the 75mm AP shells which the tanks were now firing, crashing into the dust only a few feet above our men's heads. They both had confidence in each other and worked in perfect unison. Slowly the troops advanced, closing gradually from two sides on to the top of the hill. Both companies reached the crest simultaneously. To my amazement, once again they were met by a furious blast of fire from the enemy. I could see a platoon of 'B' Company charging on to the top. Then back they would go, driven off by a hail of enemy bullets. Sergt Lee led his platoon three times on to the crest. Each time he was driven back. I then got through to both company commanders and told them not to get on to the top but to push both platoons round to the flanks and gradually surround the crest of the feature. As soon as we started this circling move, things happened quickly. The enemy, obviously already severely shaken, saw that he was almost cut off. He could stand no more. I saw little figures rushing hither and thither. The Jap was bolting. He was literally running for his life. Our lads rushed on, firing into their backs. Some fell over the precipitous sides of the hill. Others lay groaning in the dust. The Jap officer in command, already wounded, gave himself up to our big Sergt Major of 'D' Company, CSM Townsend. He spoke in English 'You English bulldogs have got us this time'. Later he tried to bolt from his escort and unfortunately was killed.

The enemy, realizing we had now captured his key position, immediately started retaliating. He shelled it intensively with his mortars.

It was now scorching hot but our lads dug like hell. They suffered few casualties from the Jap mortars because, in a very short time, they were down in their slit trenches.

The first stage of the battle was over. For the first time we had seen the Jap run. We found many of them lying dead. Dozens more must have been buried in the collapsed bunkers. Thanks to the guts of the men, and the magnificent support of the tanks and artillery, we had really scored a great victory. It was certainly the proudest moment of my life. What a wonderful thing it was to be in the Wiltshire Regiment amongst such gallant lads.

I remember thinking that England may be often governed by stupid leaders but it can never be said that she does not possess a bounty of brave men.

(Houghton Brown: Farmer – Soldier)

Col Frink also described this battle, though not at the same length as Col Houghton Brown:

The 'A' Squadron battle lasted from 0830 hours to 1500 hours when they were able to pull out unscathed. They were tucked into positions that would have been very hard for the enemy to reach. About 20 mines had been picked up by the sappers during the night. The mist came down just before action which made visibility very bad, added to which the smoke and dust brought down by a strong artillery concentration completely obliterated our targets. The result was that we did not get a good shoot to support the infantry on and consequently they failed to reach the top of their objective. They fought very gallantly but were eventually grenaded and mortared off.

Much the same happened on the right where the Sherman Squadron (149 RAC Regiment) were supporting the Frontier Force Rifles. Artillery alone simply cannot get the infantry onto a position which the Jap is determined to hold. Another attack was laid on for 1430 hours and this time with tank support from 'A' Squadron alone they reached their objective and found 82 dead Japs.

Seven clutches seized-up during the day, due mostly to excessive dust. The tanks are definitely beginning to show signs of wear.

'Camel' and 'Hump' were two peaks to the east of the main feature. The 2/13th Frontier Force Regt attacked the peaks to the west but were held up by a fake crest and heavy machine-gun fire and were unable to take their objectives. The 2/17th Rajput gained a footing at the north end of the 551 ridge and turned south onto the ridge but were pinned down. The squadron of 149 RAC Regiment were also engaged in the operation, giving fire support to the infantry. 'A' and 'B' Squadrons of the Dragoons fired the whole of their ammunition, the maximum they could carry. Despite all this and considerable artillery support and air cover and dive-bombing strikes, it became clear that the second and third phases of the attack could not be put in that day.

'A' Squadron evacuated some wounded of the Wiltshires to their regimental aid post and withdrew. They suffered no casualties either to themselves or to the tanks. They had been in action all day and, though exhausted, greatly admired the stamina and courage of the infantry. With little fuel left and seized clutches, some tanks only just reached harbour. The Regiment was not called on again to take part in the fighting for Pt 551. However the following day Col Houghton Brown inspected the positions that had been taken:

> I then went forward with my party, on to 'Camel'. When I got there I was even more amazed than ever to see the features we had captured the day before. The sides of the hill were so steep that it was almost impossible to walk up them unaided. How our chaps had stormed these strongholds, with Japs waiting for them on the top, was really miraculous.
>
> I looked round towards 'Hump'. The feature was now quite bare as all the jungle had been blown off it. At that moment the enemy started shelling and the shells came screaming through the air landing plump on to the middle of the hill. I feared greatly for Chris and his young leaders. I knew they had just arrived there and could hardly have had time to get into trenches before the bombardment started.
>
> After fifteen minutes it suddenly ceased. I moved across to see what the damage was. On 'Hump' I met Tom Dutton. He was as calm and smiling as ever. Plastered in dirt from head to foot, he looked like some prehistoric warrior. I was sorry for any Jap who tried to attack Tom in his present mood. He showed me round his positions. They were so well dug-in that they had not suffered a single casualty from the recent shelling. Chris Green's party had also got away unhurt. It was a beautiful position to hold but intolerably hot for the troops. There was no cover available over the trenches. The sun scorched down as if determined to wither up every living thing.

The Wiltshires continued with the operations on Point 551 but after eight days Col Houghton Brown was himself severely wounded. His journey to Base hospital would have been typical of many others. He was first taken by stretcher to the nearest RAP, then by jeep to the Advance DS, then again by jeep to the Main DS in the Admin Box where, after a rest, an operation was performed to extract shrapnel from the wounds. The following day he was loaded onto an ambulance and driven over the Pass. It took three weeks before he eventually reached a Base hospital in Secunderabad in South Central India.

It was a long, uncomfortable and often agonizing journey, which was one of the least pleasant features of the Burma war, when compared with the European front. The casualty proceeded by stretcher-bearer, lorry, ambulance, boat, aircraft and train. The most comfortable were boat and aircraft and the most agonizing was the jolting over primitive roads.

There were five large hospitals at Secunderabad with some 7,000 beds. Another 'hospital town' was prepared at Jallahalli near Bangalore to cope with the wounded from the final attack on the Japanese.

Col Houghton Brown was afterwards awarded the Distinguished Service Order. The citation mentions his powers of leadership, his courage, his cheerfulness and his 'magnificent example to his men'.

* * *

The reason for not using the 25th Dragoons again on Pt 551 may have been the scheduled withdrawal of 'B' Squadron from the fighting area and a consequent change in the role of 'A' Squadron who remained. On the 16th April 'B' Squadron said goodbye to the Admin Box and crossed the Okeydoke, the last we should see of either, eventually reaching Bawli Bazaar. Col Frink also returned to Bawli for two days. Meanwhile our place in the Box was taken by 'A' Squadron, who moved in that afternoon with the LAD, one D8 tractor and a patrol of Scout Troop. Their role now seemed to be to work with whatever regiment was attacking or being attacked in the area north of the Maungdaw-Buthidaung road.

A lot of Japs might be dead but there were still plenty who would not lie down and they frequently infiltrated back on to the hills which we had decisively captured. This continued to fulfil the prophecy of Messervy in the cinema at Ranchi all those months earlier that the troops of the Japanese and allied armies would interpose between each other like the layers of a Neopolitan sandwich.

Both sides realized that Pt 551 was the last vital point in the area. The Japanese held on tenaciously for many days. On the 25th April reinforcements were brought in from 74 Brigade (25th Division) and the Frontier Force Regiment were able to take the three remaining peaks by storm. On the 27th they were thrown off two of the peaks. At the end of April the position was almost stalemate. On the night of the 3/4th May the Japanese launched an attack but by the evening of the 4th the allies had taken the whole position. The enemy later tried a counter-attack but were thrown back.

Thus XV Corps had secured its main objective before the onset of the monsoon – control of the Maungdaw-Buthidaung road. The value of this effort was not fully appreciated until the advance on Akyab was commenced at the end of the monsoon, when allied troops were able to push through with little resistance. This had been achieved whilst at the same time inflicting an ignominious defeat on a key Japanese attempt to invade India, then pulling out two experienced divisions and sending them to the Imphal front, where a major battle on a bigger scale was now being fought. Meanwhile 'A' Squadron started co-operation with 71 Brigade and on one occasion with 36 Brigade.

At 1pm on the 18th April a message reached the Admin Box that the Japanese had got into positions on Pt 121 in the 'Mont Blanc' area on the west side of the Kalapanzin. The 5/1st Punjab of 71 Brigade had attacked but had been unable to dislodge them. HQ and two troops of 'A' Squadron were ordered out to deal with the situation. An attack was laid on for 4pm with Capt Munro in charge. The Squadron was able to fire on the hill from two sides and at very short range. It took a considerable amount of hand-to-hand fighting by the infantry before they were eventually able to take the hill. Nevertheless they were able to do this with few casualties to themselves but with a toll to the enemy of fifty-one dead counted on the objective afterwards. The tanks also started fires in Japanese positions east of the river and as the enemy had occupied Sinobyin village, the same was done to that. These villages concealed and fed the Japanese. The tanks did not suffer any casualties and were back in harbour by 6.30pm.

On 22nd April Regimental HQ withdrew to Bawli so there now remained at the Box, 'A' Squadron, one section of Recce Troop, one section of the Bridging Troop, the Medical Officer, and one platoon of 3/4th Bombay Grenadiers, with various staff elements on the technical and recovery sides.

The enemy continued to cause trouble in the area of Mont Blanc and Pt 121 and on the 24th April an attack was planned for late in the day. This was to be with the 8/13th Frontier Force Regt (36 Brigade) on the centre of Mont Blanc, Hammer Head and the south tip of Pt 121.

Zero hour was 1700. 'A' Squadron was in support of two companies of 8/13th FFR. One troop attacked from the north onto the Hammer Head – Mont Blanc features, two troops from the south, whilst the remaining troop attacked Pt 121 from the south. The infantry axis of advance was west-east. The Squadron was heavily shelled and mortared from Bulge, Kyaukit and Pt 162. Some 30-40 AP and double that number 75mm and mortar HE were fired on them but no tank sustained a direct hit. Squadron HQ attempted to neutralize Bulge and Kyaukit, as also Sinobyin which was still causing trouble. The infantry were successful in taking Pt 121 and the centre of Mont Blanc, where they counted sixty enemy dead and saw many more to the east, presumably on Hammer Head. They claimed to have raided Hammer Head but according to 25 Division they did not get nearer than 200 yards. However, enemy were observed on all the features attacked. A sampan on the Kalapanzin river was sunk. The action was broken off at 6.55pm by which time the infantry had withdrawn to their former positions as planned.

During these operations as on others, Vengeance dive-bombers gave support. Their accuracy was so good that the tanks were prepared to be within close range of the targets i.e. 200 yards. However the infantry were not so keen because the bombers' tail-gunners were inclined to fire back at the targets after bombing! Also during these and other operations, including the Point 551 attack, 'A' Squadron asked that two Hurricanes patrol the battle area to keep the Japanese artillery quiet, particularly the 155mm guns. The dust raised by the tanks produced targets for the long-range Japanese artillery and the presence of the Hurricanes normally silenced these guns when they circled the area. They were christened 'George' and 'Margaret' by the tank crews of 'A' Squadron.

Several RAF and USAAF pilots visited the tanks during these operations and saw the effect of their flying and bombing.

On the following day 26 Division HQ suggested further attacks in the same area but information of the enemy's activities was scanty. At a conference with 36 Brigade it was decided not to use tanks until patrol and mine-sweeping reports were complete. Nothing further of note seems to have happened until the 3rd May when it was reported that during the previous night the enemy had attacked Pt 121 in strength and succeeded in capturing it from the 8/13th FFR. A conference was held at 36 Brigade and an attack planned for that afternoon, zero hour 1600. The Squadron was to support D Company of the FFR with the infantry axis of advance north to south. All-round fire support was given with one troop in close support over the open padi. As the expected artillery support did not materialize (owing to a misunderstanding over timing), the Squadron doubled its rate of fire.

The infantry attack was successful on the east and west ends of Pt 121. Fourteen enemy were killed by the infantry in hand-to-hand fighting and twenty-six recently-killed bodies were found on top of the hill. The tanks killed fifteen enemy in the open. They had come under heavy mortar fire whilst attacking the hill but suffered no damage. At 4.45pm the infantry was observed on top of the hill and the tanks ceased operations. At 7pm the infantry, having achieved its objective, withdrew to former positions as planned without further incident.

During their return to the Admin Box 'A' Squadron came under some very accurate fire from a 75mm gun firing over open sights. Another 75mm, thought to be firing from the Bulge area, engaged the tanks at the east end of Wet Valley. In all, three tanks were slightly damaged but all were repairable by second line within 48 hours. There were no casualties amongst the crews.

During the afternoon of the following day a message was received at the Admin Box that a party of about 600 Japs had infiltrated to a position about 11 miles north-east of the Box. The defence was tightened but nothing further occurred or was reported, nor was the report ever confirmed by patrols.

The next morning an SOS was received from 71 Brigade at 9am. During the night the Japs had apparently put in a general attack over the entire brigade front. They had infiltrated in two strong parties, one on 'Jags' above Brigade HQ and the other in the centre of 'Astride' (on the Buthidaung road) held by the Lincolns. The enemy was rolling grenades down the hill into the HQ! Brigadier Cotterell-Hill considered that, as the Lincolns and the Garwhalis were both out of touch and cut off, the Squadron would be best employed going to their assistance and that HQ itself and the 5/1st Punjab on 'Jags' should deal with the situation there.

Accordingly the squadron leader with Lt Rothery and one other tank proceeded to 'Astride' and were able to clear the enemy out of the defile. With one platoon of the Lincolns they cleared a hill in enemy hands inside the Lincoln's perimeter. Meanwhile other Lincoln positions were being heavily attacked and Lt Spooner had brought up the rest of the Squadron. He took two tanks of No 4 Troop and went down to the Garwhalis HQ and brought back Lt Farquarson for a conference. At the same time Lt Durie with his troop and Lt Walker went to the Boomerang area and covered the withdrawal of 'B' Company of the Lincolns back to 'Astride'. This exercise caught the Japanese by surprise out in the open and many were shot walking about near the road or digging-in on the hills. 'B' Company received only one casualty during this withdrawal. Lt Spooner located a 75mm gun going into action in the open and his crew shot-up the gun crew at 30 yards range and then ran down the gun.

Lt Col Sinclair of the Lincolns decided that the Garwhalis should withdraw to the area of 'Astride' Box. 'A' Squadron went to cover this by attempting to neutralize the heavy automatic and rifle fire coming from the hills between the Garwhalis and Astride. Several small parties of Japs were caught in the open. They were probably trying to evacuate their dead and wounded. Those on the hills were not properly dug-in and many casualties were inflicted. The Garwhalis reported 150 Japs on the forward edge of Command Post Hill and the Squadron were able to kill about 60 of these. The last of the Garwhalis gained 'Astride' Box by 6pm. The Squadron picked up the Garwhali wounded and our 'Doc' Gaunt spent the night on 'Astride' helping the infantry wounded.

The tanks withdrew from the action at 6.30pm. During nine hours of action they had been shelled continuously by 150mm and 75mm guns and mortars. Only Sqn Sergt-Major Haddon's tank received a direct hit. It caught fire and was completely burnt out but the crew were able to escape and join other tanks. Trooper Alford was wounded slightly by a shell splinter. During the return to the Admin Box the Squadron came across a battery of 160 Jungle Field Regiment which was pulling out its guns and coming under heavy small arms and mortar fire from the south of Pt 162. Lts Rothery and Ransome remained with the battery and gave them covering fire, although it was nearly dark. Lt Ransome's tank had a track blown off but was towed out by Rothery's tank to the north of Tatmin Chaung where the D8 took over. Both these tanks arrived in harbour just before midnight.

This was a substantial battle, involving all three regiments of 71 Brigade as well as artillery and a squadron of tanks. The Japanese, no doubt, considered they had achieved their object of holding 71 Brigade down on this front but at a far higher cost in casualties than ourselves. It was reported that all the Japanese soldiers were wearing good new clothing with large packs and a lot of rice. This certainly suggested that reinforcements had been brought into the area.

The following day 71 Brigade was to withdraw from its existing line on the Buthidaung road to a line running roughly from west to east through the north of 'Abel'. Brig Cotterell-Hill decided to withdraw in daylight with tank support rather than by moonlight without. 'A' Squadron surrounded Astride, Udder, East and West Fingers and the south-west corner of Pt 162 at 4.45pm and immediately came under regular automatic fire from all these features. These guns were neutralized by 5pm except one on the south of Rabbit. The exact position of this gun could not be pinpointed and it fired spasmodically throughout the withdrawal, which took place according to plan. An exceptionally heavy artillery concentration of 150mm, 75mm and mortar was brought down by the enemy between 4.45 and 6pm. Most of this concentration was in the area of the tanks and did not delay the infantry, which completed withdrawal by 6.05pm. The only enemy actually seen by the tank crews were two Japs and a light machine-gun on the south tip of Udder, both of whom were killed. The Squadron was back in harbour by 7.20pm.

Col Frink said that both the division and brigade commanders were of the opinion that the Squadron alone made the withdrawal possible and saved the infantry very heavy casualties. It was a very fine last performance for the regiment by 'A' Squadron under their leader 'Jock' Munro.

No medical arrangements had been made by the infantry and their casualties were taken by the tanks to Tatmin Chaung where

Capt Gaunt evacuated them direct from his Aid Post to the main dressing station.

This was the last engagement our tanks were to have with the Japanese in this area. The fact that, despite a great deal of shelling from 150mm and 75mm guns, the Japanese seldom scored direct hits seems to bear out the opinion of Brig (later Gen) Evans and others that their army, at any rate, were 'bad shots'.

On the night of the 10/11th May twelve tanks of 'A' Squadron and one bridging-tank left the Admin Box, crossed the Pass and harboured south of Bawli bridge. They loaded onto the *Folkestone* at 9am, sailed at once and were able to off-load at Tumbru on the same tide, from where they proceeded to Reju Khal. On the night of 12/13th May the remaining four tanks of 'A' Squadron, with the D8 tractor and remaining bridging-tank, followed suit and also proceeded to Reju Khal. The whole regiment had now been successfully withdrawn across the Pass but in fact the monsoon came exceptionally late that year. After a number of heavy storms it did not finally break until 15th June.

12
The Way Back

For sometime Col Frink had been exercised in his mind as to how the tanks were to be got back to India. The difficulty was to find sea transport. All the LSTs had returned to Italy to be used in the Allied beach landing at Anzio and the smaller craft could not stand up to the swell.

It was some ten months ago that Gen Slim had ordered Col Atte Persse of the Indian Armoured Corps to get 25th Dragoons into Arakan but it was not so easy to get them out. Slim said:

> I knew Persse and his qualities well, having had him in command of a cavalry regiment under me. He lived up to his reputation for drive, pertinacity and ingenuity . . . and for making himself a nuisance to all and sundry until he got what he wanted.

This might account for his lack of popularity at lower levels. However he had gone back to South East Asia Command at Delhi and was battling with the Royal Navy to get the tanks out. Col Frink was definite that the tanks would not stand another campaign without refits, and 'it would appear to be an unforgivable waste to leave them here to rot, when training material is always wanted in India.' 25th Dragoons were only too aware of the colonel's meaning in the last sentence.

Col Frink said of Persse: 'He has been a very good friend of the regiment and put in an endless amount of work to help us along.'

By 29th April it looked pretty definite that the tanks would not be moved out of Arakan before the monsoon, due to lack of shipping and the inability of small craft to take the tanks from Cox's Bazaar to Chittagong for trans-shipment. Col Frink hoped he would be able to get the personnel back to India to refit and train, whilst a maintenance group looked after the old tanks, which certainly would not be fit for action unless fitted with new engines and suspensions. In the meantime he was hoping to start sending off leave parties from the 1st May.

On the night of the 8/9th April 'C' Squadron had moved back to Bawli Bazaar, where also was Corps HQ. On the 16th 'B' Squadron did the same. From here it was planned to move over the Naf River and back to our original harbour at Reju Khal. Accordingly on 18th April a large part of 'C' Squadron loaded on to the *Folkestone* which had been 'improved' – one of the centre pillars had been moved one foot forward. This gave the tanks more room to manoeuvre and quickened the loading. They arrived that evening and harboured in Debenia, proceeding to Reju Khal the next day. They were followed by B Echelon and later by the remainder of the Squadron plus 'B' Squadron and its echelon.

On the 21st April RHQ received the 'Armed Forces Maintenance Group Outline Extraction Plan for formations moving to India', i.e. how to get out of Burma.

In the meantime a new harbour had been found on the coast two miles south of Cox's Bazaar. The whole of 'B' and 'C' Squadrons made their way there, which involved crossing the Reju Khal River on a raft, which had some teething troubles. After arrival I wrote the following letter. The four words of the postscript were intended to make it clear that we were now out of the operational area and did not expect to return, at any rate not in the immediate future.

(Airmail) 21st April 1944

Since I last wrote, we have moved camp and are now very near the sea. I generally go in for a dip before breakfast besides going later in the day. The water is, of course, very warm and the waves are quite big, rather like Cornwall, only we haven't got any surf boards . . .

You may have seen some pictures of the fighting in Burma on the news-reels as there have been several cameramen in our area. I believe on one occasion one of them went into action inside a tank and took shots through the driver's vision port. Another time an Australian correspondent took a photograph of our crew sitting on the front of the tank. He said it would be published in a book he was writing on his travels in India.

Hoping you are keeping well and cheerful.

PS. Don't worry any more.

To meet 'the requirements of the 25th Indian Division', Col Frink formed a special troop made up of the following:

Troop Commander: Lt Arthur, who had recently joined the regiment from TDT (Tank Delivery Troop)
Troop Sergeant: Sergt Ernie Moore of 'B' Squadron
16 members of TDT and 9 of 'B' Squadron
2 tanks of 'B' Squadron, 1 of TDT and 2 3-ton lorries of 'B' Squadron.

On 30th April orders from Corps HQ required this special troop to move to Wabyin and harbour the night with 'C' Squadron of 149 Regiment RAC. Wabyin was near the junction of the road going south to Maungdaw with that going east to the Okeydoke Pass.

The following day they moved to the Maungdaw area with 149 Regiment, where they came under the command of 74 Brigade (25th Division) and were attached to the 6th Oxford and Bucks Light Infantry for all purposes. Ammunition and fuel had been previously dumped in the area with 74 Brigade.

On the night of the 5/6th May the troop left harbour for the purpose of supporting the infantry onto enemy positions in three villages with fairly impossible names. Mines and unprepared chaungs prevented the tanks penetrating far south. One tank was bogged crossing a chaung and was fired on by an enemy 75mm. The infantry carried out a 'recce' on this gun and the tanks shot it up. No further infantry were available and it was decided in all the circumstances to postpone the action. The tank was eventually recovered from the chaung. Whilst on the way back, the troop came under enemy mortar fire but suffered no casualties. They reached their harbour in the Maungdaw area by 7.10pm.

Nothing more is recorded of this action nor indeed of any other actions in which the troop may have been involved. Presumably 25 Division were having trouble clearing the Japanese out of the coastal area south of Razabil and Maungdaw. Col Frink says they were really there in case of emergency.

(Airmail) 1st May 1944

My Dear Auntie Gwen,

I have received your air letter-card of the 3rd April . . . for all of which thank you very much . . .

Yes, there are a good many ways of guarding against malaria now but none of them are absolutely infallible. However, they do make a difference to the average figures for people going down with malaria. So far I have escaped it. We sleep under mosquito nets, long sleeves and trousers after 6 o'clock in the evening, applying anti-mosquito cream to the exposed parts of the body, and take mepacrine tablets 6 days a week. I told Mother all about the latter in a sea-mail letter which you may have read.

News is by no means the only thing we can get on the wireless but BBC Overseas Service does not always come over too well. Mostly we rely on the broadcasting stations from Delhi and Calcutta. Delhi always relays the London News at 9.30pm followed generally by some good music. There is always an English programme from 12.30 to 1.45 with news. Apart from this the Delhi service broadcasts Indian programmes with Indian music, which I have not yet succeeded in understanding! You have to remember that we are something like 6½ hours ahead of you in time . . .

On the evening of the 3rd May Col Frink got orders to report to GHQ at Delhi on the 5th. This could just be done if he caught the plane from Comilla (Army HQ) next morning and reached Calcutta that night, taking a plane on to Delhi next day. Things however did not work out quite like that.

There was a plane called an 'Anson' which was used to drop batches of *SEAC* newspaper for all the troops in the area. Col Frink arranged to catch this 'SEAC Anson' at Ramkaphalong air strip near Cox's Bazaar at 1130 hours. The Anson then had to drop papers off at Bawli and Maungdaw before flying to Comilla. Col Frink tells what happened in his own words:

Being in very close proximity to the Japanese and the Anson being mostly composed of glass roof and sides the pilot quite rightly did all the forward part of the trip at zero feet. On returning north along the coast via Cox's I expected at any rate a slight rise in altitude. This was not forthcoming and halfway between Chittagong and Fenny we hit the sea an almighty welt with our props, doing about 150 mph. The result was a foregone conclusion. We did ducks and drakes for a few hundred yards before settling down in a lot of black mud below the high-water mark. How we got away with it without completely breaking up is just a miracle. This meant a 4-mile walk through mud on a boiling afternoon, spending a night at Chittagong and missing the Calcutta plane. Eventually I reached Delhi on the 7th May.

After two days' work I returned by air. The return trip was not quite uneventful. Flying back by night from Delhi one of the engines packed up and we had to land at Agra. On arriving back at the regiment, I found a message telling me to report at once to XIV Army HQ at Comilla!

(Airmail) 7th May 1944

We are still near the sea and I am enjoying the bathing very much. There is a river flowing into the sea close by so one can always have a fresh water bathe after going in the sea.

I have been playing some chess lately. Tonight I am playing in a competition against another squadron, not so much because I am all that good as that they had to make up a team of five men.

On the 11th May an area was selected on which to set up a monsoon tank park. As it was unlikely that the tanks would be taken out of Burma before the monsoon broke, it was necessary to get them to a place where they would not just sink into the mud. The area selected was on the road between Ramkaphalong and Cox's Bazaar, about one mile off the main Arakan road. For this purpose the whole regiment was to be concentrated at Reju Khal.

'A' Squadron arrived at Reju Khal that same day and 'B' Squadron moved there from Cox's Bazaar, crossing the river by barge. We were all in our old harbour by 4.15pm. The following day 'C' Squadron and RHQ with B Echelon followed us.

From the 16th to the 18th May all tanks were driven to the new tank park, where each squadron had to construct standings for its own tanks. These consisted of two layers of bullies laid at right angles to each other.

On the 13th May I received a letter from James Jefferies, a friend whom I had got to know on the troop-ship coming out to India. He was a solicitor and a few years older than me. He had gone to the 3rd Carabiniers, in effect the 'sister' or perhaps 'parent' regiment of the 25th Dragoons. The Carabiniers had the same type of tanks as ourselves and were now on the central Burma front, that is, the area of the Imphal-Kohima battles. Being in 'B' Squadron he may have taken part in the capture of Nunshigum Ridge on 13th April, a feat which is commemorated to this day every year. I would not have known this at the time and he says nothing of it in his letter:

'B' Squadron, 3rd Carabiniers,
22nd April 1944 S.E. Asia

Dear Tom,

I have intended writing to some of you in the 25th for a long time. I have scarcely been able to raise the energy to write home but the climate up here – you know of course where we are – seems to be reviving my energies.

[He goes on to speak of various mutual acquaintances and what had happened to them and continues] . . . Do you remember John Hague? He is 37mm gunner in 'A' Squadron Leader's tank and distinguished himself when a 40mm Jap shot stuck half-way through the turret by his head, by changing the periscope and knocking out two tankettes with two shots. Both were caught by surprise – the range was from 10–30 yards!

I have spoken to a number of men who were in the Arakan; they all are full of praise for the 25th. We had a certain amount of information about your doings but no details. I have wondered whether there were any casualties among my friends. I trust not.

When I get the chance I propose going on leave to Darjeeling. I shall no doubt have a chance of seeing Calcutta later. By report the chief attractions of Calcutta are brothels and booze: neither interest me.

We seem to be spoiling the Jap's fun and games up here; he does not appear to be invincible, in fact he is nothing like as good as his reputation.

Give my best wishes to Keith Fox, Jim Tiley and the rest. I hope to write to Les Hanman soon.

Yours sincerely,
James L.I. Jefferies

(Airmail Letter Card) 16th May 1944

My last AML was written to you on the 7th May. Since then I have received yours of the 24th April and 1st May, for which many thanks. Thanks for taking so much trouble over the clothes. You can't imagine how I'm looking forward to wearing them again. I have also received the March Law Notes and 'Hoddesdon Journal'.

. . . I have not been writing much lately because we have no light at night. We have been working during the day and after getting back we just about have time to get a wash all over, wash a vest and pair of socks or something, have a meal, make the bed down, and then it is dark. Today, I have some spare time. Hence this letter.

However we have managed to fill up the evenings. The other night there was a debate on the motion: 'That this house considers that the British people have done their best for India.' Two members of this Squadron proposed the motion and two of 'C' Squadron opposed it. The Padre was chairman. There was quite a good attendance and the debating went very well. Lots of people spoke from the house. The voting at the end showed 8 people for the motion and 26 against. The motion as it stood was rather difficult for the proposers. Many people are of the opinion that the

British have done plenty of good for India but have not done their *best*. Had the motion been: 'That the British have justified their rule in India', the voting might have been more equal. However, I was glad there was a clear majority against the motion because it was clearly untrue as it stood. Tonight there is a film show at an RAF camp nearby, to which I hope to go. The film is 'The Case of the Frightened Lady' by Edgar Wallace.

I do appreciate SEAC newspaper. It reaches us very quickly now. I imagine it is distributed by air daily.

All my love

As for the debate, I remember a senior Indian NCO, who could speak English with confidence, standing up and saying that the Indian's idea of the average British soldier had him with a bottle in one hand and woman in the other. It caused a laugh but everyone knew it was pretty well the truth. I do not remember the Edgar Wallace film, if in fact I went to it. It would have been shown on a screen erected in the open.

By the 19th May all standings for the tanks were complete and one man per tank was left with TDT to complete the final maintenance, assisted by daily fatigue parties from the squadrons. The tanks were eventually handed over to the officer commanding TDT – and that was that. One source said they passed to the Chinese army.

The Arakan monsoon dispositions had been taken up without incident and it now remained to hold the firm bases of Maungdaw and Bawli during the rains as jumping off places for any operations that might be decided on for the next dry season in this area.

Col Frink received a number of letters of congratulation on the Regiment's performance during the campaign. Amongst others these came from the Army, Corps and Division Commanders and the Armoured Fighting Vehicle (AFV) Directorate at GHQ. The latter was as follows:

D.O. No DR1/AFV.1
General Headquarters
General Staff, India
New Delhi
5th April 1944

Dear Frinkie,

We should like to congratulate you and all ranks of the Regiment for the splendid work you have done and on the recent awards.

Your experiences which represent the first material results of three years of labour and frustration give us particular satisfaction.

I have taken on myself, as one of the oldest members of the Directorate, to write this small appreciation of your efforts but I know that the others feel the same.

We hope that you will continue the good work and will continue to call on us to assist in any way we can.

Yours
Donald Ross

Lt Col H.R.C. Frink DSO
Commanding 25th Dragoons

Col Frink also received the following letter from Major General C.E.N. Lomax commanding the 26th Indian Division, which members of 'A' Squadron will be particularly interested to read:

Headquarters 26th Indian Division
c/o ABPO 18
9 May 1944

My Dear Frink

I am writing to tell you personally how very much all ranks of my division appreciate the support we have consistently received from your Regiment.

You have done us magnificently on all and every occasion and the faith and confidence which our men have in yours is unlimited.

I should be very grateful if you would pass on our gratitude, our thanks and our hopes that we may hunt together again in future seasons.

Munro has been splendid and a bond has been established between 'A' Squadron and 71 Brigade.

I have had the pleasure of meeting this Squadron today. I am very grateful to you personally for your never-failing help and readiness to come into a party with us – hope we have many more!

All good fortune to you and your Regiment.

Yours very sincerely,

Cyril Lomax.

Col Frink summed up the fighting as follows:

> It has not been a satisfactory campaign from the soldiers' point of view. They have fought hard under difficult conditions, made a few miles and killed quite a number of the enemy but now we have had to pull back from most of the forward areas we have won. The reason, of course, is that the monsoon floods make it impossible to maintain troops off the main L of C, but it is bound to have rather a disheartening effect. If the Akyab landing had been able to take place, the situation would have been different. The shipping had to be used at Anzio which naturally had priority.
>
> The job we were given to do, which was to kill Japs, we have done to the best of our ability and, from what higher authority say, satisfactorily.

This is a sober view of the fighting itself by a man not given to hyperbole or exaggeration and probably reflected the feeling throughout the Regiment. Seen in the wider context of the reconquest of Burma, the campaign was an unqualified success and a turning point in the Burma war. As such it raised morale all round, blocked the invasion of India on this front and, by freeing 5th and 7th Divisions, underpinned resistance to the Japanese thrust at Imphal on the central front.

Due to the heavy rains that were now coming on, Corps HQ decided that our camp at Reju Khal was no longer tenable because of the bad access road. The proposal was to move to a place somewhat misnamed 'Happy Valley'. On the 31st May the Regimental Quartermaster with representatives of the squadrons visited the site. There were 'bashas' for sleeping in, made mainly from dried leaves and guaranteed to let the water in. Some of these were still occupied but it was decided to move the next day. This we did.

On the same day Lt Col Frink DSO was called to XVth Corps HQ and told that he was being promoted to command 252 Indian Tank Brigade in the Middle East. He was told to fly to Delhi on 3rd June. On that day Lt Col R.D. Hearder assumed command of the Regiment.

A cavalry officer of the past, Brigadier Frink had become a popular and respected commanding officer. We assumed that his promotion was by reason of his leadership of the Regiment throughout the 'Battle of the Box' and in the battles that followed. He had taken up command of the Regiment in 1941, soon after its formation, and had seen it through a lengthy period of training and non-training and change of personnel. To quote from *SEAC* newspaper: 'In their CO the men see the true blend that goes to make up the leader. About him there is none of the stiffness associated with the regular officer, especially the cavalryman. The men feel in him that confidence which is fundamental to good morale.' He was a great regimental officer who thought of his men on all occasions whatever else he might have to think of during this time.

At first sight it seems odd that, after conducting a very successful campaign in the Burmese jungle, he was sent to command in the Middle East, where jungle was hard to find and war was retreating. The fact was that he was now approaching 45 years of age and GHQ were taking the view that this was too old for this theatre of war. In addition GHQ may well have known by now that the Regiment was to train on amphibious tanks in order to take part in the projected landing on the Malay coast, as soon as Burma was reconquered, and wanted a younger man for this task. At any rate we were sorry to see him go and were lucky to have had him when we did. His name will always be identified with the 25th Dragoons and with their achievement at a crucial point in history.

★ ★ ★

(Airmail letter) 2nd June 1944

Thank you for your AML of 15th May and sea-mail of the 23rd March with the socks. I shall be very glad of the latter. Many thanks for taking the trouble to make them.

In a letter to Auntie Lillian I mentioned repatriation and what I said may have sounded depressing. The facts are these. At present the maximum period of overseas service is 5 years. Before the end of this year it is almost certain that this will be reduced to 4 years. I have been out here 2 years and 4 months. The idea that I may be out here for another 1½ years may not be very cheering but at least it sets a positive limit on the time I may have to remain here. There is always the possibility I may be home before then . . .

On the 4th June the special troop under Lt Arthur at last returned from Maungdaw. They reached the tank park the following day despite heavy rain.

A news item about the 25th Dragoons by Tom Willcox appeared in *SEAC* newspaper giving the names of a 'sample crew' without saying the squadron to which they belonged. It is reproduced here as a matter of interest:

Tank Commander: Sergeant R.W. Crawley, aged 31, of Carter Drive, Romford, Essex, Warehouseman with a transport company.
75mm Gunner: Tpr Jack Eves, aged 38 of Birch St, Manchester 12.
75mm Loader: Tpr H. Parnell of 30 Pole St, Bolton, Lancs.
Wireless Operator: Tpr G. Broadbent, 35 Sunny Bank, Churwell, Leeds.
Driver: L/Cpl S. Alford, of 6/7 The Warren, Croydon.
37mm Gunner: Tpr E. Fairchild, aged 22, of Park St, Peterborough.
37mm Loader: Tpr J. Gibbons of 24 Mills St, Willington, Co Durham.

The addresses show how members of the Regiment came from all parts of the British Isles. Ages varied from 19 to 38 years or thereabouts. This crew was in fact No 1 Troop of 'A' Squadron. Sergeant Crawley was afterwards wounded near Buthidaung but was later able to re-join the regiment.

What of the regimental mascot? Our elephant had remained on the west side of the Mayu Range and did not go over the Pass. It was nevertheless named 'Ngakyedauk'. Eventually it died and three different causes of death have been given: (a) it died of heat stroke; (b) the proper food could not be obtained; and (c) it drank some petrol. I remember the latter being passed round the Squadron at the time. It may be that the true cause was never known and the above statements were attempts to explain the death.

(Airmail letter) 3rd June 1944

My Dear Auntie Gwen,

I have suddenly remembered that your birthday occurs very shortly. I hope this reaches you in time. Many, many happy returns of the day. I was very happy to receive your letter of the 18th May and the magazines. I have also had Auntie Lillian's letter of the 14th May . . .

We too are all waiting for the invasion and shall watch events closely when it begins. We know that the sooner Germany is defeated, the sooner will we out here get the full resources of the United Nations to drive the Japs back to Japan. In fact the sooner the war is over, the sooner I shall be home again to see you all. You say you wish it had not to take place. So do I. I wish the war had not to take place but we can't turn round now and leave it to somebody else to finish off. I do not think Germany will surrender to the tremendous bombing offensive. Only when Britons and Russians meet at Berlin will Germany be defeated. The sooner the invasion starts, the sooner will the war be over. There has been a lot of talk and publicity but still nothing happens. My own opinion is that it will be timed to take place with the opening of the Russian summer offen-sive. Let's hope Monty will be well on his way to Berlin by the time you get this.

There is really nothing else to write about as we are doing nothing of any interest at the moment. Very best wishes again and all my love.

(Airmail letter) 4th June 1944

My Dear Mother and Dad,

Many thanks for your AML of the 20th May. I'm glad to hear you read 'Picture Post' every week. Some members of my crew used to have them sent out fairly regularly so I used to see them quite a bit.

You ask about the friends I used to mention. They are mostly still with the Regiment and I see them quite often. John (Bradberry) is still with me in 'B' Squadron in the same troop. Cliff (Reeves), Jim (Tiley) and Gordon Maxwell are still in 'A' Squadron. Keith (Fox) works in the orderly room now. I'm glad of this because he's over 40 but he has always kept himself very fit. When in February our base was attacked by Jifs and only non-combatant staff were there to defend it, he was foremost in volunteering to join parties to try and retrieve kit in areas still occupied by small enemy parties.

Martin Brown left the Regiment a year ago to join the AEC. You remember he was a schoolmaster. Gerry Chance recovered from his illness, tho' it had left his stomach very weak. He also went to the AEC (another schoolmaster). (AEC = Army Education Corps.)

I have found it impossible to keep in touch with all my friends who have left the Regiment and everyone at home. I believe I mentioned Gordon Barnes once. He was in our troop and his tank was hit. He was badly burnt and died the next day – during the Ngakyedauk fighting.

The CO, Lt Col Frink DSO, has left us. I think most people regret this and I am one of them. I think we shall be lucky to find another as good.

The day after this letter was written news of the fall of Rome came through. According to Churchill the 88th British Division entered the Piazza Venezia in the heart of the city at precisely 7.15pm on the 4th June. In the absence of any Italian government Rome had been in the hands of the Germans since the previous year. On the 22nd January 1944 Allied troops had landed at Anzio some 60 miles to the south of Rome but it had taken over four months to fight through to the 'Open City'.

This news was almost immediately overshadowed by another event. At dawn on the 6th June the Allies landed on the north coast of France – D Day – an event which at last put the end of the war into focus. It was a nice coincidence that I had written about this to Auntie Gwennie at such length only three days before. Churchill later called it 'the supreme climax of the war' for the Western Powers. He wrote:

> Africa was cleared. India had been defended from invasion. Japan, over-strained and disillusioned, was recoiling on her homeland. All danger to New Zealand and Australia had passed away. Italy was fighting on our side. The Russian armies had driven the German invaders from their country . . . The Crimea had been cleared. The Polish frontiers had been reached. Roumania and Bulgaria were desperately seeking to escape the vengeance of their eastern conquerors. Russia's new offensive, timed with our continental landing, was about to break . . .
>
> Here we might pause in thankfulness and take hope, not only for victory on all fronts, but also for a safe and happy future for tormented mankind.

(Churchill: *Closing the Ring*
The Second World War, Vol 5)

(Airmail) 11th June 1944

My last AML was dated 4th June. Many thanks for the 'Hoddesdon Journal' and 'Herts Mercury' just received. What tremendous things have happened in the last few days! First Rome falls and now a Western European Front in earnest. This is great news and makes one feel optimistic, tho' I think the Germans will offer very tough resistance for some time to come. When the Russian offensive opens (and it may have already started) 'Gerry' will certainly have his hands full.

Rome's capture, besides its military significance, will clear the air in Italian politics. Victor Emmanuel (the King) has gone and the government of Marshal Badaglio has resigned. If a government representative of all the parties at the Bari Conference can be formed, they should be able to organize the Italian people beind the war effort . . .

(Airmail) 14th June 1944

Thank you very much for your AML of 29th May and for 'Everybody's', 'Illustrated' and the 'Musical Times'. When you talk about a heat-wave, meals in the garden, flowers, church on Sunday mornings, it brings back memories. I hope they will be realities for me in the not-too-distant future.

I don't expect Stephen G liked being transferred to the infantry. I'm sorry for him having to go abroad at this time but someone will have to take the place of those who have been overseas for 3 and 4 years.

You have probably been wondering why most of my AMLs have been about general topics without any news of myself. The fact is we are doing nothing of much interest just now. I had a two-day gunnery course on a different type of tank and hope I shall get a two-day course on the engine shortly. It rains on and off most of the time. I'm sleeping in a 'basha' which is rapidly collapsing but has kept the rain out so far. We eat, sleep, read, write letters, do drill and PT. That's us!

I notice in the papers that the truth about China is gradually coming out. The 'Daily Mail' says that China is far from being united and that Chiang-Kai-Shek has 500,000 of his troops watching the 'Red' regions in the North. Madame Sun-Yat-Sen says that the border regions in the North are being blockaded and no equipment is allowed to reach the armies there. Another source accuses China's rulers of withdrawing their troops before greatly inferior Jap forces in the recent fighting in Honan and deliberately preventing the armies of the North (under Mao-Tse-Tung) from taking part in the major battles. It looks as though Chiang-Kai-Shek would rather have the Japs in the country than get them out and face the possibility of a socialist revolution after the war . . .

I hope to go on leave shortly tho' it's not definitely fixed yet. All my love.

As the above letter says, the rain was beginning to get incessant and about this time the monsoon can be said to have set in for good. We were not sorry to be out of the jungle and could have only the greatest admiration and sympathy for those who had to hang on and see it out.

(Airmail letter) 18th June 1944

Many thanks for your AML of 4th June.

We have been told on the wireless, and it has been published in 'SEAC', that if we want to vote at the next general election we must fill up a certain form. If we have not got it, we have to ask for it. None seem to have reached the Regiment. Neither squadron office nor the orderly room know anything about them. The answer seems to be 'This is India and they have not come out yet.'

We have no lights at night so, if it is not raining, I sometimes go and listen to the wireless. On the whole I think the new General Forces programme is not too bad. There's plenty of it that does not appeal to me but I expect that. Some of the talks are rather tame and pointless but occasionally there are good ones.

Last night there was a talk about Italian patriots and revolutionaries and how from Garibaldi onwards they had always come from the North. I was reminded that it was the strikes and riots in Milan which brought Mussolini down.

Sir James Grigg (War Minister) announced the other day that the period of overseas service was 4 years. This might be reduced if operational conditions permitted. The period for the RAF is 4 years for single men and 3 years for married. The American soldier does only 2 years abroad. I think 4 years is the reasonable period. Grigg is not very popular over repatriation, over 'V' cigarettes (what *were* they made of?), and over his ban on ABCA's (Army Bureau of Current Affairs) pamphlet on the Beveridge Report . . . I don't smoke yet but by all accounts 'V' cigarettes are not worth the name . . . All my love.

During this period, now that we had disposed of the tanks, final preparations were being made to move back to India. Major Youens had taken the remaining vehicles to Chittagong and handed them over to the Ordnance depot. Capt Burton and party had taken all armament from the 37mm and 75mm guns to Chittagong for shipment to India. Capt Maclean left Chittagong with all the regimental baggage aboard His Majesty's Troop ship *Empire Rani*.

On the 20th June Corps HQ had said we would be going to Ranchi and the quartermaster, Capt Manners, and a small party set off for that place of evil memory. Within two days and in traditional Army style this had been changed to 'Near Poona', so a message was at once sent by cipher to the QM to change his destination. There are rather more than 800 miles between the two places!

Finally, the bulk of the Regiment moved by road through Cox's Bazaar to Chittagong and embarked at 10am on the 27th June on HMT *Varda*. At noon we sailed – destination Calcutta. Any remaining personnel left Chittagong by train on the 30th June.

With a new commanding officer and a draft of new men to replace the casualties, we were about to 'embark' on a new and unexpected course of training. Whatever the war might yet hold in store for us, this was the end of one particular phase. Now, we were all looking forward to *leave*.

Nonetheless, we remembered the friends and comrades left behind in the Arakan earth and the wounded who would never return to the Regiment. The experiences of the last six months were to become ineffaceable memories of a strange and beautiful country, a place of sudden death and bitter pain; of ruthless action and profligate killing; but it was, too, a time of courage and sacrifice; of friendship and loyalty; of sadness at the loss of friends; and despite all, of belief in the future. Perhaps above everything it was this unity of purpose and unity of spirit that made it an unforgettable moment in the lives of those who took part.

Postscript

'A' Squadron's expedition to Meiktila in April/June 1945

After coming out of Burma in the summer of 1944, the Regiment went to a camp near Poona (now Pune) from which everyone had leave. At the end of September we travelled across India to a port on the east coast, about 500 miles south of Calcutta, called Cocanada (now Kakinada) in Andhra Pradesh. We were to train with amphibious Duplex-Drive Sherman tanks with a view to taking part in the projected beach landings on the coast of Malaya. This continued into 1945.

Suddenly in the middle of April of that year 'A' Squadron was detached and sent into Central Burma. By this time the Allied forces had crossed Burma and were about to take Rangoon. What was left of the Japanese armies was attempting to escape into Siam (now Thailand) and French Indo-China (now Laos). The Squadron left Cocanada by train for Calcutta, not taking any tanks with them, under the command of Major Anderson. From there they took another train to Goalundo Ghat and then by paddle-steamer on the Brahmaputra to Chandpur. From here by train to Comilla and finally by air to Meiktila, a town some 80 miles south of Mandalay to the east of the Irrawaddy.

In the meantime, air reconnaissance had discovered that the Japanese had departed from Rangoon and on the 4th May the Allies entered the town and their main objective in Burma had been achieved. All that remained was to prevent the Japanese escaping from Burma and mop them up, a task sometimes easier said than done. Indeed this seems to have been the reason for calling 'A' Squadron into Burma.

However this triumphant news was swept off the front pages of British newspapers by the impending collapse of Germany. That country officially surrendered on 7th May and 8th May was declared by Churchill to be V E Day, Victory-in-Europe.

'A' Squadron arrived at Meiktila on 6th May, where they spent days watching the comings and goings of Dakotas. Tom Thompson was given a jeep and became a chauffeur for various officers. He was also given the job of transporting the Dakota crews to outlying villages to purchase Japanese memorabilia in exchange for American cigarettes.

They camped beside one of the lakes of Meiktila close to some pagodas which had been damaged by gunfire during the fighting to capture the city. They watched amazing and tremendous thunder storms, the beginning of the monsoon season. There was a Red Cross canteen where some white ladies were serving refreshments. The war had passed on elsewhere and there was a general air of peacefulness.

Meiktila had been the main administrative centre of the Japanese 15th and 33rd Armies. In this area were their chief supply bases, ammunition dumps, hospitals and depots. It was a transport junction with five or six airfields where road and rail routes converged. The battle for the capture of Meiktila had begun in late February. The Japanese defended it with grim determination and fierceness, so much so that, by the time the British had the whole town securely in their hands on the 5th March, the entire Japanese garrison had been annihilated. So important was the town to them that the Japanese commander immediately started operations to recapture it and especially its airfield. Yet another battle had to be fought before Meiktila was finally secured in Allied hands in the last week of March. This was General Slim's decisive stroke in the great battle for Central Burma. By the 29th April he had moved his headquarters to Meiktila.

It was whilst it was camped beside the lake that 'A' Squadron first heard the news of Germany's surrender. Geoff Anlezark remembers standing in a marquee, sheltering from the pouring rain, and listening to a crackling radio with a mug of tea to toast the victory. Eventually they were taken by truck to a tank park near the airfield. They walked round it, as round a second-hand car lot, looking for the best of a clapped-out collection of Sherman tanks that were on offer. However they were glad to have some friendly mobile homes again! When they switched on the wireless sets (those that worked) and tuned to All-India radio, all they could hear was the relay from London of pealing bells and cheering crowds celebrating Victory-in-Europe. Great news as it was, it somehow had an ironic feel for those about to go to war all over again.

The Squadron came under the orders of the 19th Division commanded by Major General T.W. (Pete) Rees, part of IV Corps. In particular they were to co-operate with the 64th Indian Infantry Brigade which consisted of the 2nd Battalion the Worcestershire Regiment, the 5th Battalion the 10th Baluch Regiment, and the 1st Battalion the 6th Gurkha Rifles.

All the tanks proceeded to a harbour some way outside the city. They were split into small groups that bore no relation to the original troups of the Squadron. One group under the command of Captain Munro went east in the direction of Kalaw and Thazi and this group included Geoff Anlezark and Jim Tiley. Two tanks were sent ahead as a reconnaissance unit to find a suitable route, as the Bailey Bridges over the chaungs along the route could not take the weight of the Sherman tanks. Eventually an order came through that they were not to cross these bridges but by that time many of them had been crossed.

Some of the banks of the chaungs were quite steep and the crossing required some low-gear driving close to the limit of the tank engines. Especially when climbing out of the chaung. Tow ropes joined together were helpful on such occasions. Eventually they were given a bulldozer to clear the chaungs in wooded areas. Stumps of trees proved hazardous as the tracks were frequently forced off the sprockets, particularly on sharp turns.

What they found difficult to understand were the numbers of smiling cheerful Indian soldiers marching in the opposite direction and waving to them as they covered them with dust. These troops soon disappeared and they had the road (and the nearby railway) to themselves.

That night they parked at the roadside and the following day the other tank returned to Meiktila. The guns and gun-sights were adjusted and the machine-gun fired. Geoff recalls that about this time he fell from the turret of the tank to the ground and Jim went down with a temperature and suspected malaria (which he had had before). At one point a staff officer appeared but could give no information.

Finally the rest of the tanks arrived and it appeared that they were to co-operate with the Worcesters and the Gurkhas in the capture of Kalaw in the hills. They were camped for several days during which they made contact with these regiments. Their camp was probably in the area of Nampandet at the foot of the hills beyond which was Kalaw. The plan was for the infantry to advance along the road to Kalaw and for the tanks to support them. This narrow road wound its way up through the jungle. In many places it was little more than a ledge cut into the hillside with sheer drops of hundreds of feet to the valley below. The surface was metalled and there were milestones along the way. They could not but remark on the expansiveness of the views and the luxuriance of the jungle foliage.

They travelled all day and eventually reached a natural lay-by, where it was decided to stay the night. The news was that several Japanese had been seen and killed nearby on the day before, so orders were given to park the tanks at the roadside under guard taking out the distributors and the machine-guns. The rain had been intermittent and they dried themselves by standing near the engine exhausts. The crews were to climb to the top of a nearby hill and dig-in for the night. 'Dig in' proved to be an optimistic assumption. The ground was rock-hard under a thin layer of grass and shale. With the tools they had, they could only manage a few inches. They mounted guard, prayed for dry weather, and got as much sleep as they could.

The next morning they continued. This part of the road was known as 'the Staircase'. They joined up with the Baluchi on 30th May, who had established themselves in the area of Milestone 43. The tanks' job was to keep any Japanese bunkers covered and under fire. On 31st May the Baluchi were able to occupy the remaining 'Staircase' positions of the Japanese without opposition. On 1st June the Baluchi and the Gurkhas joined up and 'Operation Staircase' was complete. The size and scope of the enemy's defences suggested that they had been sufficiently overawed by the encircling movements of the Baluchi and the Worcesters to abandon their positions, coupled perhaps with the presence of the tanks. By this time the Worcesters had a company at Wetpyuye near Milestone 50 and another near Milestone 53.

Two days' rest was taken while the sappers repaired the many broken bridges and culverts. The advance continued on 4th June, tanks and infantry moving forward together. At Milestone 57 the road entered a pine forest and moved upwards in a zigzag, where it was known as the 'Little Staircase'. Strong enemy opposition was expected but none was forthcoming and they reached Milestone 58 without incident. Kalaw was now 2 miles away. At this point the reader may wish to refer to the map.

It began to look as though the enemy was pulling out altogether. No such luck. At this moment some machine-guns on the ridge, on the opposite side of the valley to the road, opened up on the column, which was extremely exposed and without cover from that side. At the same time a company of the Worcesters was attacked by the enemy high on a ridge overlooking the road from the west. The advance was held up and the column on the road suffered casualties. At this point, says the Worcesters' account, the 25th Dragoons came swinging round the very narrow road and brought their guns to bear on the enemy positions. The machine-guns were soon silenced.

However it was considered unwise for the whole column to continue along the road. While 'B' Company of the Worcesters and the tanks remained on the road the remainder of the Battalion moved back half a mile beyond Milestone 58. Leaving their animals there, they ascended a track onto the ridge to the west of the road. This was followed through the pine forest, keeping parallel to the road. Thus there were now two columns advancing together, one with the tanks on the road and one on the ridge above.

Things proceeded without much incident until the column on the ridge reached a cemetery and that on the road Milestone 59. Here the Worcesters on the ridge met up with a well-dug Japanese position blocking their approach to Kalaw. A long way down the hillside the tanks were halted by a culvert which had been blown up and which the tanks could not cross. At this point the road bent sharply to the right with a big drop to the left and a high cliff face to the right. Geoff Anlezark was driving the tank immediately behind that of Captain Munro. The latter appears to have climbed out of his tank and gone forward on foot to investigate. He came back waving his arms, implying it was 'kaput' – no good. As he got back into his tank a hale of bullets descended on him. Jim Tiley remembers his voice on the 'B' wireless set saying: 'Give them all you've got, "A" Squadron' – but even as the words were spoken, his voice faded. He had been mortally wounded in the head.

SKETCH MAP: THE APPROACHES TO KALAW, JUNE 1945

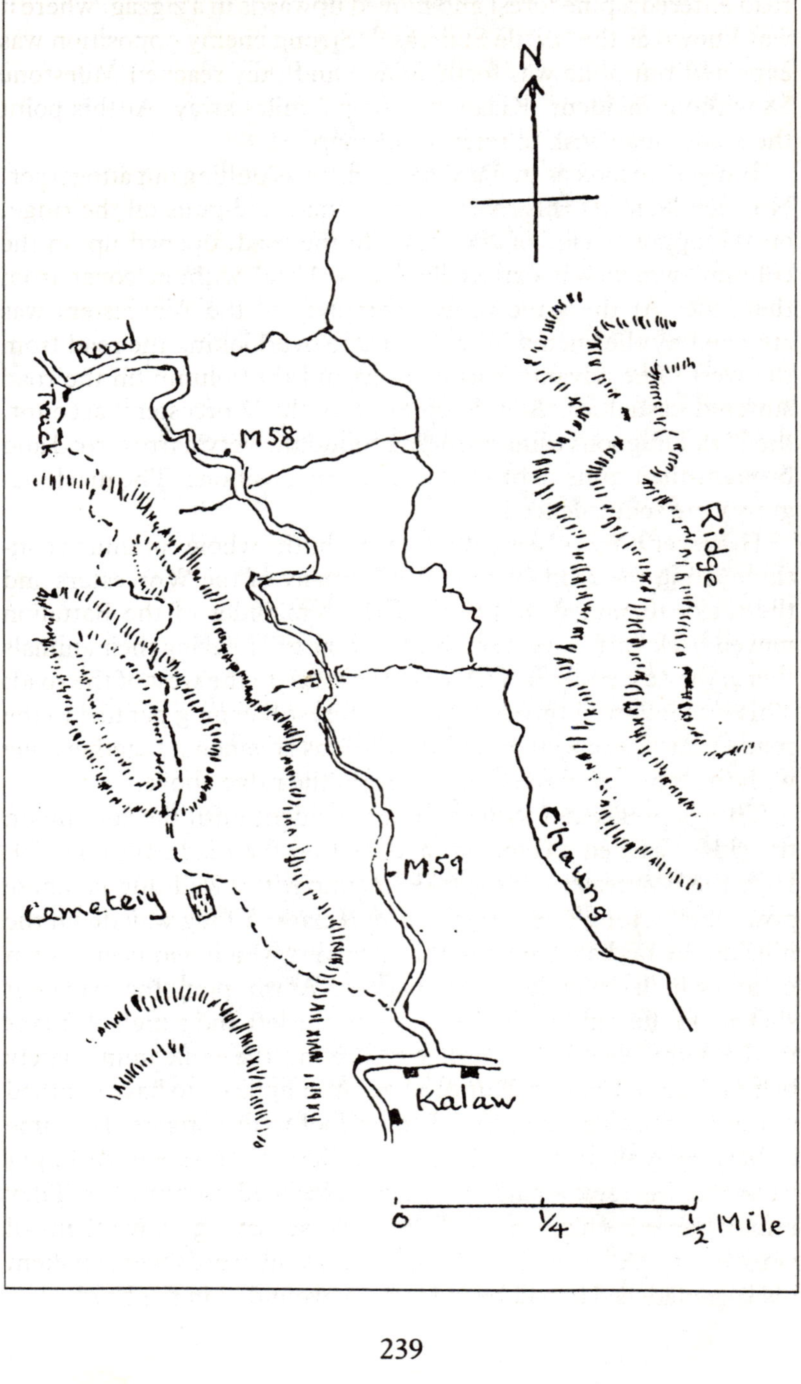

The infantry were all round the tanks and under fire from the east ridge – the same machine-guns as in the previous encounter but moved further along the hillside. It proved impossible to locate their new positions. The column was in the centre of an arc of fire, the advance was completely held up and heavy casualties were suffered. It was too late in the afternoon to launch an attack to clear the east ridge, so the order was given to disengage. The Worcesters were to rally on a position on the west ridge some 300 yards back from the point where they had been held up near the cemetery. Great difficulty was experienced in getting the wounded away under fire and eventually the casualties were brought out by the tanks, who were able to cover the withdrawal of the company in the evening. Unable to turn due to the narrow road, they reversed all the way back to the point where the track to the ridge joined the road.

The Worcesters suffered five fatal casualties and twelve wounded. 'Jock' Munro did not die until the following day, the 5th June. He was a popular, brilliant and respected officer of 'A' Squadron and his death a shock for many. *SEAC* newspaper had the previous year described him as 'fair, boyish-faced, and a newspaperman in civil life'. He received posthumously the Military Cross for his bravery and leadership. He was 26 years old at the time.

Lt S. Walker of the 25th Dragoons, who had also dismounted from his tank was wounded in the hand but not seriously.

On the following day the Gurkhas took the east ridge which, at its southern end, overlooked Kalaw. The Worcesters also moved forward on the west ridge and patrolled quite close to the city. The information gleaned from intensive patrolling over two days indicated that Kalaw was not now occupied in strength. It was assaulted in the early morning of 7th June, the Gurkhas coming in from the north-east and the Worcesters from the north-west. The latter were divided into two columns as before, the tanks being on the road. By 5.30 in the afternoon the two regiments had linked-up without opposition. The city had fallen and the Japanese were fast disappearing to the east.

That night the tanks were to harbour on a flat piece of ground for a change, probably just outside the city. It was the end of the operation as far as the tank crews were concerned. Rumours began to circulate that 'A' Squadron was required back in Cocanada to prepare for the proposed amphibious landings on the Malay coast for Operation Zipper. They were to be relieved by an RAC Regiment (No 116 The Gordon Highlanders). They listened for the skirl of the pipes for quite a long time before they arrived. They then returned to Meiktila.

* * *

In the meantime another group of tanks, under the command of Major Anderson with Lt Ray Rothery, left Meiktila by the south road making towards Toungoo. At some point after Meiktila they were driving along a tarmac road with thick jungle either side. They were co-operating with and supporting a platoon of Indian infantry which was clearing out pockets of Japanese. Tom Thompson was driving the second tank behind that of Lt Goldsworthy who was leading the column and the infantry walked on either side of them in single file. The road was barely wide enough to allow two vehicles to pass.

Suddenly at a bend in the road the leading tank was hit by an armour-piercing shell at close range from a 75mm gun. The shell drilled a very neat hole in the turret of the tank and on entry into the turret split into three segments. These whistled round the inside, killing Lt Goldsworthy, the tank commander and L/Cpl Peter Dell, the wireless operator and wounding Thornley, the gunner, in the legs. This happened on 19th May.

After this they made their way to the main Mandalay-Rangoon road. The terrain changed completely from thick jungle to open grassland reminiscent of home. They now 'toddled along' well in rear of the infantry who were on their mopping-up operation. In fact the retreating Japanese seemed to be going faster than the tanks and infantry. They were able to get a good night's sleep by the side of the tanks with only a minimum number on guard duty. They carried on south along this road, passing Toungoo, and were well on the way to Pegu when a halt was called. There was no further purpose for the tanks and they returned to Meiktila.

Tom Thompson thinks they travelled some 300 miles down the road from Meiktila. After the Goldsworthy incident they did not encounter any other opposition but they did see quite a few burnt-out tanks and trucks from earlier actions.

* * *

All members of 'A' Squadron had now returned to Meiktila. They had done what they had been told to do but had a feeling that they had lost some valued comrades-in-arms without a lot to show for it. During these operations they had existed entirely on 'K' rations. The main improvement since the Arakan days was the provision of two-man tents for sleeping, rather than ad hoc arrangements for keeping out the rain with tarpaulins. They all lost weight and, they felt, must have looked like concentratrion camp survivors.

There was little organization about 'A' Squadron's return to Cocanada. Each man was left to do the best he could and they arrived singly or in dribs and drabs – by road and air to Chittagong and by rail and paddle-steamer to Cocanada. Most of the personnel were due for repatriation to Britain. The rest would be wanted for the impending and finally cancelled expedition by sea to Malaya.

Epilogue 1947

In the autumn of 1945 Compton Mackenzie, the writer and novelist, was approached by the Government of India (then British) to write a history of the contribution of India to victory in the Second World War. After some hesitation, due to age and ill-health, he accepted.

The Government of India laid on a tour for him of all the battlefields through which Indians had fought, from Tunis to Hong Kong. He eventually set off in October 1946 and by mid-February 1947 he was at Chittagong where he was met by, amongst others, Brig M.R. Roberts, formerly commander of 114th Brigade, 7th Indian Division. Brig Roberts was to escort him through the fighting areas of Arakan, which we had come to know so well exactly three years before. He described it as follows:

Brig Roberts . . . and I boarded Motor Launch 1110 to go to Maungdaw 14 miles away. The last mile or so was up a creek or chaung of the Naf river. I noticed several little bitterns poking about in the mud. On the jetty at Maungdaw we were met by Lt Comdr L. Burness Burma RNVR who had helped in the complicated arrangements for re-visiting this extremely complicated land of Arakan. The luggage was sent on to Buthidaung and we enjeeped in the hope of getting a glimpse of the Ngakyedauk Pass from west of the Mayu Range.

Most of the gardens in Maugdaw had a beautiful small tree, bare of leaves, and covered with flower spikes of deepest scarlet which I think must be some variety of erythrina. I noticed also one or two cotton trees, one of which I described at Tiddim when I did not know what it was called. Birds seem to use the cups of rosy blossom as cocktails. Another beautiful floral effect was the fields of Indian-yellow flax, protected against cattle by formidable bamboo fences. Thin spiky canes called pangis, six feet high, stick up every yard, and these are interwoven with thicker horizontal canes. The barrier is very effective. The Japs used to put these spiky canes round possible landing places for parachutists and several of these gallant men in Force 136, who were dropped in Burma, were wounded by them.

The level country along the coast, mostly padi but growing flax and other crops, is bounded on the east by the Mayu Range which writes a zigzag line along the sky and rises practically sheer from the plain to about 2000 feet. I had seen this range from the air and at the south end of it I had noted the wide elephant track which runs along the top for some way.

I heard a grim elephant story. A machine-gunner took a shot at an elephant. The elephant charged and knelt on the LMG which being nearly red hot burnt him and made him more mad than ever. The rash machine-gunner was picked-up in his trunk and smashed to death.

We turned off to the left from the Maungdaw-Buthidaung road on which the Public Works Department had scattered a quantity of stones without laying-on a steam-roller. We were relieved to get off this hellish surface and jeep in comparative comfort through the dust. We got a glimpse of Hill 1301 with its fringe of blasted trees along the top. Finally we came to what was known as Piccadilly Circus where the road through the Ngakeydauk Pass began. There is a mound in the middle which the traffic used as a roundabout. Unluckily we found that the bridge over the first chaung was down which put an end to the hope of getting any way along the road from this side.

We had just decided to turn back when we met the District Commissioner, Mr L. Lees, who was visiting this part of his district for the first time . . . He asked if he might join us on our expedition to the Admin Box (the following day). . . . We sat under a tree, drank beer and gin and ate some cheese sandwiches at 13 o'clock, while Brig Roberts gave a clear account of 5th Indian Division's fight on this side of the Range. Then we drove back to have a look at the Razabil fortress, which is a huddle of low hills covered with elephant grass and low scrub. This was damnably difficult country from which to eject Japs because as soon as they were put off one hill they would get on to another, and, when put off that, the company working on them would find they were back on the hill from which they had just been put off.

We left Lees to go to one of the teas prepared for him on his progress . . . At the jetty at Maungdaw we embarked in sampans to return to our ML which was waiting for us off the creek . . .

February 19th:

We boarded ML 1110 at 7.30, transferring at Maungdaw to ML 1304 of the Royal Burma Navy. The District Commissioner hopped on board with extreme agility at 9.30, followed by a welcome consignment of beer. We reached the Maungdaw jetty to enjeep at 10. Our kit was to proceed straight to Buthidaung in a lorry when we turned off to the Admin Box. The surface of the road improved as we drew near the Mayu Range. The clumps of wild and quite uneatable pineapple gave way to jungle. We passed a memorial to the 19th Hyderabad Regiment and another to the York and Lancasters. The road was originally the permanent way of a light railway built in 1918 but soon abandoned because it did not pay. I find the country most difficult to describe.

We entered a valley between the precipitous hills of the Range, full of smaller pointed hills with streams and a very rich vegetation of innumerably various greens. The effect resembled an elaborate laid-out super-landscape garden. After a few miles we reached the west tunnel which pierces the steep range for 300 yards. The tunnel was used as a store by the Japs and there is much evidence of attempts by the RAF to seal it with heavy bombing. The two east tunnels are much narrower. A stone over the arch of the second records that it was built by J. Martin of Rangoon in 1918.

We came down into the wide plain between the Mayu Range and the Arakan Yomas. The long low hills known as Cain and Abel rise from the plain on either side. Abel was the scene of desperate fighting in January 1944 when it was taken by 33 Brigade. The 4th/1st Gurkhas held it for six weeks and it was never lost but Cain remained in Japanese hands much longer. After passing Cain and Abel we reached a point on the road where a dust track turned off to the left across the padi. Here we were met by the taxi which was to lead the way to our destination – the village of Ngakyedauk. The villagers in this part of Arakan did not leave their homes during the fighting. We reached the village of Tatmingyaungwa where we had to cross a deep chaung by a rickety bridge. I don't know how the taxi negotiated it. When we got to the village our taxi guide was out of sight and we had some trouble finding the right track.

The landscape became more attractive bounded by the Mayu Range to the west and level as a billiard-table except for a small ridge prodigally clothed with trees on which there were more orchids than I had seen anywhere else. Alas, they were not in bloom; Michael Roberts told me they were mostly the yellow and brown kind, the name of which eludes me. There were also white ones.

We stopped for a few minutes to eat some chocolate. . . . I turned my attention to watching a water-buffalo enjoying a glorious wallow. At last we reached a dyke across the padi and, after driving over that, we came to an end of any road negotiable, even by the most optimistic jeep. Half-way across the dyke, Brig Roberts pointed out the trees, away to the right, where General Messervy and his Divisional HQ were suddenly overrun by the Japs in February 1944.

The villagers of Ngakyedauk had fenced in with bamboo a space beneath a spreading peepul tree and there set out deck-chairs and a table for our reception. Outside the fence they were gathered to the number of about 200 – almost all Chittagonian Mussalmans – to gaze at the rare visitors. A deck-chair slung on a bamboo pole had been arranged to carry me along the two rough miles from the eastern gate to the western gate of the Admin Box. I was borne across three streams up and down a very rough path and I felt sorry for the four villagers who took turns with the burden. The sun was blazing down and another villager walked beside the chair, holding an umbrella over me. From time to time we were refreshed by the shade of some really magnificent trees. It was fantastic to think that along this track only three years ago hundreds of every kind of motor transport were passing.

Sinzweya, in which three years ago there were thousands of vehicles and pile upon pile of stores, resembles an expanse of common land in a sylvan area at home and is surrounded by large wooded hills with one higher conical hill to the south-west known as Artillery Hill which was completely blasted by our guns firing at point-blank range, but is now green again with the rapid growth from three monsoons since that February of 1944 . . . We sat beneath a tree and surveyed a scene of Arcadian peace. The local inhabitants have found a use for most of the debris which once covered the place. I was carried as far as a point from which one could see the road our sappers had cut through the Ngakyedauk Pass but it is rapidly falling to pieces, so that even its trace will hardly be discernible after another couple of monsoons.

It was on February 19th 1944 that the Jap attack on Sinzweya began to weaken and here three years later to the very day we were standing on the spot which marked the end of the beginning to destroy the military power of Japan. This green enclosure in its decisive influence on the course of human history may stand beside the Mound of Athenian dead at Marathon. In the middle of the common we saw where Lord Louis Mountbatten stood on a soap-box and addressed the visitors of the Admin Box, having been flown there from his HQ at Kandy.

I left this inspiring spot conscious that very few Europeans were likely to see it again and immensely grateful to the energy and determination of Brig Michael Roberts which had made possible what everybody told me would be an impossible expedition to carry through.

When we reached the pavilion of the peepul tree where we were to eat our lunch, we found the bamboo fence surrounded by a throng of villagers prepared to enjoy the spectacle. The officials began to hurry them away but we intervened and they were allowed to come back and watch our demonstration of drinking gin, lemonade and beer, and the rapidity with which we could put away the hard-boiled eggs provided by the headman. We left Ngakyedauk grateful for the hospitality of the villagers.

On our way back we missed the track to Tatmingyaungwa and had some difficulty in picking it up again. Our jeep jibbed at a ridge in the padi and had to be lifted off, which for a jeep is a pretty humiliating experience. We reached Buthidaung about tea-time. . . .

Our basha for the night was a rat-infested primitive building with a mud floor and sanitary arrangements at which even Adam and Eve might have raised their eyebrows. Certainly Eve.

February 20th:
I was awake at 4, watching the morning star winking through the roof of the basha, and through the 'walls' the kindling of a fire by the bearer, the admirable Abdul. It was still dark when we left the basha and stumbled down the bank to the water's edge. In the east Lucifer was showing his incandescent lamp to guide the sun up and the Great Bear's snout was below the western horizon. The dawn was beginning to break in rose and orange when we boarded the Unit Craft provided by the Graves Concentration Unit. Wisps of mist were rising from the water like cold smoke but the shades of the morning dusk were warmer than at home and more like the dusk of evening. Flights of egrets broke into the patterns of a Chinese painting on rice-paper as they winged their way to the feeding grounds. The trees on either side of the Kalapanzin were loud with bird-song.

A Unit Craft is not designed for comfort but to carry the remains of those dead soldiers which are to be concentrated in certain cemeteries. Those who fought in Arakan will rest in Akyab. The members of the Graves Concentration Unit are all volunteers and the work they are doing in these remote spots deserves a tribute. These men are living hard. They have to explore the remotest parts of the jungle, which on these Arakan hillsides is particularly dense and their labour is arduous. Lt D. Gilday of the Royal Welsh Fusiliers commands this unit and Brig Roberts was able to tell him where he would find some bodies not yet gathered in, and that was to him and his crew a rich reward for their kindness in taking us up the creek and back.

After the sun rose to starboard, the mist gathered more thickly. It was a typical Arakan morning of early spring, Brig Roberts told me. Going upstream we passed Kyaukit where there was much heavy fighting. We passed the funnel of a Jap steamer sunk by one of our Hurricanes. This used to serve as a mark for our patrols. We saw where a Polish officer called Lubeck, who was attached to 114th Brigade, launched his fire ships full of explosives against the bottom of the hill held by the Japs. His originality in devising trouble for the Japs was inexhaustible until at last he was killed. Peace to his bones where they rest far from his own tormented country.

Kingfishers flashed through the trees. A couple of monkeys stared at us from the branches. Suddenly a 25lb rohu was sighted on the mud of the bank and the craft slowed down to allow one of the sampans we were towing to investigate. The big fish was not dead and the chap who landed to get it sank up to his thighs in the mud. The rohu was put in the pot and was to be served for breakfast the next day.

After moving upstream for about half an hour we reached the mouth of the Myan Chaung which runs eastward from the right bank of the Kalapanzin. We transferred to a couple of sampans and made our way up the chaung which was about the size of the Cherwell where it runs along Addison's Walk at Oxford. A peasant carrying a large bunch of golden pumpkin flowers beamed at us from the bank. The chaung grew narrower, darker and shallower. The sampans, which require only 18 inches of water, always seemed on the verge of going aground. The left bank was fringed with abutilons in flower, their brick-red bells swinging gently over the black slimey mud. We passed under a crazy bridge consisting of one bamboo cane and a handrail across which a party of cultivators were passing in single file. A couple of hundred yards beyond this the sampans went firmly aground. Planks were taken out of them and we scrambled up the steep bank without getting much of the mud on our clothes. We walked across a stretch of padi to a small village called Paledaung.

The sun was blazing. I sat down on the outskirts of the village. The others walked on for a mile or more to see Brig Roberts' old HQ, the full extent of 114th Brigade's Box, and the airstrip from which casualties were evacuated. After a while John D and I walked across the padi fields, having left word for the others to follow us when they returned. After a laborious trudge of about half a mile we came to one of those formidable bamboo fences which we had to break through to reach the point where the chaung enters the river. We hailed the Unit Craft which was backed-in and with the help of the planks we managed to get aboard. The others arrived soon afterwards and we were back in Buthidaung by 11.15.

Here Brig Roberts left us. At 11.30 we set off down the Kalapanzin in ML 1304. The river was sometimes very wide, sometimes very narrow. To left of us the Arakan Yomas, to right the Mayu Range, slowly turned from green to blue and at last to misty grey. I recall a sampan with an orange sail and three hpoongyis in their orange robes crouched amidships. Just after 17.30 we were in the war-shattered harbour of Akyab. I felt rather tired but it had been another day of days.

(Compton Mackenzie: 'All over the Place')

Appendix No 1

ORDER OF THE DAY: 29th February 1944

To the XIVth Army, Eastern Air Command and Arakan Naval Coastal Forces: You have come victoriously through your first battle since the formation of XIV Army and the E Air Cmd.

You have given the Japanese a crack they will remember.

They are learning that, just as wars cannot be won by sudden treacherous assaults, so too battles are not decided by surprise attacks.

Three weeks ago the enemy sent a large and formidable force through the jungle to cut your lines of communication and attack you in the rear.

They launched a major offensive in the Arakan in the hope of defeating you and sweeping on into India.

You have met the onslaught with courage, confidence and resolution.

Many of you were cut off and encircled, dependent on supplies dropped from aeroplanes, but everyone stood firm, inspired and strengthened by the knowledge that powerful support was at hand from land, sea and air.

Now after bitter fighting in the jungle and in the skies, the Japanese attack has been smashed.

The enemy forces which infiltrated into your rear have been destroyed or scattered. The threatened passes are clear, the roads are open.

You have gained a complete victory.

Mountbatten
Supreme Commander,
South East Asia

SEAC

Appendix No 2

25th Dragoons
Medal Awards

Distinguished Service Order

Major (temporary Lt Colonel) Herbert Ralph Cuyle Frink. RAC (Dragoons) Thurlow, Suffolk. Commanding Officer, 25th Dragoons

Captain (temporary Major) Nial Vernon Johnstone. RAC (Dragoons) Sketty, Glamorgan. Squadron Leader, B Squadron, 25th Dragoons

The Military Cross

Lt Norman Johnson. Royal Tank Regiment. RAC (Kings Lynn) Troop Leader, B Squadron
Capt William Alexander Hay Munro, A Squadron

The Military Medal

Trooper John Monger. (Basingstoke) B Squadron
Trooper William Henry Williams. (Poole) C Squadron
Sergeant Major Ernest Frank Dennis Haddon. (Glyneath) A Squadron

Certificate of Gallantry (Gen Giffard)
Trooper David Vagg. HQ Squadron

Mentioned in Despatches
Major (temp) C.W.D.W. Alexander
Capt (acting) E.J.R. Foxwell
Lieut H.I.H. Grant
Sergt D.M. Robertson
Corpl H. Busfield
Trooper W. Taylor

Appendix No 3

25TH DRAGOONS

BATTLE HONOURS

BURMA: 1944–45

NORTH ARAKAN:	1st January to 12th June 1944
BUTHIDAUNG:	16th January to 3rd February 1944 5th March to 8th April 1944
RAZABIL:	19th to 30th January 1944 10th to 17th March 1944
NGAKYEDAUK PASS:	4th February to 4th March 1944

Appendix No 4

A ROLL OF 25th DRAGOONS KILLED IN BURMA 1944-45

We died . . .
Far from the lands we loved, that gave us birth,
Our sepulchre this whole tormented earth.
(J.W.L. Forge, Royal Signals)

ARAKAN, 1944

26 Jan	Tpr John Swinburn, C Sqn. Age 22
6 Feb	Tpr Ernest Walter Brock, B Sqn. Age 33
7 Feb	L/Cpl Walter Heesom, B Sqn. Age 24
10 Feb	Tpr Reginald Albert Widger, HQ Sqn. Age 24
11 Feb	Tpr Walter Francis Mowle, B Sqn. Age 32
11 Feb	Tpr John Stainbank, B Sqn. Age 32
12 Feb	L/Cpl Gordon Arthur Barnes, B Sqn. Age 22
14 Feb	Tpr Frank Percival Myers, B Sqn. Age 20
15 Feb	Capt Edward George Winters, HQ Sqn. Age 36 Technical Adjutant
17 Feb	Capt James Keith Copeland, B Sqn. Age 28 Second-in-Command, B Sqn
25 Feb	Sergt Clive Ali Chimmo Branson, B Sqn. Age 36 Troop Sergeant
26 Feb	Tpr William Tosh Graham, C Sqn. Age 35
6 Mar	Tpr William George Foote, A Sqn. Age 36
12 Mar	Sergt Herbert Greatorex, A Sqn. Age 27
12 Mar	Tpr William Albert Eastham, A Sqn. Age 22
12 Mar	Tpr Norman Lionel Wagstaffe, A Sqn. Age 22
12 Mar	Tpr Edward James Hammond, A Sqn. Age 23
12 Mar	Tpr Albert Thomas Woolmer, A Sqn. Age 21
25 Mar	Capt David Arthur Robertson, HQ Sqn. Age 35 Regimental Signals Officer
7 April	Tpr Henry Newman, A Sqn. Age 25
8 April	Tpr Archibald Mitchell, A Sqn. Age 34

KALAW AND TAUNGOO, 1945

19 May	Lt Dennis George Goldsworthy, A Sqn. Age 25
19 May	L/Cpl Peter Francis Dell, A Sqn. Age 23
5 June	Capt William Alexander Hay Munro, MC, A Sqn. Age 26

Sergeant Greatorex and Troopers Eastham and Hammond were missing believed dead and they with Trooper Wagstaffe are commemorated on Face 1 of the Rangoon Memorial at Rangoon. All the remainder are buried in the Taukkyan War Cemetery at Rangoon.

Appendix No 5

THE 25TH DRAGOONS
MEMORIAL FUND COMMITTEE.
MINUTES OF MEETING
HELD ON THURSDAY NOV. 23RD 1944.

The following Committee was elected :—

President :—The Commanding Officer.
Vice-President :—A Warrant Officer.
Treasurer :—The P.R.I.
Secretary :—The Padre.
together with one B.O.R. representative from each squadron.
Home Representative :—Mrs H.R.C. Frink (wife of Brig. H.R.C. Frink D.S.O. late Commanding Officer of the Regt.)
Address —Thurlow, Newmarket, England.

1. Objects of the Fund.

The Committee outlined the objects of the Fund to be as follows :—

(*a*) To assist to the fullest extent of its resources the provision of financial support to dependents of regimental casualties on active service.

(*b*) To assist any member or ex-member of the Regiment who in the opinion of the Committee needs financial support.

(*c*) To make contact between any member or ex-member of the Regiment with the Ex-Cavalryman's Association until such time as a Regimental Old Comrade's Association is formed.

(*d*) To provide a permanent memorial at some future date.

2. Money will be raised for the Fund in the following ways :—

(*a*) Individual Donations.

(*b*) Annual Subscriptions.

(*c*) Annual Memorial Service Collection.

(*d*) Proceeds from entertainments etc. organised by the Memorial Committee.

(*e*) Proceeds from such other Funds as are directed by the Commanding Officer.

P.T.O.

3. Applications for Assistance.

Application may be made as follows :—

(*a*) By direct application to the Committee through the Commanding Officer.

(*b*) By the application of any member of the Regiment on behalf of anyone known to be in need of assistance.

(*c*) By any home representative whose name will be published from time to time.

N.B.— i. Assistance from this Fund will be irrespective of aid from official sources

ii. For the purpose of report the names of those receiving help will be anonymous.

4. Administration of the Fund.

i. An a/c has been opened with Grindlay & Co., Ltd.. 54 Parliament St. London SWI. to be called The 25th Dragoons Memorial Fund Account.

ii. Money subscribed outside the Regt. should be sent direct to this account or through the P.R I.

iii. No money shall be paid from this account without written approval signed by the President and Vice-President after the consent of the majority of the Committee.

iv. The Committee are empowered to make an immediate grant of not more than £ 3-3 (three guineas). Further grants will be paid on investigation according to the merit of the case or reliable evidence. Investigation will be carried out by representatives of the Committee or by such agencies as are nominated by them.

v. An Annual Balance Sheet will be published and distributed.

vi. As far as possible no expenses will be deducted from the Fund in connection with its administration, and all work will be voluntary.

vii. An Official Receipt will be sent in respect of all postal donations.

These minutes are being circulated to all ex-members of the Regiment whose addresses are known. It will be appreciated if any member can assist the Committee by giving other addresses.

All correspondence should be addressed to :—The President of the Memorial Fund,
25th Dragoons, R.A.C.
India Command.

Appendix No 6

Subsequent History of the 25th Dragoons

After withdrawing from Burma the Regiment was chosen to train on amphibious DD Sherman tanks or 'swimmers' as they were sometimes called. These tanks had taken part in the D-Day landings in Europe but were still on the secret list and remained so until the war in the Far East ended. The training was done at Cocanada (now Kakinada) on the east coast of India about midway between Calcutta and Madras.

During this training 'A' Squadron was called back into Burma in May 1945. They were flown to Meiktila where they collected somewhat battered Sherman tanks and came under the command of 19th Division. Their experience is described in the Postscript. Two officers and a lance corporal were killed. Two officers and four troopers were wounded. The Squadron returned to Cocanada in mid-June.

It was now clear that the Regiment was to take part in the proposed large-scale landing on the Malay coast known as Operation Zipper. One squadron got so far as to be loaded on board ship at Madras harbour but the operation was forestalled by the Japanese surrender.

The Regiment continued in India but did not take part in the Victory Parade in Delhi, being on security duties at the time. Perhaps in compensation they received a visit from the commander-in-chief, Field-Marshal Auchinleck, the following month, when a parade and march-past were held, the Field-Marshal taking the salute. Two members of the Regiment, John Kitney and Tom Grounds, were in the Royal Armoured Corps Contingent of the Victory Parade in London on the 8th June 1946, the latter being in Lt Col R.G. Byron's Comet Command tank at the head of the Army Mechanized Column.

The Regiment remained in India until disbandment in August 1947 on the granting of Independence to India and Pakistan. Such members as were left then returned to Britain.

Appendix No 7

Brigadier H.R.C. Frink, DSO
Biographical Note

Brigadier Frink was born in 1899 in Thurlow, Suffolk. The family was of Dutch and German Huguenot descent, having emigrated to Canada in the 17th Century. He was educated at Sherborne and entered the Royal Military College at Sandhurst. He joined the 4th Royal Irish Dragoon Guards at Cologne early in 1919 and served continuously with them until they were amalgamated with the 7th Dragoon Guards to become the 4th/7th Dragoon Guards.

These regiments were still true cavalry, having not yet been 'mechanized'. Throughout his career he took an active part in all regimental sports and was a good strong horseman making a name for himself both in this country and in India, where he served with his regiment from 1921 to 1929. He was the last survivor of its polo team which won the Subaltern's Cup in 1928 and he played several times for the regimental team.

Before the Regiment returned to England, he met and married Jean Conway-Gordon whose father was in the Indian Army. A daughter Elisabeth (later Dame Elisabeth Frink) was born at Thurlow in 1930 and five years later a son Timothy.

In 1936 the 4th/7th Dragoon Guards held their last mounted parade in Edinburgh prior to being mechanized. They did not receive their first tank until March 1939. In September war was declared and the Regiment was at once sent to France where, thanks to the 'phoney war', they were able to complete their training.

After the Germans broke through the Allied lines and retreat became necessary, he was left commanding a squadron of the Regiment after the main body had been withdrawn. They were required to fight a rear-guard action to delay the enemy and they were some of the last of the Allied troops to reach Dunkirk in June 1940.

In 1941 Brigadier Frink was sent to India to command the newly-formed 25th Dragoons at Sialkot. In December of that year Japan attacked Pearl Harbour and in the early months of 1942 captured the whole of Burma to the Indian border. After training on a selection of vehicles at various stations in India, the Regiment eventually went into

Burma in December 1943 equipped with Gen Lee medium tanks. Before long they were at the centre of the Battle of the Admin Box in Arakan. Despite being wounded at one point Frink remained in command during the whole battle and received the immediate award of the DSO from General Messervy on the field. This battle was at once recognized as the first decisive land defeat of the Japanese and thus a turning point in the war.

He continued to command until the Regiment was withdrawn with the onset of the Monsoon. He was then promoted to brigadier and sent to command 252 Indian Armoured Brigade in the Middle East. At the end of the war he had a short spell commanding the Queen's Own Hussars in Italy and then took over the command of a Territorial Brigade in Yorkshire.

Suddenly it was found that he had tuberculosis. After two years in hospital, he was invalided out of the Army in 1949.

He returned to his native Suffolk and led as normal a life as was possible, running the local landowners' sport and taking an active part in local affairs. His last years were a constant battle against ill health which he bore with great courage. He eventually died in his sleep on 2nd March 1974. A Memorial and Thanksgiving Service was held on 1st May 1974 at St James' Church, Piccadilly, London, where the address was given by the former Padre of the 25th Dragoons, Captain the Reverend Wallace F. Cox.

Appendix No 8

Major N.V. Johnstone, DSO
Biographical Note

Major 'Tony' Johnstone was educated at Eton and attended the Royal Military College, Sandhurst. He joined the 3rd Carabiniers in India in the late 1930s. In 1941 he, with a number of other officers, NCOs and men were detached to form a new armoured regiment, the 25th Dragoons, in Sialkot. He was appointed to command 'B' Squadron and, after some two years training on a selection of vehicles and in various stations in India, the Regiment went into Burma (Arakan) in December 1943. In early February 1944 the Japanese out-flanked the 7th Indian Division on the east side of the Mayu Range and 'B' Squadron under Major Johnstone's command were the first to cross the Ngakyedauk Pass to go to their assistance. The Regiment remained at the centre of the Battle of the Admin Box and its tanks turned the tide of battle against the Japanese during the weeks of siege. Major Johnstone received the DSO for his gallantry and command of the Squadron.

He continued in command in the subsequent operations until badly wounded. He eventually returned to active service and commanded 'C' Squadron of the 25th Dragoons during their amphibious training at Cocanada on the east coast of India in preparation for the landing on Malaya. The Japanese however surrendered in August 1945 and the landing never took place.

After the War he saw service in Korea and retired from the Army shortly thereafter. He trained as a teacher and went to South Africa to become a master at Ridge School, Johannesburg. Later he became headmaster at Pridivin Preparatory School. A cricket enthusiast, he coached and organized cricket in both schools. After leaving 'The Ridge' he stood as an accredited umpire in the Transvaal League and later became personal assistant to Dr Ali Bacher, Managing Director of the South African Cricket Union. Tony Johnstone and his wife Sheila had no children. Schoolboys are said to have seen Tony as a disciplinarian but to have respected him greatly. A small group of firm friends saw him as unassuming, courteous and considerate. He died in Johannesburg on 26th January 1989 shortly after his wife.

Glossary

Charpoi: light wooden string bed

Chaung: waterway, stream, in Arakan often tidal

Chota: little

Havildar: Sergeant (Indian Army)

Khana (Konna): food

Maidan: open space, usually grass, in or near town

Naik: Corporal (Indian Army)

Nullah: large ditch, dried-up watercourse with steep sides

Peepul: large fig tree

Pukka: genuine, permanent

Rickshaw: light 2-wheeled hooded vehicle drawn by one or more persons

Rupees, Annas, Pice: Indian currency

Sabib, Memsahib: the titles by which Indians (when no disrespect was intended) addressed or spoke of British or other European people

Sources

Unpublished

Personal recollections, Letters home.

Papers of the late Brig H.R.C. Frink, DSO

War Diary of the 25th Dragoons, 1943-1944

Here and There – William Nicholson

Farmer-Soldier – J. Houghton Brown, 1945

Defence of 7th Indian Division HQ by Signals Personnel – Patrick Hobson

History of 139 Jungle Field Regiment – William Harding

A contemporary account of the Siege of the Admin Box – R.Q.M.S. Murgatroyd, RA

The Turning Point – Peter Ascham

Published

The Story of 25th Dragoons – Oliver C. Horne

The 25th Dragoons – Appendix 1 to the History of 3rd Carabiniers

SEAC Newspaper

British Soldier in India – The Letters of Clive Branson, 1944

Far East – Cecil Beaton, 1945

Journal of 25th Dragoons, July 1946

The Campaign in Burma – Frank Owen HMSO, 1946

All over the Place – Compton MacKenzie, 1948

Report my Signals – Anthony Brett-James, 1948

Ball of Fire, History of 5th Indian Division – Anthony Brett-James, 1951

Golden Arrow, History of the 7th Indian Division – M.R. Roberts, 1952

Defeat into Victory – William Slim, 1956

The Desert and the Jungle – Geoffrey Evans, 1959

Spearhead General (Biography of Frank Messervy) – Henry Maule, 1961

Tank Tracks to Rangoon – Bryan Perrett, 1978

The Battle of the Box – Patrick Turnbull, 1979

XIV Army at War – George Forty, 1982

Burma – The Longest War – Louis Allen, 1984

Personal Diary of the Lord Louis Mountbatten, 1943-1946. Ed Philip Ziegler, 1988

Dekho, The Magazine of the Burma Star Association

Index

Ablett, Capt H.G. (Mich) 56, 68-9
Alexander, Capt C.W. 46, 123, 125, 141, 250
Allason, Maj J. (3 Carbs) 143, 144
Allison, Capt (REME) 105, 106
Amery, Leo (Sec for India) 14, 26
Anderson, Capt C.D. 148, 165, 167, 168, 234, 240
Anlezark, Geoffrey 235, 236, 238
Arthur, Lt 220, 227
Auchinleck, Lt C.J. 150

Baig, Tara Ali 1
Banbury, Alf 150
Banerjee, Lt 81
Barnes, Gordon 111, 121, 122, 229, 252
Basu, Lt (IAMC) 90-92
Beaton, Sir Cecil 3, 5, 18, 42, 46, 50
Blair, Cmdr (US Navy) 28
Bose, Subhas Chandra 42, 93
Bradberry, John 8, 16, 229
Branson, Sgt Clive A.C. 22, 31, 151, 252
Brett-Janes, Capt 71-3, 87, 88
Briggs, Maj Gen H.R. 45 70-1, 115, 121, 147
Briggs, Lt (Sappers) 55, 56, 137, 138, 150, 169, 187
Brock, Cpl E.W. 105, 252
Brookfield, Lt (US Navy) 28
Brunet, Lt Col (RAMC) 89
Bryant, Lillian and Gwennie 6, 51, 220, 228
Burrell, Maj (IE) 123, 130
Burton, Capt R.H. 123, 232

Chadburn, Paul (SEAC) 117-8
Charles, Lt R.J. 141,150
Cherry, Graham (7 Div) 162
Chiang Kai-Shek, Generalissimo 15, 177, 231
Choudhury, Subadar (IAMC) 91
Christison, Lt Gen Philip 45, 87, 160-1, 164, 198, 201
Churchill, Rt Hon W.S. 7, 19, 116, 159, 230
Cole, Lt Col R.B. (RA) 57, 78, 163
Copeland, Capt J.K. 130, 252
Cotterill-Hill, Brig R.C. (71 Bde) 214, 216
Cox, Rev F. (Padre) 8, 16, 37, 46, 97, 111, 116, 117, 159, 196
Crawley, Sgt R.W. and crew 228
Cree, Lt Col (W Yorks) 78, 88, 163
Crowther, Brig (89 Bde) 125, 147

Dean, Lt C.H. (W Yorks) 113
Dell, L/Cpl Peter 241, 252
Devenport, (SSM) G. 130
Dinwiddie, Brig H.W. (114 Bde) 188
Doi, Col 84, 107
Dow, Sir Hugh 15
Dunlop, Maj Alec (W Yorks) 78, 119
Dunlop, Maj (Bombay Grenadiers) 35, 165
Durie, Lt L.A. 215

Eastham, William A. 174, 252
Evans, Lt (REME) 47, 130, 131, 134, 136, 147
Evans, Brig Geoffrey 70-3, 78-9, 80, 85, 86, 87, 88, 102, 115, 137, 144, 147, 163, 192, 217
Evans, Ray 111

Fairweather, Charles 105, 106, 150
Farquarson, Lt (Garwhal)

Ferguson, Capt R.H. (REME) 155
Foote, William G. 167, 252
Fox, Keith S. 8, 105, 223, 229
Foxwell, Capt E.J.R. 188, 250
Frink, Lt Col H.R.C. (later Brigadier) 22, 23, 26, 28, 29, 30, 31, 32, 33, 37, 38-9, 45, 47, 48, 49, 51, 55, 56, 73, 77, 79, 87, 97, 100, 101, 110, 115, 123, 148-9, 159, 160, 163, 165, 167, 168, 171, 173, 174, 179, 180, 181, 183, 187, 188, 193, 196, 201, 203, 205, 209, 211, 216, 218-27, 229, 250, 257-8
Frink, Mrs J., Elisabeth and Timothy 33, 257

Gabriel, Sgt Philip 58
Gandhi, M.K. (Mahatma) 27
Gaunt, Capt B. (Doc) 101, 217
Giffard, Gen George 156
Goldsworthy, Lt D.G. 241, 252
Graham, William T. 154, 252
Grant, Lt H.I.H. 149, 169, 193, 250
Gray, Lt Ian 48, 193
Greatorex, Sgt Herbert 173, 252
Griffin, Ken 193, 195
Grigg, Sir James (Sec for War) 34, 232
Grounds, Mr and Mrs W. (Mother and Dad) 1, 6, 8, 16, 17, 20, 21, 43, 53, 154, 157, 162, 177, 178, 196, 200, 219-24, 229, 230-2

Haddon, (SSM) E.F.D. 194, 215, 250
Hammopnd, Edward J. 174, 252
Hanaya, Lt Gen 156, 161
Harding, Bill (RA) 76, 99, 124, 180, 195
Harrington, Maj 94
Hasim, Driver 92
Heesom, L/Cpl Walter 86, 252
Hely, Brig T. (CRA) 65-6, 75, 76
Hobson, Lt Col P. (RCS) 59, 62, 65, 74, 75, 163
Hodgson, Cpl 103
Hoey, Maj C.F. (Lincolns) 126
Holdaway, Freddie 140
Holgate, Ralph 26, 27
Horne, Maj O.C. 9, 33, 46, 48, 57, 120
Houghton Brown, Lt Col J. (Wiltshires) 98, 108, 127-9, 135-6, 145-6, 152-4, 157, 197, 201-11
Howden, Cpl 'Curly' 111, 121, 122

Irwin, Capt A. ('V' Force) 124

Jefferies, James L. (3 Carab) 222
Johnson, Lt N. 119, 170, 171, 173, 175, 187, 250
Johnstone, Maj N.V. (Bumper) 'Tony' 29, 57, 58, 81, 103, 131, 139, 150, 164, 169, 170, 171, 176, 187, 250, 259

Kershaw, Eric 24
Khadilka, Lt (IAMC) 91
King, (RQMS) Harold G. 121
Kubo, Col 82, 104, 107, 134, 164

Lewis, Lt Alun (6 SWB) 70
Ley, Maj H.M.H. 30, 35, 49, 52, 72-3, 78-9, 87, 88, 96, 97, 100, 102, 114, 123, 133, 163, 168, 191, 192
Leyin, John 58, 103, 119
Lilwall, Maj B. (RAMC) 133
Loftus-Tottenham, Brig F.J. (33 Bde) 102, 167, 184
Lomax, Maj Gen C.E.N. (26 Div) 185, 197, 201, 225
Lowther, Brig (4 Bde) 148, 197
Lubeck, Capt 191

McCaig, Lt Col R. (RA) 74-5
McConnell, Lt Col D. (KOSB) 179
Macfarlane, Lt L.J. 120
MacDonald, 'Mac' & Joyce 8, 26, 33, 34, 199
MacKenzie, Sir Compton 161
McLaren, Lt Col (KOSB) 143
McVicker, Lt J. 74
Mair, Lt J.M. 140, 186
Maloney, RSM (W Yorks) 102
Manners, Capt W. 43, 232

Mao-Tse-Tung 15, 231
Marwood, Capt Malcolm 114
Maxwell, Gordon E. 229
Mazumda, Subadar (IAMC) 91
Messervy, Maj Gen W. (7 Div) 52, 55, 58, 59, 60-1, 62-3, 64-5, 73, 78, 81, 82, 87, 88, 97, 101, 102, 121, 147, 148, 156, 163, 164, 168, 176, 189, 191, 192, 197, 201, 211
Messervy, Mrs Pat 96
Miles, Lt Eric 111
Mitchell, Archie 127, 193, 252
Manger, John 111, 112, 187, 250
Montgomery, Gen Sir B. 60, 61, 120, 229
Moore, Sgt Ernest 220
Mountbatten, Admiral Lord Louis 3, 7, 15, 18, 19, 20, 34, 39, 40, 51, 60, 101, 107, 112, 120, 159, 172, 185, 197, 198, 249
Mowle, Walter F. 111, 252
Munday, Sgt 104, 106
Munro, Capt W.A.H. 48, 139, 140, 147, 178, 186, 192, 212, 216, 225, 236, 238, 240, 250, 252
Murgatroyd, RQMS (RA) 76, 113
Myers, Frank P. 111, 121, 122, 252

Nand Singh, Naik (11 Sikh) 171-2
Nehru, Jawaharlal 27
Newman, Henry 193, 252
Nicholson, Sgt W. (Bill) 24, 25, 30, 104, 115, 127, 155, 194

O'Hara, Maj C. (W Yorks) 78
Owen, Frank (SEAC) 34
Oxtoby, Sgt Fred 158

Padre, the *see* Cox, Rev F.
Pain, Capt 105
Paul, Capt (RAMC) 91
Peake, Cpl 111
Persse, Col S.H. 'Atte' 22, 30, 35, 77, 119, 150, 182, 188, 218
Poole, Sgt 'Taff' 111

Rayfield, Sgt 106
Reeves, Cliff 16, 105, 229
Reeves, Taffy 24
Roberts, Lt B. O'C. 126, 130, 148-9
Roberts, Brig M.R. (114 Bde) 67, 182, 188
Robertson, Capt D.A. 73, 183, 252
Robinson, Capt (RAMC) 94
Robson, Sgt (QM) 106
Roosevelt, Franklin D. 19, 112
Rothery, Lt R. 215, 216, 241
Rulia, Labourer 92, 93, 94
Ryan, Lt 196

Salomans, Brig 70-1, 163
Sarbjit Singh Kalha, Maj 141
Scaramanga, Capt Raymond 68, 75
Sinclair, Lt Col (Lincolns) 129, 215
Slim, Lt Gen William 19, 22, 38, 77, 99, 107, 156, 160, 172
Sloan, Maj Charles ('Tod') 48, 102, 178
Smiles, Cpl R. and crew 127
Smith, Capt (Peter Ascham) 63-5, 73, 85, 137-8
Somerville, Lt P.C. 23, 40
Spooner, Lt K.S. 48, 188, 192, 195, 215
Stainbank, John 111, 252
Stalin, Joseph 19
Stevens, Capt Wilson 54
Stilwell, Gen J. (US Army) 38
Swinburn, John 47, 252

Tanahashi, Col 50, 82, 104, 105, 107, 119, 156, 160
Thompson, Tom 235, 241
Tiley, James 16, 193, 223, 229, 236, 238

Vagg, Tpr David 156, 250
Vaughan, Lt 23
Verghese, Naik 92
Vyner, Cmdr C.G. (RN) 30

Wagstaffe, Norman L. 173, 252
Walker, Lt S. 215, 240
Warren, Brig D.F.W. (161 Bde) 47
Watt, H. Munro 25
Wavell, Lord (Viceroy) 20, 172
White, Chalky 105
Whittle, Grp Capt 34
Widger, Reginald 110, 252
Williams, William H. 86, 187, 250
Wingate, Gen Orde 38, 112
Winters, Capt E.G. 25, 123, 252
Wood, Capt (7 Div) 67
Woolmer, Albert T. 173, 252

Youens, Maj S.B. 104, 150, 232

Ziegler, Philip 3